CHAOS, CONTROVERSY
AND THAT
KUNG-FU
KICK

CHAOS, CONTROVERSY AND THAT KUNG-FU KICK

ROB FLETCHER

94/95
THE PREMIER LEAGUE'S MOST DRAMATIC SEASON

First published by Pitch Publishing, 2024

Pitch Publishing
9 Donnington Park,
85 Birdham Road,
Chichester,
West Sussex,
PO20 7AJ
www.pitchpublishing.co.uk
info@pitchpublishing.co.uk

ISBN 978 1 80150 746 2

Typesetting and origination by Pitch Publishing
Printed and bound in India by Thomson Press

Contents

The Beginning

NINETEEN NINETY-TWO was English football's modern 'Big Bang'. The birth of the Premier League changed the structure of the domestic game and created a new 'Super League' in everything but name. Money flowed into the top clubs' bank accounts through the bumper television deal with Sky Sports. Transfer fees spiked, wages increased and new talent arrived from abroad. Although the football looked similar to the old First Division, there was a clear change.

The biggest league in Europe was Serie A. Every Italian team had expensive foreign talent and some of the best domestic players money could buy. So, what better way for Premiership clubs to compete with Serie A than to bring over talent showcased in the biggest football event on the planet? By 1994, English clubs were flush with cash and scouted players over the summer months by turning on the television and watching a game from the USA.

Across the squads at USA 94, there were only 18 players who played their football in England. The pre-season of 1994 changed all that. Subsequent summers and World Cups consistently featured huge numbers of international players from the Premier League. A shift had started in the summer of 1994 in the way that teams spent their money and the amount they had to invest. Most clubs had begun work to make stadiums all-seater after the recommendations of the

Taylor Report, but now it was time to have the quality to draw in the fans.

Football in England had changed with the advent of the Premier League, now known, for sponsorship reasons, as the FA Carling Premiership, and there was a new team on top – Manchester United. Clearly, Alex Ferguson's team wanted to challenge for the title again. Many quickly installed them as favourites to win a third consecutive crown, but the challenge was certainly much stiffer and varied than in 1993/94, when United won with some style.

The reigning champions' preparations got under way when they allowed a legend to leave the club. Middlesbrough, led by young chairman Steve Gibson, had approached Bryan Robson, on the recommendation of outgoing manager Lennie Lawrence, to take up the post of player-manager at Ayresome Park. The ambition was to get Middlesbrough back into the Premiership and showcase top-flight football at their new state-of-the-art stadium on the banks of the River Tees. Robson accepted that his future was away from Old Trafford and made his first step into management.

Ferguson was not in rebuilding mode – far from it. The only addition to the side was defender David May, signed from the previous season's runners-up, Blackburn Rovers. The deal cost £1.4m and both player and manager were happy to join forces. May wanted to earn a place at Manchester United and thought the long-term prospects were better than remaining at Ewood Park. Rather than turning to the transfer market, the United boss bolstered the squad with a number of his youth players. The likes of Gary Neville, Paul Scholes, Keith Gillespie, Nicky Butt and David Beckham had a chance to play meaningful minutes as squad players and Ferguson did not want to jeopardise that.

Although Kenny Dalglish's expensively assembled squad of stars at Blackburn had pushed United closer than Aston

Villa had in the inaugural Premier League season, they still finished eight points adrift. They wanted to compete at the top table of English football and decided that the only way to do that was to invest heavily in the squad.

The first three summers of the new Premier League featured transfer battles between United and Blackburn. In the summer of 1992, Blackburn beat United to the signing of Alan Shearer and broke the English transfer record, paying £3.6m. A year later, Dalglish was furious not to repeat the feat when Ferguson and Manchester United stole Roy Keane from under his nose. That deal was almost signed and sealed until a late intervention from Ferguson made sure the Irishman played his football at Old Trafford.

Arsenal had tracked Chris Sutton even before the summer, when they tried to prise the striker away from Norwich City. They had allowed Andy Cole to leave in 1992, while neither Alan Smith nor Kevin Campbell had been able to become a consistent partner for Ian Wright. Smith and Campbell had contributed vital goals for Arsenal, but Sutton was seen as a long-term solution. George Graham, with a preference for English players due to UEFA's insistence that Welsh, Scottish and Irish players were 'foreigners' in European competitions, put Sutton ahead of Queens Park Rangers striker Les Ferdinand on his wish list and sent his bid to Norwich chairman Robert Chase, who had initially been reluctant to sell his star asset.

Another runner in the race were Arsenal's North London rivals Tottenham Hotspur, who were keen to find a partner for Teddy Sheringham and entertained the idea of signing Sutton, but chairman Alan Sugar baulked at the player's wage demands.

A major impact of the new television money flowing through the Premiership was the increase in player wages. Transfer fees were nowhere near those paid for stars on the continent, but they were on the up at a rapid rate, as were salaries. The going rate for Sutton was rumoured to be £12,000 a week. Sugar did not entertain that and said that paying those wages 'to an unproven player was out of the question for Tottenham. It's not greedy asking for it, but how would the others react?' The idea of more established stars getting wage increases followed the boom in modern transfers.

Arsenal fought Blackburn fiercely for Sutton's signature and in the ensuing auction the bidding started at £4m. Ferguson and Manchester United obviously wanted a piece of the action, too, so matched Arsenal's bid, but claimed that was the limit of what they were prepared to spend on such an unproven player. Norwich acknowledged the bids, but set a price of £5m and a deadline of the 14 July for any club to match the valuation. Sutton would have the deciding vote on where he played his football.

The bidding continued and, despite his insistence that £4m was the maximum he could offer, Ferguson increased his bid to £4.2m. Clearly, money was no object to Blackburn, who were poised to pay the £5m if all of the other clubs could not meet Norwich's valuation. Next, it was Arsenal's turn to up their offer, which trumped United's and reached £4.5m. The story kept the press interested all summer and certainly provided plenty of headlines that were usually reserved for the demolition of the England team's performance at a World Cup.

An interesting wrinkle to the whole transfer saga came when Everton joined the bidding race at the last minute. Their manager, Mike Walker, had led Sutton through the reserves at Norwich and into the first team. Sutton was loyal and one of the reasons he wanted to leave was the fact that Walker had left the club and Norwich were now in decline. Although aware that Norwich wanted and would accept £5m, the Everton boss declined to meet that price and offered £4.75m.

As Norwich's deadline approached, Arsenal's managing director Ken Friar announced that Arsenal had withdrawn their offer for the striker. Blackburn had their man. Chris Sutton became the most expensive player in English football history at a fee of £5m. It was a huge moment for domestic transfers, but it barely made a ripple in the wider context of the game. The transfer record remained at £13m after Gianluigi Lentini's move from Torino to Milan in the summer of 1992 and Sutton's transfer was only the third highest of the last year, with Luca Marchegiani and David Platt commanding higher fees after moves to Lazio and Sampdoria respectively.

Blackburn used a similar transfer policy as some of the biggest Italian sides with their huge outlay on transfers, comparative to other English clubs, to transform a second-tier side into one challenging for a Premiership title. By the time Sutton had the pen in his hand to sign for Blackburn, Dalglish had spent more than £25m in less than three years.

Jack Walker had bankrolled one of the most successful players and managers in British football to elevate the club he had supported as a boy into a force in the Premiership. Money was spent well and the plan was working. If not for an injury to Alan Shearer on Boxing Day in 1992, Blackburn might have competed with Manchester United all the way to the last day for the title. In the end, they finished fourth – a fantastic achievement for a side who had just returned to the top flight. The 1993/94 season was a different story. Disheartened but not defeated by the Keane transfer disappointment, Blackburn pushed United further than any team had the previous season. A victory at Ewood Park in April 1994 closed the gap to three points and gave Dalglish and his side hope, but the United juggernaut rolled on and victories up to the end of the season allowed them to pull clear and lift the title again.

The signing of Sutton was seen as a gamble by many. It was a huge fee for an English club at the time. It was well over a million pounds more than United had spent on Roy Keane for a player who, at age 21, had scored 35 league goals in his career and no less than 18 months earlier had been playing as a central defender. Despite Sutton's age and track record, the amount of clubs who coveted him was telling.

Once Sutton signed on the dotted line, his new strike partner, Shearer, immediately received a call from the Blackburn hierarchy while he was at Ewood Park with his adviser Tony Stephens. The Rovers chairman Robert Coar called a meeting with the pair and they discussed their new record signing. It was a frank and open conversation and Coar revealed that the new striker was getting a higher salary than Shearer, who earned around £8,000 a week. Shearer notes in his autobiography that he was told by the chairman he was Blackburn's 'best player and should always be treated as such. We would like to give you a pay increase.' Shearer dutifully accepted and was surprised that there was no requirement to extend his contract. Blackburn had a big-money strike force ready to deliver on their big promise. 'The SAS' was born.

At the opposite end of the transfer spectrum were those who had not enjoyed the spoils of the first Premier League seasons. The inflated prices were sometimes a challenge for clubs who did not have the big budgets found near the top of the table.

For the three promoted teams, the goal was to stay in the league. Due to the Premiership reducing from 22 to 20 teams, four teams were relegated at the end of the season. In turn, this meant that only two promoted teams joined the Premiership from the Endsleigh First Division. There was, as always, a lot at stake without a lot of money to go around. That was certainly true in the case of Crystal Palace and

Leicester City, but Nottingham Forest wanted to do things differently.

Frank Clark first arrived at the City Ground in 1975, not long after Brian Clough took his place in the dugout. Clark was already a veteran then, having signed on a free transfer, and made his final appearance for the club in the 1-0 victory over Malmö in the 1979 European Cup Final in Munich. Now, in the summer of 1993, he was back after Clough's retirement. Clough had mentioned Clark to the chairman Fred Reacher, who took heed of the great man's recommendation when another Forest legend, Martin O'Neill, dropped out of the running.

Once installed, Clark set about reshaping the Forest squad with funds from the sales of star players Roy Keane and Nigel Clough. He splashed out a huge £2.25m on the Southend striker Stan Collymore. A fee of that size for a player who had cost Southend only £150,000 was a gamble, but one that paid off immediately as the club got back into the Premiership at the first time of asking. That season, he also added reliable defender Colin Cooper and Norwegian midfielders Alf-Inge Haaland and Lars Bohinen. The transfers were a big success and Forest finished well clear of third-placed Millwall, securing their place in the Premiership for 1994/95.

Back in the big time, Forest's main transfer target was an attacker to complement Collymore. Bryan Roy of Foggia, who regularly sold star players to keep the club afloat, was identified as the man who fitted the bill. He did not come cheap. Roy was coming off the back of a strong season, finishing with 12 goals and a place among the top ten goalscorers in Serie A. Forest had to break their transfer record to bring the Dutchman to the City Ground. Having agreed personal terms with Roy before the start of the World Cup, a fee of £2.5m was negotiated and the attacker left sunny

Serie A for a new career in England. Forest looked like they had a strong squad and could compete in the top half.

Having been relegated from the Premier League on goal difference, Crystal Palace were able to hold on to most of their established first-team players. The only player they lost after relegation was Eddie McGoldrick to Arsenal. That left manager Alan Smith with the likes of Nigel Martyn, Gareth Southgate, Richard Shaw, John Salako and Chris Armstrong to form the nucleus of a side that ran away with the title. They ended up finishing seven points ahead of Forest and a massive 16 ahead of Millwall. Smith added a few bargain signings in the summer, including Darren Pitcher and the experienced Ray Wilkins, but his hopes of a top-six finish looked lofty.

The third promoted team were Leicester City, who finished fourth at the end of the season, but earned their promotion in the most dramatic way possible with victory in the play-off final. Steve Walsh was the final hero as Brian Little's Foxes overcame big-spending Derby County to end seven years outside the top flight. The chairman, Martin George, made funds available to Little, but attracting players to the club proved difficult. They did, however, manage to sign the highly rated Mark Draper from Notts County, but a lot more quality was needed to make the side competitive.

One player to watch at Leicester was Julian Joachim. A forward blessed with blistering pace, his form for England Under-18s in the victorious European Championship campaign marked him out as a talent. His international team-mates included the Manchester United trio Nicky Butt, Paul Scholes and Gary Neville, Sol Campbell of Spurs and Robbie Fowler of Liverpool. With Darren Caskey, Mark Tinkler and Chris Casper also featuring, England had a brilliant side who defeated nations who could boast young talents such as Olivier Dacourt, Clarence Seedorf, Patrick Kluivert and Dani.

wider comment on the state of the market, Hoddle suggested that any decent striker cost a minimum of £2m.

Another player hopeful of making Chelsea the top side in London was Scott Minto, who moved to Stamford Bridge from Charlton Athletic. The £775,000 fee was small change for a player wanted by Arsenal and rated as one of the top young prospects in English football. Minto was convinced the Hoddle effect separated his new side from Arsenal. First-team football was another carrot that the manager dangled in front of the young Minto, something George Graham would not have been able to do with such an established pro as Nigel Winterburn looming large in the left-back role.

Chelsea had another link to the Gunners that summer, with the arrival of David Rocastle from Manchester City for £1.25m. Having only moved to Maine Road in December 1993, it was a real shock to the player to move again. Since leaving Arsenal for Leeds in 1992, Chelsea were Rocastle's third club in as many seasons. He had come a long way from being a core part in the Arsenal side that won the title in the iconic game at Anfield in 1989. But, with a four-year deal in his pocket, a move back down to London and the prospect of European football, Chelsea seemed like a great place for Rocastle to rediscover his best form.

Staying in the capital, Tottenham Hotspur were about to have the kind of summer that became typical of Premiership teams. Not content with buying the best talent in England, such as Teddy Sheringham and Darren Anderton, Spurs brought in some of the best talent the continent had to offer. They certainly had their scouts' eyes firmly fixed on what was going on across the Atlantic, with the eventual signing of three World Cup stars.

Before all of that, there was the small matter of the legal wranglings that dogged the club and a very public war of words between owner and Amstrad supremo Alan Sugar and former manager and chief executive Terry Venables. Both parties were not the kind to go quietly and their battle was in the public eye for the next few years. Before the two of them could bring lawsuits against each other, Spurs were punished for financial irregularities under former owners.

The FA came down hard on the club and proposed a punishment in the form of a £600,000 fine, expulsion from the 1994/95 FA Cup and, most alarming of all, a 12-point penalty for the upcoming season. After surviving relegation by only three points, the future did not look bright. With the genuine prospect of relegation looming large, an appeal was quickly lodged. Starting on minus 12 points when the league was reducing in size was certainly not helpful.

Once Spurs' appeal was heard, with Sugar particularly vociferous in his opinions on the way the FA had acted, the punishment was reduced. Now, Spurs faced a six-point deduction, but the fine had been increased to a massive £1.5m, which at that point was the price of a Premiership footballer. Sugar was apoplectic. He felt like his club were being made an example of, claiming that at least 70 per cent of clubs in the top flight were involved in taking improper payments. This included his own ex-manager Venables, in the form of a cash exchange at a service station on the completion of Teddy Sheringham's transfer from Nottingham Forest to Spurs in the early stages of the 1992/93 season. A light shone on the dark side of football.

Still fighting his corner, Sugar spent money to ensure his team would not flounder at the wrong end of the table. First up was Ilie Dumitrescu, who was one of the best performers for Romania as they surprised many with their progress to the quarter-finals of the World Cup. Gheorghe Hagi and Florin Raducioiu were Romania's two other standout performers and, despite being linked with Spurs, signed for Barcelona and Espanyol respectively.

Dumitrescu was an intelligent player who provided Spurs with more creativity and attacking intent in the final third. The fee was £2.6m, which was a sensible investment for a 25-year-old player who had the potential to reach his peak at Spurs. It certainly added more depth to the squad and showed the club's ambition. Manager Ossie Ardiles tried as much as he could to add to his side to avoid a repeat of the relegation-threatened performances of the previous season.

Taking an almost exclusively international approach to scouting, Ardiles had dinner with Brazilian striker Muller in São Paulo with a view to him signing for Spurs. Another member of the Seleção to be linked with a move to White Hart Lane was powerful centre-back Marcio Santos, a consistent feature in the Bordeaux line-up and a member of the team of the tournament at USA 94. Santos was more interested in a move to Serie A and Fiorentina eventually signed the Brazilian.

Spurs' search for a star took them on a month-long pursuit of one of the most recognisable stars of European football, Jürgen Klinsmann, tracking him down to a boat in Monte Carlo. Although Germany had failed in their bid to reach a fourth consecutive World Cup Final, their No.18 scored five goals and was an integral part of their team; his tireless running and predatory instincts ensured he was a constant problem for opposition defenders. Transferring this to the fast-paced Premiership seemed to be a logical move, but there were detractors from his native Germany, with *Kicker* remarking that his 'displays in the World Cup were exceptional, but he is not such a good player as those observers in America assume'.

Klinsmann was bullish about his chances in England and did not let the doubters back home stop him from succeeding. This was a player who had excelled after moving to Italy in 1989 and he was not about to let his age or an unfamiliar style

Joachim was the breakout star for England. He had been compared to the Brazilian striker Romario during the tournament by his manager Little and *The Guardian*'s Patrick Barclay. He was touted, along with Caskey, as an England prospect for the 1998 World Cup. His star was rising and Leicester hoped he would translate his promise to the Premiership.

Some teams were destined to avoid a relegation battle but not have the quality to compete for a title. However, Premier League riches meant they could afford to be bold in the transfer market. Where the promoted teams were still conservative in their ambition, a group of clubs looked to make a splash and be more competitive.

One of the clubs happy to spend money were Chelsea. Glenn Hoddle had been brought in with the hope of moving the club out of mid-table mediocrity, but a finish three places below what they had managed the previous season hardly provided the fans with a sense of promise. Reaching the FA Cup Final against Manchester United helped. It meant that Hoddle's men competed in the UEFA Cup Winners' Cup, as United's league victory gave them a place in the European Cup.

Chelsea prioritised investing in a striker to lead the line. Paul Furlong was the man they chose and had the task of getting them goals. The deal cost Chelsea £2.3m, which was a huge sum of money for the club but roughly half the price of Chris Sutton. In 1991, Furlong had joined Coventry City for just £150,000 and his time in the First Division was far from a goalscoring success. A return of four goals in 37 league appearances hardly suggested a move back to the Premiership. But Hoddle was happy enough to break the club transfer record after seeing his exploits for a struggling Watford side. The Chelsea boss liked Furlong's 'good touch, pace and [the fact he] is genuinely two-footed'. Making a of football get in the way of his continued success. It was true that Spurs had paid a premium in wages for the German, somewhere between £8,000 and £15,000 a week. There were also suggestions of a £500,000 signing-on fee and a bonus of £1,000 per goal, which were subsequently denied, but probably the going rate in leagues like the wealthy Serie A.

Whatever the financials involved, signing Klinsmann was a coup for Spurs and they now boasted a forward line made up of the German, new signing Dumitrescu, England Under-21 star Nick Barmby and two signings from the summer of 1992 in Teddy Sheringham and Darren Anderton. With the ability to play such an attacking line-up, the odds on Spurs' fortunes for the season quickly shifted from possible relegation candidates to top-six contenders.

Shifting to the other half of North London, Arsenal plotted another assault on the top six and more. In transfer terms, the Gunners were firmly in the shadow of their local rivals throughout the summer. Ossie Ardiles's side splashed the cash on European stars while Arsenal lost the struggle to pry Chris Sutton from Norwich and were beaten to Scott Minto by Chelsea. The strict wage policy at the club proved to be a stumbling block during negotiations. It was also clear that George Graham and the club did not have the same pulling power as the likes of Manchester United and Blackburn.

Despite their difficulties in the transfer market, Arsenal already possessed quality at both ends of the pitch. Not only that, they had just finished fourth in the league and had defeated Parma 1-0 in the Cup Winners' Cup Final in May 1994. It looked, from the outside, like Arsenal were genuine title challengers who, alongside Blackburn, were most likely to cause the most problems for Manchester United. A defence that featured Lee Dixon, Winterburn, Tony Adams, Martin Keown and Steve Bould and an attack of Wright, Kevin

Campbell and Paul Merson suggested tinkering and not restructuring was required.

The star man who arrived at Arsenal was Stefan Schwarz. A fee of £1.75m was agreed with Benfica and, despite George Graham being on holiday, the deal was completed in early June, which meant there was no post-World Cup inflation of the fee. Schwarz was a creative midfielder who had starred against Arsenal in the 1991/92 European Cup for the Portuguese champions. He was the only player of note signed by Arsenal before the season got under way.

Another team looking to mount a title challenge were Newcastle United. Although not quite at the level of Blackburn in terms of spending power, Kevin Keegan had the backing of his board to build on his side's impressive showing back in the top flight. Powered by the phenomenal goalscoring exploits of Andy Cole and his strike partner Peter Beardsley, Keegan knew his side had a chance to challenge for Europe again and that he was in a position to build a squad which could compete at the top end of the table every season.

After scoring a league-high 82 goals, Keegan focused his transfer attention on his defence. Having already signed Darren Peacock for a sizeable fee from QPR a few months earlier, Keegan added £2.6m Philippe Albert to his central defensive rotation after being impressed by his performances for Belgium at the World Cup. Albert took the No.27 shirt to match his age on the day of signing – his birthday, no less. A defender who was as good on the ball as he was stopping it, Albert gave Keegan's side depth and an additional ball player to enhance the impressive attacking unit. Before Albert's arrival in August, defender Marc Hottiger had already signed from Sion for a fee of £600,000.

Liverpool stayed quiet in the transfer market over the summer months, despite being linked to numerous players, as had become the case for most teams. Instead, Roy Evans, taking a much different approach to managing Liverpool than his predecessor, Graeme Souness, wanted to wait until the right players became available. It was likely that defence was the area Evans wanted to improve, as the impressive duo of Robbie Fowler and Ian Rush provided more than enough firepower up front.

Off the pitch, an indiscretion involving nudity and a Budweiser bottle in Ayia Napa ended with Don Hutchison being transfer-listed. It followed a similar event the year before when he had used a particular area of his body to draw a group of girls' attention. There had been no interest in the young attacker as yet, but it looked like the writing was on the wall. Julian Dicks was another player that seemed to be on his way out of Anfield if the right deal came along.

After just missing out on European football in 1993/94, Leeds bolstered their squad with the expensive signing of midfielder Carlton Palmer from Sheffield Wednesday. At £2.6m, Palmer was the big-name summer signing in the vein of Brian Deane and David Rocastle in the preceding two seasons. Howard Wilkinson hoped that he could fit into the centre of defence and help his side remain towards the top of the table. The manager also added another player from his former club, with the addition of experienced defender Nigel Worthington. Unlike Palmer, Worthington had played under Wilkinson at Wednesday.

At the other end of the pitch, Wilkinson took a risk on South African striker Philomen (Phil) Masinga for a fee around £275,000. The tall striker was granted a work permit, which often proved difficult to acquire, and joined Leeds in pre-season training. Masinga's fellow countryman, highly rated defender Lucas Radebe, joined Leeds in another low-cost deal rumoured to be a similar fee to that paid for the big striker. With the league moving towards investing in overseas talent, Wilkinson had two relatively low-risk/high-reward signings.

Ron Atkinson was another who took a risk on unknown talent when he signed Nii Lamptey from PSV Eindhoven. The Ghanaian attacker added to Aston Villa's up-and-coming young talent, with the likes of Dwight Yorke and Ugo Ehiogu already in the first team. There was plenty of excitement around Lamptey, but the signing of striker John Fashanu was more about experience than potential. The strong and physical striker had fitted perfectly into Wimbledon's ethos for a number of years, but his £1.35m move to Villa meant an adjustment in playing style.

Having won the League Cup but finished in mid-table, Villa hoped for a good European campaign and better form in the league to take them towards challenging for the top six. The signings they had made, compared to some of their rivals, suggested that was a tough ask.

Transfer deals continued to be discussed and negotiated as clubs worked through their friendly schedules and prepared for the new season. Even without new signings, it was clear that Manchester United were favourites to regain their title. Last season's runners-up, Blackburn, were next on the list. On paper, the £5m capture of Sutton provided the perfect foil for Shearer, but becoming a second striker could be a challenge. Arsenal had a disastrous 1992/93 season that saw them finish tenth, their lowest position for ten years, but bounced back in 1993/94 with a fourth-place finish and victory in the Cup Winners' Cup.

The title winners were not decided in pre-season or before a ball was kicked. There were plenty of teams in the race, ready to challenge Manchester United at the top.

The Attackers (August)

THE CHARITY Shield is the season curtain-raiser. The importance of the game ends there. Despite some heavily fought contests in the 1970s, by 1994 the game had become much more sanitised and a glorified end to pre-season. If anything, it got fans excited that football was back.

The sun-bleached Wembley turf and fans decked in new shirts signified the start of the season, but not the competition that was about to develop between the two sides involved that August.

Leading the challengers on to the hallowed turf was Blackburn Rovers owner Jack Walker, while a smiling Kenny Dalglish, decked out in full training gear, looked on alongside his backroom team, Ray Harford and Tony Parkes. Alex Ferguson stood alongside Walker as he strode out of the tunnel with his double-winning side behind him. The classic Manchester United club suit, an iconic image of Ferguson's reign, was pride of place here as he aimed to expand the bulging trophy cabinet at Old Trafford.

Blackburn on the other hand were nowhere near the side that would take the field in their first league match of the season at The Dell. Injuries mounted up to such a desperate point that Dalglish, without £8.6m duo Chris Sutton and Alan Shearer, was forced to field a strike force of Ian Pearce and Stuart Ripley. Added to that, the core of his side was depleted by Mike Newell, Kevin Gallacher, Paul Warhurst and David Batty all being on the treatment table. Coming into the side were two new signings in Robbie Slater and Tony Gale.

Ferguson had some selection issues of his own. Due to their famous exploits across the Atlantic with the Republic of Ireland, Roy Keane and Denis Irwin had returned back to the club later than the rest of the squad. Rather than risking them both, Ferguson turned to Lee Sharpe to fill in for Irwin at left-back and Brian McClair took up Keane's position in central midfield, a role the veteran Scotsman had filled on many occasions. United included summer signing David May in their line-up. He made his debut against his former club, replacing Paul Parker, who had problems with his ankle.

The game itself did not live up to any pre-match promise as a meeting between two possible contenders for the title. Ferguson wrote a diary of the 1994/95 season titled *A Year in the Life* and he was quick to note that he did not believe that Blackburn were one of United's main challengers for the title. Instead, he preferred the football of Newcastle and believed the 'hunger for success up there' gave them more chance of winning the title than Dalglish's expensively assembled side. An Eric Cantona penalty, taken with trademark nonchalance, started the scoring for United halfway through the first half. Paul Ince's goal confirmed the win in the final ten minutes and the first piece of silverware for the season was heading to Manchester United. They hoped it was a sign of things to come.

One contentious area of the game, from the managers' point of view, was the liberal use of yellow cards. Charity Shield games are by no means a kickaround, but for Philip Don to dish out seven cards over the course of the game irked Ferguson and confused Dalglish. The Manchester United manager wrote in his diary that because the referee had 'booked three Blackburn players, he had to come down on us'. Dalglish was also suitably unimpressed with the referee, saying that 'when you come to a game with no malice in it and you end up with seven or eight bookings, it isn't good'. The new mandate for referees, handed down by FIFA, was that the best players deserved more protection and this meant more bookings for tackles from behind. The FA refereeing chief, Ken Ridden, was determined to see it implemented effectively and called all the managers in for a meeting a few days before the season started.

Football continued to evolve and FIFA wanted the game to be more creative, with more goals, which meant more eyes in front of television screens as part of lucrative deals that were being made across the game. The World Cup had much stricter laws imposed and, despite FIFA president Joao Havelange stating that anyone who tackled from behind would be sent off, a notion dispelled by the then general secretary Sepp Blatter, more goals resulted from the new directive. Transferring that to the Premiership was not easy. Traditional defenders, in the most complimentary sense, still operated at most clubs and needed to adapt their style of play to make sure they stayed on the pitch. Further to the tackle from behind, FIFA wanted to clamp down on the liberal use of arms and elbows when challenging for the ball. Reducing contact in these duels between defenders and strikers was supposed to favour defenders, who often received robust treatment from opposing No.9s.

On the opening day of the season, all eyes were on one of the stars of the World Cup – Jürgen Klinsmann. Ossie Ardiles took his Spurs side to Hillsborough for their first game after a summer of high-profile transfers and endless legal battles. Eyes certainly widened when the teams were announced as Ardiles opted for all-out attack. The side featured not only Klinsmann, but Teddy Sheringham, Nicky Barmby, Darren Anderton and Ilie Dumitrescu, a front five that rivalled anyone else's in the division. It was left to Colin Calderwood to mop up behind the 'Famous Five' and somehow provide protection for a back four that featured a young star in Sol Campbell alongside Stuart Nethercott at the heart of the defence, with Justin Edinburgh and David Kerslake as the full-backs.

Patterns of play can quickly emerge in games and this one was no different. Spurs attacked in waves, with players pouring forward at every opportunity. Sheffield Wednesday withstood a number of early attacks and, with Calderwood already becoming an isolated figure inside the first 15 minutes of the game, created chances themselves. Despite this somewhat kamikaze approach to the game, Spurs' attacking intent paid off and they were two goals in front by half-time.

Anderton created numerous chances for Spurs and he was a brilliant crosser. His trademark delivery into the box found Sheringham in space and, with a touch into the box, the striker fired a shot past Kevin Pressman and into the corner. Roles were reversed for the second as Anderton drove from midfield, played a neat one-two with Sheringham and found himself in the box. Striding clear of the Wednesday defenders, Spurs' No.9 stabbed the ball into the bottom corner. Ardiles's five-man attack was firing on all cylinders. The defence just needed to hold out.

Sheffield Wednesday had signed another USA 94 star, Dan Petrescu, who was not in the same stratosphere as Klinsmann, but was a core part of the Romania team and a goalscorer, too. He got his new side back in the game with a well-taken goal, a right-foot shot slotted into the bottom corner past Ian Walker. Just over ten minutes later, Wednesday were level, after great work in the box from Chris Bart-Williams resulted in Calderwood hammering the ball into his own net. Chaos reigned so far and Spurs only had one way to get themselves back into the game and that was to continue to attack. After a great goal by 20-year-old starlet Barmby, the stage was set for Klinsmann to make his mark on English football with a goal and an iconic celebration.

Now much more balanced in system and formation, Spurs continued to attack. A good passing move got the ball out wide to Anderton again. His perfect delivery found Klinsmann at the back post. The defenders misjudged the flight of the ball, but Klinsmann did not. He hung in the air and generated incredible power as his header flew into the top corner. Pressman had no chance.

The German peeled away to the touchline, euphoric after his first goal for Spurs. It was further proof of his ability as a fantastic striker and he also made a statement and addressed some of his critics. As he wheeled away from the box, his team-mates following a few strides behind, he turned to them, started to slow himself down and then threw himself head first on to the turf. See, Klinsmann *does* dive. Once he hit the ground, Sheringham did the same, diving, arms outstretched to hit the ground. And Calderwood. And Barmby. Klinsmann had already bonded with his team-mates and the fans. Critics started to love him, too.

Klinsmann's goal proved to be crucial, as his side conceded again, coming away with what was, on paper, a less than convincing win. Ardiles had to address the defensive set-up of his team, but the attacking flair and drive shown in this game gave hope that the points deduction would not have a detrimental effect on Spurs' prospects in the long term. After hovering above the relegation zone the previous season, they did not want a repeat and, with the addition of two star signings, the pressure was on.

The German striker tended to his wounds after the game thanks to a clash with Wednesday defender Des Walker. A nasty clash of heads meant Klinsmann required medical attention. He spoke to the *Daily Mirror* after the game, 'I'm fine – there are seven or eight stitches inside the mouth, but I'm very happy to have started with a victory, especially away from home.' Spurs had certainly set a marker down for others, not just with their transfer business, but their swashbuckling performance.

Sheffield Wednesday manager Trevor Francis told the same paper, 'When you have world class players like Klinsmann and Ilie Dumitrescu, you'd expect them to do well. But I was surprised when they announced a team with five attackers.' Francis's surprise at the attacking intent of the Spurs' line-up was much more obvious to his opposite number Ardiles, 'With that sort of talent, how could you leave any one of them out?' He had a point.

Roy Evans joined the Liverpool 'Boot Room' as a coach under Bill Shankly after an injury-hit career before serving under Bob Paisley, Joe Fagan, Kenny Dalglish and Graeme Souness. Not a bad way to learn how to be a football manager. His chance as manager came in January 1994 after the disastrous Souness reign came to an end. Liverpool finished eighth at the end of the season, their lowest position in more than 30 years. Evans had started to change the style of play and used a crop of up-and-coming youngsters in order to bring success back to Anfield.

The first game of the season for Liverpool was at Selhurst Park against Crystal Palace and their line-up clearly showed that this was a club in transition. Experienced players, who had cemented their legacy at the club with continued success, featured alongside academy graduates and young players with burgeoning reputations. On paper, Evans had a team with plenty of ability to challenge at the top end of the table, but consistency was key. If young striker Robbie Fowler continued to develop his partnership with Ian Rush, Liverpool had a big chance of success.

On the pitch, the performance was vintage Liverpool. Sometimes, everything clicks for a football team and, on that day, it did for Evans's team. Fantastic performances from Steve McManaman, Rush and Fowler blew Palace away. Playing with freedom, McManaman was a joy to watch. His gangly frame moved so smoothly with the ball at his feet. The goal he scored encapsulated the youngster's immense talent.

Evans decided that McManaman needed a freer role in the side, so allowed him to drift during the game. Dribbling was his elite skill and he used it to devastating effect.

The goal against Palace, Liverpool's second after a Jan Molby spot kick, summed it up. Ball at his feet, McManaman sprinted towards the Palace goal, then expertly slowed down, the ball still under total control. He faced up the defender, who was terrified of making the wrong challenge. With a touch inside, he fired his shot past Nigel Martyn and into the net. A superb goal to put Liverpool 2-0 up and on course for an opening-day victory.

Fowler's goal put Liverpool three up at half-time, but they were not done. The goals flowed in the second half and, after Chris Armstrong pulled one back for the home side, Ian Rush found the net twice, either side of another Steve McManaman goal. A clear statement of intent for the season ahead, Liverpool's 6-1 win put down a marker. For Palace, their return to the Premier League was not going to be easy. After the game, Eagles manager Alan Smith lamented the fact that his side's shots were continually repelled by David James. The other sour note for Smith was an injury to new signing Ray Wilkins, who broke his foot.

The two seven-goal games were the most eye-catching results of the day. There were home wins and clean sheets for Manchester United and Arsenal, two of the early-season favourites. Newly promoted Nottingham Forest travelled to

Ipswich full of confidence and Bryan Roy's debut goal was enough to see them victorious.

Chelsea's expensive new striker Paul Furlong also found the net on his debut as he scored the second goal in a 2-0 win at Stamford Bridge against Norwich. Four draws completed the remaining fixtures, with Shearer scoring an equaliser for Blackburn against his former side Southampton. Sutton provided the assist to christen the new strike partnership.

Finally, the first *Super Sunday* of the season featured newly promoted Leicester against Kevin Keegan's Newcastle. In the starting XI for the first time for the Magpies were Philippe Albert and Marc Hottiger with Foxes manager Brian Little giving debuts to Nicky Mohan and Mark Draper.

Andy Cole and Peter Beardsley wasted no time in renewing their prolific partnership from the previous season with a goal each just before the hour mark. Twenty-year-old Robbie Elliott scored the third to bring Leicester back down to earth. Newcastle showed promise in 1993/94 and wanted to continue that with another positive campaign. Keegan had strengthened the defence and, with a formidable strike force, was looking to close the gap on Blackburn and Manchester United.

A full round of fixtures completed in two days meant that the next round of games began immediately. Sky Sports' *Monday Night Football* started the second set of matches, with Manchester United travelling to the City Ground to face Nottingham Forest just 48 hours after the two clubs' opening games. Such a quick turnaround was not unusual, but one that clubs preferred to avoid.

Like Newcastle a season earlier, Forest hoped to prove they could excel in the top flight after a season away. After relegation in 1993, Brian Clough left the club he had built into European champions and he was replaced by ex-Forest full-back Frank Clark. He had a short spell at Sunderland

and took the reins at Leyton Orient, where he stayed until Forest came calling after the double blow of relegation and Clough's departure. Clark galvanised the club and, with some additions, formed a side that finished second to Crystal Palace and earned an instant return to the Premier League. The star of the side was Stan Collymore, who hit the back of the net 25 times in the promotion season after signing from Southend. Thanks to a clause in the deal, his former club netted £250,000 for his goalscoring exploits. The next task was to prove himself in the Premier League.

Manchester United were the reigning champions and their routine opening-day win at home to Queens Park Rangers did not shine any light on their potential for the new season. Eric Cantona was suspended, so the experienced duo of Mark Hughes and Brian McClair led the line with a talented midfield of Lee Sharpe, Paul Ince, Ryan Giggs and Andrei Kanchelskis behind them. Roy Keane started on the bench against his former club as he made his way back to fitness after his World Cup exertions.

United, wearing the iconic black away kit that launched a year earlier, took the lead after 22 minutes thanks to an excellent volley at the back post from Kanchelskis after Sharpe's cross found him in acres of space.

It wasn't long before Forest threatened United's goal, with a long-range effort from Collymore testing Peter Schmeichel. It was a warning for United. Minutes later, Collymore found himself in space again. This time, he had United defenders in front of him but, after he managed to wriggle away, he powered towards goal with Gary Pallister facing him down. It didn't matter, as he let fly from the edge of United's box and beat Schmeichel at his near post.

Both sides created chances, with Forest's Mark Crossley and Schmeichel able to showcase their ability with some great goalkeeping. The Dane, in particular, showed off his distinctive technique in one-on-one situations. The almost starfish-like shape he took up to double the size of his body stopped both Bryan Roy and Collymore, who showed signs of developing a strong partnership. In the end, the goalkeepers kept the scores level and, at this stage of the season, both sides were happy with a draw.

Collymore featured on the back pages of the daily newspapers the day after he announced himself to the league. 'Colly wobbles Fergie' was the headline from the *Daily Mirror* but the local paper, the *Nottingham Evening Post*, anointed the striker 'King Stan'. Alex Ferguson praised the 23-year-old striker and insisted that even though Klinsmann was a world-class player, 'He can't give us any more problems than Collymore did last night.' The Manchester United manager broke down the impressive facets of the Forest number 10's game: his pace, powerful running one-on-one and his love for a shot off either foot.

Tuesday, 23 August featured three more games. Blackburn beat Leicester at Ewood Park with the Foxes conceding another three goals, this time without reply. A familiar pattern was starting to form for Dalglish's Rovers, too. In the opening game at The Dell, Blackburn's 1-1 draw with Southampton featured a Shearer goal assisted by Sutton. This time, Blackburn's £5m striker got on the scoresheet, assisted by his strike partner. Sutton then set up defender Henning Berg for the second before Shearer got in on the act to make it 3-0. A good start at home for the title contenders.

In the other two games, a late Noel Whelan goal for Leeds inflicted defeat on Arsenal at Elland Road, while Wimbledon and Ipswich played out a 1-1 draw.

The remaining four games featured four home wins and two draws. Newcastle and Manchester City made quick work of Coventry and West Ham, recording 4-0 and 3-0 wins respectively. Newcastle were playing without Beardsley in attack, but that did not stop them scoring three goals within the first 35 minutes. Rob Lee put in a classy performance in central midfield, full of energy and running from deep, finding the back of the net twice.

City had been taken apart at Highbury, but Brian Horton's side impressed against the Hammers with goals from Paul Walsh, Peter Beagrie and Uwe Rösler. Beagrie was the star, having a hand in all three goals to leave West Ham with one point and no goals from their first two games. Newcastle had a perfect six points from their opening two games with seven goals scored and only one conceded.

QPR recorded a home win against Sheffield Wednesday with the impressive 19-year-old Kevin Gallen getting on the scoresheet with the winner and his first league goal. Having made his league debut at Old Trafford, Gallen showed the QPR fans what he was capable of at professional level after breaking Jimmy Greaves's long-standing goalscoring records at youth level. A striker at the other end of his career, Jürgen Klinsmann, bagged two goals at home to Everton to give Spurs their second consecutive win of the season. Nick Barmby gave another excellent performance as Ardiles's attacking quintet proved too much for Mike Walker's Everton.

A trademark long-range Matt Le Tissier effort in the last minute gave Southampton something to cheer about against Aston Villa. It was an almost nonchalant effort curled past Mark Bosnich in the Villa goal. Le Tissier barely seemed to exert any effort with the strike. A simple touch out of his feet and a swing of the right boot, he sent the ball high, looping over Bosnich, who stood no chance. It was a good point for the Saints, who had to travel to Newcastle and host Liverpool in their next two. The aim for Alan Ball and his team was to avoid a relegation fight at all costs.

The theme of summer spending in the Premiership was a focus on stars who had performed well during the World

Cup. Everton decided that they were going to get in on the act. After the early season capture of non-World Cup star Vinny Samways, Nigeria's Daniel Amokachi was the man manager Walker turned to. The striker had starred for Club Brugge after his breakthrough in the 1990 African Nations Cup and also scored the first goal in the new Champions League group stage in 1992/93.

After rejecting overtures from Spurs and reported interest from Juventus and Ajax, Brugge's price for Amokachi was £3m, which was a new record transfer for Everton, and Walker hoped that it would turn around his team's fortunes after only a last-day victory against Wimbledon kept them in the Premiership. Further links to Bulgarian striker Emil Kostadinov of Porto, Mark Hateley of Rangers and Jan Age Fjortoft of Swindon emerged in *The Independent*, clearly showing that Walker was interested in finding a big man to partner the pacy Amokachi. Once the Nigerian agreed personal terms, the plan was to unveil the striker in front of the home fans against Nottingham Forest, days after a visit to Maine Road.

The previous season, Brian Horton had taken over Manchester City after a terrible start under Peter Reid. After weathering the storm of losing David White mid-season, Horton set about building a side to finish higher in the table. In came Nicky Summerbee to add pace out wide and provide the ammunition for the attacking talents of Uwe Rösler, Niall Quinn and Paul Walsh. Everton were hit with the full force of City's attack as Horton's side, fresh from a 3-0 victory at home to West Ham, put four past the hapless Toffees. The 'cut-price Klinsmann', as Rösler was dubbed by Dave Hadfield in *The Independent*, scored twice, while his strike partner Walsh scored the other two. Luckily, Amokachi was not able to watch his new side be torn apart by City. Walker knew all too well that the performance was not good enough.

Elsewhere in the league, Newcastle continued to steamroller allcomers with an emphatic 5-1 victory against the hapless Southampton. Keegan loved his team to attack and the Geordies did just that. An unlikely brace from Steve Watson put Newcastle 2-0 up before a routine brace from Andy Cole extended the lead to 4-0 after 70 minutes. Rob Lee found the net again, coming off the back of his own brace in the home win over Coventry City three days early. Watson also had three goals for the season, with Cole ahead of them both on four. 'The Entertainers' truly was the correct moniker for a side who had scored 12 goals in their opening three games.

Blackburn kept up their good start to the season with a 4-0 home win over Coventry that featured a Sutton hat-trick. Coventry had held off Blackburn for an hour until Micky Quinn's two quickfire yellow cards meant he received his marching orders after 65 minutes. Two minutes later, Blackburn were 1-0 up and didn't look back. Jason Wilcox added a goal between Sutton's second and third as Kenny Dalglish's £5m man quickly silenced any doubters about the transfer fee.

The striker said as much in his post-match comments. Not one to shy away from the criticism, Sutton asked for patience, 'I feel I should be judged at the end of the season and not the start.' Looking at his performance against Coventry, the start was pretty good too. The league's new record signing also paid tribute to his strike partner Alan Shearer, 'Everyone's watching him and that allows me more room. I can learn a lot from a player of his class.'

In his account of the season, Shearer referred to Sutton's predicament and stated that 'the only way for a striker to silence criticism – score goals.' Shearer knew all about the pressure of a record transfer fee and despite his new partners quiet and reserved personality, he acknowledged, even after a few games, that Sutton was 'a great lad and a good partner to play alongside.'

Leeds raced into a 2-0 lead after just 20 minutes against Chelsea. New signing Phil Masigna scored his first goal in English football inside five minutes, followed by a brilliantly taken overhead kick in the six-yard box from 19-year-old starlet Noel Whelan. Howard Wilkinson's team looked on track for a second consecutive win at home against London opposition. Chelsea had other ideas.Before the break, a clumsy Carlton Palmer challenge on John Spencer gave Dennis Wise the opportunity to score a well-taken penalty that found the top corner. In the second half, Spencer notched the equaliser after John Lukic failed to keep out a routine free-kick. Not content with a draw, Chelsea continued to push forward.

There were chances aplenty. Spencer hit the post, Masinga hit the bar and Frank Sinclair kept out a David White effort. Minutes before the end, the deciding goal came. A Spencer volley looked too straight to trouble Lukic, but the Leeds goalkeeper got his footing wrong and almost toppled over the ball. His hands did not hold firm as the powerful shot came in, so the ball wriggled through his body and over the line. Euphoria for Spencer, but total disappointment for Leeds.

Around the rest of the league, Norwich and Nottingham Forest recorded 1-0 wins at home, while Manchester United and Sheffield Wednesday repeated the feat on away soil. Ipswich beat QPR 2-1 at Loftus Road and the only draw came at Villa Park where an 87th-minute Gareth Southgate goal rescued a point and secured a second consecutive draw.

The Sky Sports cameras arrived at Anfield on Sunday, 28 August to watch Liverpool take on Arsenal and see a different side to the famous Kop. The end of the 1993/94 season saw the end of The Kop terrace as recommendations from the Taylor Report were implemented.

Fans on probably the most famous end in world football sang The Beatles' songs as they took over Europe, roared and rocked with the incredible rise to success in the 1970s and were wowed by incredible football during the 1980s. The Kop was the heartbeat of Anfield. As games ebbed and flowed, so did the crowd. Young children were swept up off their feet as the excitement rippled through the terrace. And there was nothing more powerful than seeing flags held aloft as 'You'll Never Walk Alone' echoed around the famous ground.

In the build up to the game on Sky Sports, Richard Keys described The Kop as 'the most famous football terrace in the world...it was a daunting sight for visitors when it was full, awesome when it was empty. But it is gone now, to be replaced by a brand new stand. The seats in the front will be used for the first time today'.Robbie Fowler was the new local lad in the Liverpool side. Born in Toxteth in 1975, Fowler was a natural goalscorer. His passage through youth football and into the Liverpool first team was brisk and memorable. Introduced into the squad by Graeme Souness, Fowler made his debut at Fulham, scoring in a 3-1 win in the League Cup. The second leg announced Fowler to the rest of English football when he scored five goals at Anfield in only his fourth appearance in professional football. The Kop had a new hero.

Arsenal were more concerned with defence than attack. Any combination of Dixon, Winterburn, Adams, Bould and Keown in front of David Seaman provided the opposition with the task of breaking down one of the most organised defences in Europe. In the previous season, Arsenal had conceded a mere 28 league goals across a 42-game season. It made what happened at Anfield all the more remarkable.

The summer sunshine lit up the Anfield turf the way only August football can. Liverpool were in their adidas shirts, three stripes on either side of the body. Arsenal were in blue, a kit designed by Nike, who were pushing the boundaries of kit design across Europe, led by the innovative and inventive Drake Ramberg. It was an early season clash between two sides who had fought for the title years earlier.

Goalless in the first 25 minutes, Liverpool won a free kick on the right-hand side of the pitch. Defenders came up from the back and Rush and Fowler occupied the space in the centre of the box. As the free kick was lofted towards the penalty spot, Rush challenged for the ball in the air, a flailing Martin Keown launched himself at the Liverpool striker and the ball, getting neither. As Keown lay strewn on the ground, a slight touch from Rush wrong-footed Dixon and the ball bounced down to Fowler. The young striker, eight yards out, struck the ball with the inside of his foot past Seaman, who had anticipated a shot in the other direction. Liverpool and Fowler were one up.

The next goal arrived two minutes later. Steve McManaman picked up the ball in his own half and drove at the Arsenal defence. Panic set in. Defenders backed off as Liverpool's No.17 charged towards them. Fowler made his move. Drifting from right to left, he created space for McManaman to attack and got himself in a position on the edge of Arsenal's box. Dixon was bamboozled. Track McManaman and leave Fowler? Leave McManaman and track Fowler? An impossible choice.

In space, and free of Dixon, Fowler waited for the pass to arrive. Perfectly weighted by McManaman, the ball passed across the 19-year-old's body and on to his left foot. Those Puma King boots knew how to do only one thing. Score. With one strike of his left boot, no backlift, the ball caressed the turf as it beat Seaman again. Two goals in two minutes.

At this point, everything went right for the men in red. Anfield is electric. The atmosphere at a football ground when the goals come quickly is a sight to behold. The goals lifted the mood in an instant and when John Barnes floated the ball over the Arsenal defence into the path of Fowler, Anfield knew what was coming.

The scruffiest of the three goals? Maybe. But Fowler didn't care. For once, Arsenal's defence were able to stop Fowler, but only momentarily. His first shot was smothered by a collision between Keown and Seaman. While the two Arsenal players looked for the ball, Fowler stayed on his feet, darted towards the ball and, with a quick touch from his left to keep the ball in play, fired the ball into the empty net with his right, avoiding the desperate attempt by Winterburn to keep it out.

The reaction of Tyler and Gray to the attack as it built and ended was fitting for such a special moment. Tyler's voice lifted as the pass came in: 'Barnes!' The Anfield crowd noise surged in expectation. 'He's away again, is this going to be the hat-trick?' as Fowler burst through. That commentator's pause played perfectly amongst the scramble on the edge of the six-yard box, followed by a euphoric: 'It could still be, IT IS!' The Anfield noise filled the silence in the commentary booth, Tyler and Gray amazed by what they had seen; a hat-trick in the space of four minutes and 33 seconds.

It was an incredible day for Fowler, who acknowledged his efforts after the game to Sky Sports, noting Arsenal's usual solidity at the back and what an achievement it was for him to score three. In classic goalscorer's fashion, he added: 'It also makes up for the miss against them last year.' His simple explanation of his feat: 'I just erm…had three chances and three of them seemed to go in.' An economical use of words to go with his economical prowess in front of goal.

Newspaper loved a souvenir special after a great sporting moment. The *Liverpool Echo* did not pass up the opportunity to showcase the images they captured of Fowler's big day. An image of 'Fowler 23' arm in the air, having scored his second of the game. They even went as far as creating a detailed diagram of how Fowler completed his incredible feat.

To add colour to the images and match reports, the striker himself shared his thoughts. Talk of a difficult second season for the young striker was not far from the lips of many football pundits and those around the game. They had seen players explode into life, only to fade away before their potential had been realised. Fowler thought differently. 'Everyone has been saying the second season is harder than the first, so I went out there to prove to people that I can still do it.' A calm head on young shoulders. He did not shy away from praising his team-mates either with a nod towards the experience of Rush and Barnes, who created space and occupied defenders so the quality of young players like Redknapp and McManaman could take advantage.

After all the excitement at Anfield, *Monday Night Football* was somewhat of an anti-climax as an early Dwight Yorke header, thanks to hapless Coventry defending, gave Aston Villa their first league win of the season at the fourth attempt. Three draws kept Atkinson's side unbeaten, but far from in form.

The battle at the top of the goalscoring charts continued. Klinsmann netted another two at Portman Road in a 3-1 win for Ossie Ardiles's expansive side. Spurs' attacking five shone, with Ilie Dumitrescu getting his first of the season, assisted by that man Klinsmann. A late Chris Kiwomya goal prevented Spurs from recording their first clean sheet of the season, but Ardiles was not too concerned about that. Nottingham Forest and Leeds United also recorded away wins in this round of midweek fixtures, beating Everton and Crystal Palace respectively.

Wednesday, 31 August rounded out the league fixtures for the month before Terry Venables took his England side into the international break with a friendly against the USA to begin preparations for Euro 96.

Wins for Liverpool and Chelsea put them fourth and fifth in the league table. Another goal for Fowler and one for Barnes at The Dell meant Liverpool had a perfect record, as did Chelsea, with Gavin Peacock and Dennis Wise finding the net before Michel Vonk's own goal completed a disappointing night for Brian Horton's Manchester City. Despite that defeat, City were in ninth place in the table. Draws for the rest meant the league table was complete for August.

Kevin Keegan's side were the clear pacesetters at this early stage, not just because of their four wins, but the impressive 15 goals scored while conceding only three. Champions Manchester United side earned ten points after three wins and a draw. They were buoyed by the return of Eric Cantona from suspension and he scored the opening goal in the 3-0 win over Wimbledon.

The surprise package were Nottingham Forest. Eye-catching performances from Collymore and Roy up front meant they were able to match Manchester United on ten points. They had, briefly, led the league table after their 2-1 win at Goodison Park. Liverpool, Chelsea and Spurs rounded out the top six, with all three of those teams on nine points, Spurs having played one game more.

At the wrong end of the table, Everton, Leicester, West Ham and Coventry could only muster a single point from their opening four games. Not scoring enough and conceding too many was the story for those teams so far. Reinforcements were needed for all of these sides, with Everton stealing a march on their rivals with the signing of Amokachi.

Pos	Team	P	W	D	L	F	A	GD	Pts
1	Newcastle United	4	4	0	0	15	3	+12	12
2	Manchester United	4	3	1	0	7	1	+6	10
3	Nottingham Forest	4	3	1	0	5	2	+3	10
4	Liverpool	3	3	0	0	11	1	+10	9
5	Chelsea	3	3	0	0	8	2	+6	9
6	Tottenham Hotspur	4	3	0	1	9	6	+3	9
7	Blackburn Rovers	4	2	2	0	8	1	+7	8
8	Leeds United	4	2	1	1	5	4	+1	7
9	Manchester City	4	2	0	2	7	6	+1	6
10	Aston Villa	4	1	3	0	5	4	+1	6
11	Norwich City	4	1	2	1	1	2	-1	5
12	Sheffield Wednesday	4	1	1	2	6	7	-1	4
13	Arsenal	4	1	1	2	3	4	-1	4
14	Queens Park Rangers	4	1	1	2	5	7	-2	4
15	Ipswich Town	4	1	1	2	4	6	-2	4
16	Wimbledon	4	0	2	2	2	6	-4	2
17	Crystal Palace	4	0	2	2	3	9	-6	2
18	Southampton	4	0	2	2	3	9	-6	2
19	Everton	4	0	1	3	4	10	-6	1
20	Leicester City	4	0	1	3	2	8	-6	1
21	West Ham United	4	0	1	3	1	7	-6	1
22	Coventry City	4	0	1	3	1	10	-9	1

The Challengers (September)

A ONE-GAME international break spanned the first ten days of September. Clubs kept themselves busy with a flurry of transfer activity to act quickly after the early games of the season. Teams at both ends of the table decided that it was time to splash more cash and worked quickly to fill problem places in their sides.

Liverpool wasted no time in adding two new defenders to their squad. Phil Babb signed at the end of August after a transfer saga that had dragged on since the middle of the month. It seemed that a deal had been agreed with Coventry so that Babb would be a Liverpool player for the opening game of the season at Selhurst Park. It was not to be, as the saga dragged on and on.

The day before the transfer was confirmed, *The Independent* reported that the situation around the transfer was unresolved. Coventry manager Phil Neal was quoted as saying: 'That story is getting to be like Emmerdale Farm.' Transfers often resemble long-running soap operas and this one was no different. Babb was left confused by the situation but, whatever the issues, they were finally resolved and the defender headed for Anfield. Prices were rising in English football and the £3.6m Liverpool paid for their new No.6 was a club record and a British record fee for a defender.

Alex Ferguson was always a busy man, but he was particularly busy in early September. First, he had a chat with Wimbledon manager Joe Kinnear, after his side beat the 'Crazy Gang' 3-0, about getting involved in the John Scales transfer, with the player about to sign for Liverpool. In his book *A Year in the Life: A Manager's Diary,* Ferguson writes that he had previously enquired about Scales but had been knocked back. The fact he had signed David May in the summer also forced him to opt out on Scales. Kinnear also asked Ferguson if he could recommend a centre-back, so he mentioned Alan Reeves from Rochdale.

With Manchester United out of the picture, Roy Evans completed the deal for Scales. He cost £3.5m, only a fraction under Babb's price and a sizeable investment for Liverpool. For the selling club, it was a massive return on an initial cost of only £50,000 from Bristol Rovers in 1987. He was the second high profile sale by Wimbledon that summer after John Fashanu left for Aston Villa. Competing in the top half of the table came at a price for Wimbledon and that was seeing your best players picked off by the league's richest clubs.

Next on Ferguson's 'to do' list was addressing the issue around his strikeforce once chairman Martin Edwards told him that Coventry had made an inquiry about Dion Dublin. Ferguson was not convinced he should leave, stating: 'We really can't let him go, we might need him for Europe.' The main issue Ferguson had was that he was only able to field three players who were not English in European competition. This meant he had to pick between Peter Schmeichel, Denis Irwin, Roy Keane, Andrei Kanchelskis, Ryan Giggs, Brian McClair, Eric Cantona and Mark Hughes. An impossible task for any manager. Dublin was English, so that was one reason to keep him around. Another Englishman at Old Trafford was a young player named Paul Scholes. He was on Ferguson's radar as someone who was already around the first team and could possibly be part of a push for the Premiership, but not Europe.

As at most football clubs, there was a list of targets to replace players and, if someone bid close to £2m, Ferguson was going to be happy to let Dublin leave. Ferguson had already identified Teddy Sheringham as a possible alternative but, at £5m or a £4m swap deal that included Mark Hughes, Ferguson was not convinced. The player he really wanted was Andy Cole, but Kevin Keegan laughed at the prospect of losing his star man to one of his biggest rivals.

Before Liverpool had resolved their defensive issues, they let someone leave to add some funds to the Anfield coffers. West Ham decided that Don Hutchison's past indiscretions did not mean he could not be a valuable player in their squad, so they signed the promising attacker. Hutchison was reflective about the incidents when he gave *Match* magazine an interview after his transfer, saying that 'everyone makes mistakes … [and] the important thing is to learn from your mistakes'. He was positive about his experiences with the management at Anfield, too, saying that 'the club and the manager stuck by me and I really appreciated that'. It probably was not the memory Hutchison wanted to leave behind at Anfield, but he got a fresh start at West Ham to prove he could do it on the pitch.

Across Stanley Park, Everton found themselves with a player they didn't want in Tony Cottee. The striker had spent six years at Goodison Park, scoring almost 100 goals. New signing Daniel Amokachi was set to be the main focal point of Mike Walker's attack, so it was time for 29-year-old Cottee to move on. Just like Hutchison, Cottee moved to West Ham, the club where he had made his name. Always one to make a deal, Redknapp allowed David Burrows to swap places with Cottee. The defender had not always been happy in the capital and the move to Merseyside suited him and his family. Everton paid a small fee to balance the valuations of both players.

Ferguson, on his return to Heathrow from a short break to Rome with his wife Cathy during which he took in Roma v Foggia and a first-team training session, Ferguson checked his mobile and received a message from Martin Edwards, who he immediately called. Coventry had offered £2m for Dublin. Ferguson notes that he had an 'uneasy feeling' about the situation and, despite 'a lot of confidence in Scholes', letting go of an established player was not an easy decision.

England at Wembley in midweek provided a short break in league action. The United States had gone football mad for a summer at the World Cup, with the cavernous stadiums and colourful fans providing the backdrop for a great tournament. For Terry Venables, it gave him the opportunity to employ his much-vaunted 'Christmas tree' formation which had enraptured the football press.

The game itself was a classic friendly two years away from a tournament under a new manager with nothing really at stake. The USA did not really show why they had achieved such support in the World Cup, producing a limited performance. England used an experimental line-up, with defenders Rob Jones, Graeme Le Saux and Barry Venison, called up for the injured Paul Ince, boasting a combined total of only ten caps at this point. Teddy Sheringham's good form and compatibility with Alan Shearer got him a place in the starting line-up. Blackburn's No.9 was undoubtedly the star of the night with the two goals that gave England a convincing victory to nil.

Spurs decided that only the best was good enough for them and, unconcerned with where their best players came from, decided that a Romanian from the Dutch league would resolve some of the defensive frailties that came with playing five forwards. Signing Gheorghe Popescu for £2.9m took Alan Sugar's spending to £7.6m on three foreign stars. Klinsmann was already making waves and Dumitrescu was showing promise in attack. Now, bringing in Popescu, a versatile defender or midfielder, added further quality. The pressure was on manager Ossie Ardiles to deliver and, with nine points from the opening four games, the potential was there.

Further north, Dion Dublin was back from Coventry without a deal in place as Alex Ferguson pondered whether he was doing the right thing in selling his striker. To add further complexity to the deal, Paul Scholes had been injured in a reserve game. It was not looking good for Coventry, who desperately needed a new striker, not just because of their league position, but because Micky Quinn had managed to get himself a four-match ban for a sending-off. After meeting Ferguson at The Cliff to talk through the deal, Dublin eventually left Manchester United for the agreed £2m before the Premiership started up again.

Joe Kinnear was also doing some business that day and, clearly influenced by his discussion with Ferguson and boosted by the funds from the sale of John Scales, he dipped into the market within days of selling his best defender. The new central defender Kinnear had convinced to join the 'Crazy Gang' cost just £200,000. His name? Alan Reeves.

Relative sanity returned amidst all the transfer dealings of the last ten days with a full set of weekend fixtures including *Super Sunday* and *Monday Night Football* on Sky Sports. The intense midweek schedule of the August fixture list was replaced by the introduction of European competition for English sides and the Coca-Cola League Cup second-round games.

St James' Park hosted two teams with 100 per cent records to start the season; Newcastle and Chelsea. Before the game, Keegan was presented with the Carling manager of the month award, which he accepted alongside club physio Derek Wright, who had been at the club for ten years and was now on to his seventh manager. A nice gesture from Keegan, who was building a club with a fervent fan base and close links with the city.

Keegan was still without forward Peter Beardsley, who had a broken cheekbone, but having Andy Cole fit and firing was all he needed to spearhead his potent attack. Pavel Srníček was suspended, so Mike Hooper started in goal with 42-year-old John Burridge, the much-travelled goalkeeper-coach who had been first choice keeper under Keegan's predecessor, Jim Smith, on the bench.

The Geordies had a habit of scoring early goals at home and this game was no different. Putting opposing defences under immense pressure in the early stages of matches was key to Keegan's style of play. The teams exchanged goals in the first half to go in at the interval level at 2-2. Ex-Newcastle player Gavin Peacock found the net for Chelsea before Ruel Fox reacted quickest to Rob Lee's penalty miss and put Newcastle back in front. Before half-time, Chelsea equalised, Paul Furlong's looping header creeping over Hooper despite his best efforts.

As the teams came out for the second half, Newcastle had one thing on their mind; goals. Steve Watson hit the bar and Newcastle upped the pressure. Rob Lee slotted in the third into the corner of the net with his left foot. It was the midfielder's fifth goal in as many games.

Now it was the turn of Newcastle's No.9 to score. Turning provider, Lee collected Cole's initial pass and the striker headed for the box. Getting the ball tangled under his feet, Cole saw the opening was not in the middle of the goal. With a slight dummy to give him some extra space, Cole darted right. Lee pirouetted and slid the ball through to Cole. Now the striker had Chelsea's defence where he wanted them; he was in on goal with the keeper to beat. With the ball between defender and goalkeeper, Cole lashed it with his right foot into the bottom corner. That made it 4-2 to Newcastle and Cole took the lead over Lee in the goalscoring charts. Another win for Keegan's men. The defeat ended Chelsea's 100 per cent record and to make matters worse, Dennis Wise was sent off 20 minutes before the final whistle.

Liverpool were the only other side with a 100 per cent record and they welcomed West Ham to Anfield in the sunshine. The new Kop structure allowed the sun to cast shadows that showcased the new structure being erected. West Ham defended their goal as best they could, with the crossbar and Ludek Miklosko stopping Liverpool scoring. New signing Tony Cottee's second debut didn't go to plan, despite his side eventually earning their second point of the season with a 0-0 draw. His sending-off for violent conduct for a lunge on Rob Jones overshadowed a good away point and the end of Liverpool's perfect record.

Blackburn, Nottingham Forest and Aston Villa all came into the Saturday schedule with unbeaten records. All three of them proved to be too much for their opponents. Aston Villa made hard work of beating Ipswich, but a goal and assist for Dean Saunders gave them a 2-0 win. Nottingham Forest hit four past a woeful Sheffield Wednesday, with Bryan Roy scoring his second goal of the season to finish the scoring in the 82nd minute.

Alan Shearer inspired his side to record a 3-0 home victory over Everton. England's No.9 scored twice and made another to take his tally to four for the season and equal his striker partner Chris Sutton's total. 'The SAS' had scored eight of Blackburn's 11 goals to start the season and showed no signs of slowing down. Colin Hendry, the outstanding defender, marshalled Daniel Amokachi expertly to ensure the Nigerian had no chance of getting a goal on his Everton debut.

Manchester United and Leeds United had been the two main challengers for the title in 1991/92. Leeds won the battle but now Manchester United were winning the war. They faced off on *Super Sunday*. It was the type of big match-up made for Sky Sports' bombastic coverage of the Premiership.

Leeds started the game at a fierce pace. Howard Wilkinson's side pressed United on the ball and created chances. It was not long before they scored the first goal of the game, thanks to the feet of David Weatherall. Not necessarily the man you'd want to have the ball at his feet. Pandemonium at Elland Road as fans vaulted over the advertising boards and on to the pitch in celebration.

The second half started much like the first. Leeds pressed Manchester United and searched for another goal. Another Leeds attack found Noel Whelan stuck in a dead end and marshalled by Andrei Kanchelskis. The Leeds forward dribbled his way into the box and, a yard from the byline, cut the ball back into the six-yard box. Ready and waiting was substitute Brian Deane, who stabbed his shot up and over Peter Schmeichel and Denis Irwin; 2-0 to Leeds and the game under control.

One player who had excelled for Manchester United in the two title wins was Paul Ince. His surging runs from midfield had become one of his trademarks. Determined and driven, he could break through defences and create space for other attackers or score goals of his own. In this game, he made a run between the lines and found himself on the edge of the box after being tracked by Brian Deane. The big striker lunged at Ince. The referee blew his whistle. Penalty.

Absolute shock washed over the faces of the Leeds players. Weatherall's arms were outstretched in total disbelief. Referee Elleray was adamant as he called Deane over and issued a yellow card for the Leeds No.9, Boos rang out around Elland Road, but not for the referee's card. The fans had seen who had picked up the ball to take the spot kick – former Leeds hero Eric Cantona. The Frenchman calmly placed the ball on the spot. With his usual nonchalant approach, he slid the ball calmly past John Lukic and got United back into the game.

Typical of Manchester United under Alex Ferguson, his side were galvanised by the goal and it created a thrilling final 15 minutes of the match. It was not enough, though, and Leeds recorded their third victory of the season and matched their rivals' points total.

Ferguson was not happy with his side's performance, noting that: 'They out-fought us, they ran faster and harder and their supporters carried them over the hill.' A bright spark in the defeat was Nicky Butt. The young midfielder was in the frame to start more games in Europe due to the restrictions on the foreign players and Ferguson stated he was the only positive to come out of the game. It was not the best preparation for their first game in the UEFA Champions League against IFK Göteborg.

The final game of this round of fixtures was at White Hart Lane where Tottenham took on Southampton. Before the game, Klinsmann was presented with his Carling No.1 player of the month trophy as a reward for his five league goals and Spurs winning three of their opening four games. His signing was inspired and Spurs, who were listed on the Stock Exchange, had seen their value increase by £9m in the days since he was recruited. Alan Sugar's trip to Monaco proved to be fruitful off the pitch as well as on it.

Spurs' football was attacking-focused and exciting. The 'Famous Five' of Klinsmann, Sheringham, Dumitrescu, Anderton and Barmby were given attacking roles with minimal defensive expectation. Now the international break was complete, the players and fans wanted to take the next step and emerge as title contenders. Sky Sports' cameras were there to showcase the incredible attacking football in the club's first televised game of the season. Unfortunately, it didn't happen quite that way.

Klinsmann got his customary goal after six minutes and it looked like Spurs would blow away a Southampton side who had only two points to their name. However, Saints dominated the midfield, as they could outnumber Ardiles's men at every turn. Paul Allen, Jim Magilton and Neil Maddison may not have been names that rolled off the tongue when thinking about Premier League talent, but Spurs allowed them to dominate. It led to Southampton recording their first win of the season thanks to two goals from their talisman Matt Le Tissier.

There were six Premiership teams in European competition in the 1994/95 season. Champions Manchester United represented England league in the UEFA Champions League, the first time the whole competition had the new name for the whole tournament. Aston Villa, Newcastle and Blackburn earned UEFA Cup places, with Arsenal and Chelsea in the Cup Winners' Cup.

A good performance from United against a strong IFK Göteborg got their group stage campaign off to a good start. The 4-2 victory featured a double from Ryan Giggs and goals from Andrei Kanchelskis and Lee Sharpe. The previous season had been a challenge in Europe for Ferguson, so he was pleased to have started 1994/95 in more confident fashion.

A thumping 5-0 win for Newcastle was the only bright spot in the UEFA Cup. Aston Villa's poor form continued in the San Siro with a 1-0 defeat to Inter Milan. Dennis Bergkamp hit the only goal. At Ewood Park, Blackburn were embarrassed in defeat against Trelleborg. The Swedish side made life difficult for Rovers, who were poor all game. It was a huge wake-up call for a team with title ambitions. There was better news in the Cup Winners' Cup as Arsenal and Chelsea recorded more straightforward victories.

Fresh from their European victory, Manchester United faced Liverpool at Old Trafford. With John Scales in the starting line-up and Phil Babb on the bench, Roy Evans hoped his defensive reinforcements would help knock United out of their stride. Ferguson was still without Keane, so Ince had extra work to do alongside Sharpe in the middle. Giggs and Kanchelskis were always a threat and Cantona and Hughes formed an experienced front two. Liverpool had the creativity of Barnes and McManaman behind the lethal strikeforce of Rush and Fowler. The game was evenly matched, but Liverpool fancied their chances to extend their unbeaten record.

Liverpool started brilliantly and dominated the first hour. Peter Schmeichel was the busier of the two goalkeepers and made a superb save from Neil Ruddock in the first half after great build-up play by John Barnes. An inventive free kick from Liverpool gave Jamie Redknapp the freedom of the box but Schmeichel was alert and smothered the effort. At the opposite end, David James matched Schmeichel with saves of his own from Kanchelskis and Cantona. United tried to stem the flow of Liverpool's attacks with quick counter-attacks. Ferguson made a change and brought on Brian McClair for Hughes to provide reinforcements in midfield. It worked brilliantly.

Growing into the game, United created more and more chances. The one that led to the opening goal was created by a long ball from Ince towards a backpedalling Scales. As the defender leaned back and misjudged the flight of the ball, he flicked his head back, only for Kanchelskis to appear and latch on to the ball. The winger stabbed the ball past the spreadeagled James and, despite the best efforts of Neil Ruddock, the ball crossed the line.

The killer goal came from a fantastic piece of interplay between Kanchelskis, Cantona and the goalscorer, McClair.

Drifting in from his position on the right wing, Kanchelskis found McClair on the edge of the box. Cantona peeled away from his defender, creating space in the middle for McClair, who was on the ball. A sharp one-two between the Scot and the Frenchman puts United's No.9 through on goal. David James took a step forward, shifting his balance, so McClair slid the ball into the net. An inspired substitution from Ferguson had put the game out of Liverpool's reach. It was a first defeat of the season for Roy Evans's side and a return to winning ways in the league for United after the disappointment at Elland Road.

Spurs travelled to Filbert Street and met a Leicester side who, like Southampton on *Monday Night Football*, had been searching for their first win of the season. Spurs duly obliged with a shambolic performance that provided Ardiles with further selection headaches. A complete absence of defensive structure allowed Julian Joachim to run riot and he put the Foxes into the lead on the stroke of half-time. The rest of the goals came in a frantic four-minute spell at the end of the game, which saw Leicester win 3-1. Two goals for Joachim and three points for Leicester. Brian Little was a relieved man after the victory. Spurs had suffered two defeats in two and Ardiles made the decision not to start his 'Famous Five' again.

Three strikers who moved at the start of the month were all on target on their home debuts for their new clubs. Dion Dublin, newly installed as captain of Coventry, scored in a first victory of the season against Leeds with a glancing near-post header past John Lukic. USA international Cobi Jones was another impressive performer after a drawn-out work permit application had delayed his start for his new club. *The People* admired the American for, 'putting himself about in determined fashion.' Just the way the English game liked it.

Another import, Daniel Amokachi, got his first goal for Everton in a home draw with QPR, an easy tap-in from a couple of yards out. But the Nigerian was overshadowed by two trademark Les Ferdinand goals; the first was a perfect looping header over Neville Southall, who had no chance despite his despairing dive, and the second showcased his pace and calmness in front of goal. At Upton Park, Tony Cottee was more than at home scoring goals. Eleven years earlier, Cottee made his professional debut at Upton Park, where he opened the scoring in a 3-0 victory over Spurs. His second home debut resulted in a goal and a win against Aston Villa. Coventry and West Ham were delighted to have picked up wins to move them in the right direction, but the pressure remained on Mike Walker in the Goodison dugout.

In the remaining Saturday afternoon fixtures, Crystal Palace and their tenants Wimbledon faced off in the Selhurst Park derby, but failed to entertain either set of fans with a 0-0 draw. Sheffield Wednesday and Manchester City drew 1-1 in an entertaining game at Hillsborough. At The Dell, Southampton and Nottingham Forest also entertained the fans with a 1-1 draw. Stan Collymore and Matt Le Tissier provided the goals for their respective sides, which became a common theme through the season. Collymore's impact on games was continuing to increase. His strength and excellent dribbling ability meant his movement across the front line made him difficult for defenders to track. Just before half-time, he showed exactly that. He made a powerful run down the right-hand side, cutting in between Francis Benali and Simon Charlton, who tried to get a foot in but did not stand much of a chance, before firing low with his left foot to beat Bruce Grobbelaar at his near post. Le Tissier's response was less spectacular, a penalty slotted home against the only goalkeeper to ever save a spot kick against him; Mark Crossley.

At the top end of the table, Blackburn were aiming to go one better than the 1993/94 season and win the Premiership crown. Although that title race did not go to the wire, Blackburn had been Manchester United's nearest challengers. It built on their form from a season earlier which, but for an injury to Alan Shearer on Boxing Day, could have resulted in an even tighter race.

Still unbeaten, they travelled to Stamford Bridge for the televised *Super Sunday* fixture, with title challengers Newcastle also in the capital to face Arsenal. The Geordies were looking for a club record six straight wins and Blackburn were hoping to exorcise the ghosts of Trelleborg.The game at Highbury started at a frantic pace. Newcastle always knew sides could create against them, but their firepower meant they knew they could turn a game quickly. George Graham's side already carried the 'boring, boring Arsenal' tag, so going 383 minutes without scoring a goal did not help his reputation. Normally, their defence could hold strong against teams, but Newcastle were a different proposition. It wasn't long before they were in front.

Having returned from injury in the midweek demolition of Antwerp, Peter Beardsley's first league action brought him back to the forefront of Newcastle's attack. Keegan's skipper didn't think twice when the ball arrived at his feet on the edge of the box. He unleashed a fierce drive towards goal which was diverted past David Seaman and into the back of the net. Unfortunately for Beardsley, it went down as an own goal by Martin Keown.

Seven minutes gone and Newcastle were in familiar territory. Their blitzkrieg attack blew teams away, so much so that the own goal from Keown was their 11th in the first half of league games so far, more than half of their 20 goals. An incredible stat and the truest representation of Keegan's vision for his side coming to life.

When Ruel Fox received the ball out wide, he had only one thing on his mind; get the ball in the box. Philippe

Albert's thoughts were similarly positive. He arrived in the box ready for Fox's cross. Lee Dixon was touch-tight to the big Belgian, maybe too tight. Once the ball reached the back post, Albert crumpled into a heap on the floor. Penalty to Newcastle. Affirmative nods from Albert as he got to his feet amidst protestations from the Arsenal team and boos from the Highbury crowd. Beardsley slotted the penalty past Seaman. He definitely had his goal now and Newcastle were back in front after Tony Adams equalised. Before the game, Arsenal had not conceded a league goal at home; now they had conceded two in a half.

The three players who featured in Newcastle's second goal – Albert, Fox and Beardsley – were involved in the third. As was becoming customary, Albert charged upfield to support the attack, while Beardsley worked his magic with the ball. His incredible footwork bamboozled two Arsenal defenders. His shot was poor, but as it spun up off an Arsenal defender, Fox reacted quickest. He wrapped his foot around the ball and hooked a powerful strike into the roof of the net. Late in the game, Ian Wright scored a second for Arsenal, which made the score more respectable, but Newcastle's victory was well-deserved. Six wins out of six for Keegan's men and they were proudly perched at the top of the table.

After the game, Wright quickly anointed Newcastle as the leading team in the league. He said that, 'The Premiership is in your hands now – as long as you believe in yourselves.' Reported in the *Newcastle Journal*, the Arsenal manager echoed his striker's comments. George Graham thought that, 'Newcastle will be there at the finish. They are definite championship material.' Predictably, the Scot felt that Newcastle's defence was their weakness and highlighted their vulnerabilities in defence.

Blackburn may not have been as gung-ho as Newcastle in attack, but their attacking play was equally impressive.

Two direct wingers with boundless energy supplied balls into the box for two targetmen. Obviously it helped that the targetmen were Alan Shearer and Chris Sutton, but Stuart Ripley and Jason Wilcox, as well as new signing Robbie Slater, provided constant width. Behind Wilcox was Graeme Le Saux, who was the full-back given licence to get forward. On the opposite flank, Henning Berg was a central defender playing at right-back, so he did not have the same attacking instinct as Le Saux.

Ray Harford drilled the side on the training ground, with Dalglish watching on, firmly in the role of man in charge of the club. Players were put into formation again and again so that they could perfect the combinations for matchdays and build connections between positions. The arrival of Sutton also changed Shearer.

In his first two seasons at the club, Shearer had been the focal point for all Blackburn's attacking play. His partner, Mike Newell, was the link man, dropping deeper to pick up the ball and build attacks. All Shearer wanted to do was score goals. He delivered on that promise with 47 goals in 61 league appearances in his first two seasons. Clearly, playing alongside Sutton meant Blackburn and England's No.9 had the chance to evolve and increase his assist numbers as both strikers worked off each other. Blackburn hoped it would develop Shearer into an even more effective and well-rounded player.

Against Chelsea, Dalglish and Harford's plan provided the basis for Blackburn's two goals. Coming against the run of play, the first goal was a brilliant piece of play on the left wing. Le Saux's cross caused carnage at the back post for Chelsea's defenders. Shearer lurked between the defenders, watching the chaos unfold, when the ball dropped on to the knees of Erland Johnsen and into the back of the net.

After ten minutes of the second half, Chelsea were level thanks to John Spencer. It wasn't long before Blackburn got themselves back in front thanks to more good work down the left wing. This time, summer signing Robbie Slater sprinted towards the Chelsea byline and arrowed over a cross, low and hard in front of goal. It missed Mark Atkins at the front post, but Chris Sutton was there and flung himself at the ball. His fourth league goal of the season drew him level with Shearer. A great recovery from Rovers after the disappointment in Europe, with 14 points collected from the first six games, settling them into second place behind Newcastle.

Norwich could have done with Sutton for the derby visit to Portman Road to face Ipswich on *Monday Night Football*, as they had only scored one league goal. Their local rivals had not started the season well, either. One win, one draw and three defeats was not the best way to prepare for a game against your local rivals.

Despite their loss of firepower, Norwich had been solid in the early rounds of fixtures. They continued to be so in this game in which defender Jon Newsome opened the scoring for the Canaries. A penalty from John Wark on the stroke of half-time levelled the scores, but Carl Bradshaw's goal just before the hour meant Norwich had recorded their first away win of the season and a first away victory in the derby since 1982.

In Yorkshire, Sheffield Wednesday manager Trevor Francis was dealing with a mole in the camp. After just one win in the first six, reports emerged in the tabloids that senior players were calling for Chris Waddle to replace the manager. Francis was furious. He addressed the rumours directly: 'We are in danger of giving all this tabloid gossip too much credence. Possibly it is a player that has left the club, but then it can happen at any club.' In front of the television cameras as his team prepared for their next game, Francis praised his squad as 'the best bunch of lads' he had had and insisted the spirit among the players, 'despite the results not being good, it's been excellent'. He brushed off the reports and vowed to identify the source.

In a break from the league programme, League Cup games formed the midweek action. All 22 Premiership teams entered the competition at this second-round stage, with first-leg ties played over two nights on 20 and 21 September. There were big wins for Aston Villa, Arsenal and Norwich, plus a crazy victory for Spurs at Vicarage Road, where they came out on top with a 6-3 victory over Watford. Klinsmann bagged a hat-trick to take his goal tally to ten and Gheorghe Popescu made his debut.

The first thing to look out for when checking cup results are any upsets. Premiership clubs had more money to invest in their squads, but some Football League clubs kept pace with spending of their own. A string of Premiership sides – Everton, Manchester City, Leicester, Ipswich, Crystal Palace, Leeds and West Ham – all lost to lower division sides.

There were a few that squeaked past their opponents.

Manchester United's win against Port Vale came after going behind after seven minutes, but the use of five teenagers in the side certainly contributed to that. Blackburn put two past Birmingham thanks to another goal from Chris Sutton and one from Jason Wilcox.

Making his first appearance for Aston Villa in a 5-0 win was the teenage prodigy dubbed 'the New Pele', Nii Lamptey. A better-known English youngster, Ugo Ehiogu, captained the Villa side at just 21 of age. Dwight Yorke, also 21, started on the left, with the 19-year-old Lamptey taking up a role on the right. It proved to be Lamptey's night, his one-man counter-attack with a mazy run announcing the starlet to Villa fans with a bang.

A youngster linked with a Premiership move was County Durham-born Paul Kitson of Derby. His protracted transfer to Newcastle caused friction in the Derby boardroom over the fee they should demand. Majority shareholder Lionel Pickering was outvoted by a majority of four to one, so a bid of £2.25m, and not the £4m he wanted, was accepted.

That was not the end of the story, though, as the transfer saga dragged on. Derby manager Roy McFarland decided that, amid the speculation, it was in the best interests of the player and club that Kitson did not feature at Reading in the cup. That decision may have been the wrong one after Mark McGhee's side beat expensively assembled Derby 3-1.

After his own team's unconvincing 2-1 win over Barnsley, Kevin Keegan was positive that Kitson would be a Newcastle player within 24 hours. The manager was pleased to have 'overcome massive internal problems at Derby to get the player'. A deal was not done, however, and Kitson stepped away from negotiations. Freddie Fletcher, the Newcastle chief executive, said the deal was 'dead and buried'. Having made it clear that he wanted out of Derby, Kitson's future looked uncertain.

In no time at all, Kitson made an about turn and decided that Newcastle was the place to be. Keegan spoke before the home game against Liverpool and made it clear that the financial terms had not been changed and that Kitson had just taken his time to make his decision. The player confirmed as much when he spoke about the move, saying: 'I'm disappointed with what was written the next day. I mean, to be honest, it was just a load of rubbish.'

With the Kitson deal done, Newcastle welcomed Liverpool and lost their 100 per cent league record in the process. Rob Lee scored with a rocket past David James after some excellent build-up between the lines. Both sides then had chances before the evergreen Ian Rush beat Pavel Srníček with a straight drive that caught the keeper off guard and bounced over him. The 1-1 draw was a fair result, but Philippe Albert's sending-off for two bookable offences did not help Newcastle.

Blackburn continued their excellent form with a win at home over Aston Villa, two goals from Alan Shearer and one from Chris Sutton giving them a 3-1 victory. The strikers laid on the goals for each other and brought their combined goal tally to 11 for the season. Sutton was looking like a bargain at this point. A last-minute consolation goal from Ugo Ehigou was the first that Blackburn had conceded at home.

At Portman Road, Manchester United could not beat a side who hadn't won at home since February with John Lyall's recording their first win of the season. Paul Mason was the star for Ipswich, beating stand-in goalkeeper Gary Walsh twice in the first half. Roy Keane's marauding runs down the right wing quickly got United back into the game in a spell similar to their burst of goals last time out against Liverpool. Keane crossed for Eric Cantona and then young prodigy Paul Scholes to bring the scores level. Keane, though, was involved in the winner for Ipswich, with Steve Sedgeley's shot ricocheting off him on to the post and Walsh before hitting the back of the net. How United lost that game is anyone's guess. Twenty-five shots and 22 corners showed their total domination. Ipswich's keeper Craig Forrest was the Ipswich hero.

When Nottingham Forest travelled to White Hart Lane, Spurs manager Ossie Ardiles took a more cautious approach to selection. Instead of the 'Famous Five', it was a 'Fantastic Four' with Dumitrescu, Anderton, Sheringham and Klinsmann featuring. The set-up was a much more sensible version of a 4-4-2, but it did not matter too much as Forest blew away the home side, inspired by Steve Stone and Bryan Roy, to record a 4-1 win. Frank Clark's side played some excellent football and their total of 17 points matched that of Blackburn and put them in third place.

Crystal Palace remained winless after Chelsea's Paul Furlong notched his third goal of the season. The pressure was mounting on Palace manager Alan Smith and the same could be said for Mike Walker at Everton, who could only draw 1-1 with fellow strugglers Leicester. The Toffees were dealt another blow with the news that Brazilian striker Müller was not able to agree personal terms on a £2.5m move. He ended up going to Japan and signed for Kashiwa Reysol.

Alan Ball's Southampton had Iain Dowie to thank for victory over Coventry, who remained in the relegation places. Dion Dublin notched another goal early in the game, with a lob over Bruce Grobbelaar, but it wasn't enough. Dowie fired back with two goals of his own, one created from the cultured boot of Matt Le Tissier and his second a diving header after a superb cross from the impressive Dane Ronnie Ekelund, a £700,000 buy from Barcelona. Not content with an assist, Ekelund scored a brilliant goal after some quick passes with Jim Magilton saw him through on goal. His finish arrowed into the bottom corner and put Southampton in mid-table.

Manchester City claimed victory over Norwich thanks to goals from Niall Quinn and Uwe Rösler, which saw Brian Horton's men end the weekend in seventh place alongside Liverpool and Leeds. Alan Reeves, Wimbledon's replacement for John Scales, scored the winner at Loftus Road, which saw Gerry Francis's side lose their first in 13 against a team from London, with Wimbledon recording their third win in a row. The Dons were more than happy with their mid-table position after losing two of their key players in the summer.

On Sky Sports the next day, in an opening section featuring the *Super Sunday* theme mixed into the pulsating DJ Miko house remix of 4 Non Blondes, presenter Richard Keys laid out the problems that had plagued George Graham's Arsenal side in the early part of the season. The list was exhaustive; the worst start the club had made to a league season since 1953, the record-breaking Fowler hat-trick scored against them at Anfield, no goals away from home and the incredible lack of club blazers for new signings Vince Bartram and Stefan Schwarz. All of this played out over a montage, set to that pulsating Euro dance beat, of Arsenal players in various states of alarm and distress. In the studio, Andy Cole and Tony Cottee did their best to mask their confusion.

Despite the build-up, Arsenal beat West Ham thanks to two headers. Tony Adams, more like a goal poacher, got the first and then a far-post header from Ian Wright looped over Ludek Miklosko to seal the win for the Gunners. Harry Redknapp's Hammers only had one win to show from their opening seven league games, dropping to 19th in the league. For Graham's Arsenal, it was a first win since the opening game of the season and gave them a positive performance to build on before they welcomed Omonia Nicosia to Highbury for the return leg of their Cup Winners' Cup tie. Their place in the league table after seven games, a disappointing 14th, was a stark contrast to their scintillating start to the previous season.

So far, Premiership referees had come in for criticism from all quarters over their approach to tackles from behind. A new directive was in place for the season and referees were intent on cleaning up bad tackles. There had been mixed results. In the *Monday Night Football* game at Hillsborough between Sheffield Wednesday and Leeds, Gordon Watson tested out the new rules in extreme fashion.

After a relatively quiet opening five minutes, Dan Petrescu hoofed a clearance up into the air from close to his own right-back spot. The ball found its way to the centre of the pitch and the feet of Mark Tinkler. Watson had never been sent off and didn't really have a history as an ill-disciplined player, but his tackle on Tinkler almost cut the Leeds midfielder in half. Commentator Ian Darke's voice lifted as the red card was brandished by Alan Wilkie and co-commentator Andy

Gray quickly stepped in to explain why. 'Look how high it is; two-footed it was,' said Gray. No matter the new directives, that was a red card in any season.

In the face of being a man down, Sheffield Wednesday battled valiantly. They cancelled out a clinically taken Gary McAllister opener with a well-worked goal of their own. Chris Bart-Williams dribbled at the Leeds defence and Mark Bright curved his run to stay onside. Bart-Williams's weighted through ball put Bright in on goal. The striker eased past the onrushing John Lukic to slide the ball into the empty net. A positive result in the end for ten-man Wednesday, but one that kept them at the wrong end of the table. Leeds dropped two places down to eighth.

By the end of September, things had opened up at the top of the table, with Newcastle two points ahead of Blackburn and Nottingham Forest. Manchester United were four points behind that in fourth. At the bottom, Everton were rooted there with only three points from their opening seven fixtures. In the other three relegation places sat Crystal Palace, Coventry and West Ham, who were desperate to get points on the board. New signings up front in Amokachi, Dublin and Cottee gave three of those four teams some hope. Crystal Palace, meanwhile, needed to do something quickly to stop the decline.

Before the month ended, Football League teams played the second leg of their Coca-Cola Cup ties as European action took precedence for Premiership teams. Confident after their victory over IFK Göteborg, Manchester United travelled to Istanbul to face Galatasaray in a rematch of the hostile meeting between the two teams the previous season. Then, Eric Cantona's sending-off in the second leg, after the Turkish side notched three away goals at Old Trafford, had caused a near-riot which Bryan Robson later recalled was partly due to the police who 'more or less joined in' as tempers boiled over. This time, there was no repeat of those antics. A professional performance from United earned them a point and a clean sheet.

Embarrassment for Blackburn continued in the UEFA Cup with a 2-2 draw in Trelleborg, which meant their home defeat proved costly and knocked them out of the competition. Newcastle again made light work of sorry Antwerp as they hit another five goals. The result of the round was for Aston Villa, who eliminated Inter Milan on penalties. Phil King earned himself a place in Aston Villa folklore with the winning penalty after misses from Davide Fontolan and Rubén Sosa. In the Cup Winners Cup', Chelsea and Arsenal both progressed with routine wins.

A busy month of a hectic league schedule, a cup match, possible European games and a first international of the season meant that some players had notched up 11 or 12 games in little over six weeks. The relentlessness of the English football schedule was not about to let up, with the promise of five weekends of Premiership action, more League Cup and European games and another international fixture planned for October.

The Challengers (September)

Pos	Team	P	W	D	L	F	A	GD	Pts
1	Newcastle United	7	6	1	0	23	8	+15	19
2	Blackburn Rovers	7	5	2	0	16	3	+13	17
3	Nottingham Forest	7	5	2	0	14	5	+9	17
4	Manchester United	7	4	1	2	12	6	+6	13
5	Chelsea	6	4	0	2	12	8	+4	12
6	Liverpool	6	3	2	1	12	4	+8	11
7	Manchester City	7	3	2	2	11	8	+3	11
8	Leeds United	7	3	2	2	9	8	+1	11
9	Aston Villa	7	2	3	2	8	8	0	9
10	Wimbledon	7	2	3	2	5	7	-2	9
11	Norwich City	7	2	3	2	3	5	-2	9
12	Tottenham Hotspur	7	3	0	4	12	15	-3	9
13	Southampton	7	2	3	2	9	12	-3	9
14	Arsenal	7	2	2	3	7	7	0	8
15	Ipswich Town	7	2	1	4	8	12	-4	7
16	Queens Park Rangers	7	1	3	3	9	12	-3	6
17	Sheffield Wednesday	7	1	3	3	9	13	-4	6
18	Leicester City	7	1	2	4	7	12	-5	5
19	West Ham United	7	1	2	4	2	9	-7	5
20	Coventry City	7	1	2	4	6	16	-10	5
21	Crystal Palace	7	0	4	3	4	11	-7	4
22	Everton	7	0	3	4	7	16	-9	3

The Defeated (October)

ALL OF the transfer talk in the summer was around the influx of players from around the globe to the Premiership. After the huge commercial success of USA 94, and the players on show, spreading the net as wide as possible became a key focus for teams. Rather than limiting themselves to the often overpriced players from rivals, negotiating with clubs abroad could bring more value for money. There was obviously opposition to these signings, as there always is, but the early success of Jürgen Klinsmann and the impact of Eric Cantona showed that players from abroad could fit into the English game.

Spurs had spent freely in the European market with the additions of Romanians Dumitrescu and Popescu under a manager in Ossie Ardiles who had been one of the most famous early imports to English football. Alan Sugar's spending spree was also a clear two fingers to the FA, who had banished his club from the FA Cup and placed a six-point deduction on them. After a few early months of booming season ticket sales and increased share prices, he didn't mind too much.

Other overseas players had made a good impression on their clubs, too. Dan Petrescu had quickly settled in at Sheffield Wednesday, Bryan Roy had surprised many with his stellar performances for Nottingham Forest and Philippe Albert was strutting around Tyneside like a Belgian

Beckenbauer. Even with some being a relative success, the poor showing of others would bring the value of imports into question. Although most commentators would agree that bringing in players from around the globe was good for the domestic game, there were still detractors.

In his role as PFA chief, Gordon Taylor had many words to say about the predicament in the league. He viewed the increased number of players arriving from abroad as a clear block for homegrown talent to thrive. No doubt some of the members of his union thought the same.

Fans, on the other hand, loved the buzz created by exotic talents in their teams. Imagine the excitement for fans of Aston Villa being able to field a player like Dwight Yorke or sign 'the Next Pele' in Nii Lamptey. At Portman Road under Bobby Robson, Ipswich fans had marvelled at the ability of Dutch pair Arnold Muhren and Frans Thijssen in their glory days, now they had Claus Thomsen, Mauricio Taricco and Bontcho Guentchev in the squad, hoping to bring some much-needed quality.

The arrival of USA World Cup poster boy Cobi Jones at Coventry was another landmark moment in the arrival of imports in the league. Hair recognisable from anywhere around Highfield Road and an enormous number of international caps under his belt. After difficulties obtaining a work permit because he came from outside Europe, Jones arrived with a style that seemed suited to the speed of English football.

Work permits were an issue around this time, as players from European Union countries were waived through automatically, but non-EU players had to be 'established' internationals before they could sign. This meant playing 75 per cent of their country's recent fixtures. Taricco, an Argentinian, had his application accepted, but Jones had to wait much longer for his. Fellow American international Brad

Friedel had the same issue. Wanted by Kevin Keegan all summer, he was not granted a work permit, despite having 20 caps. The fact that Newcastle already had Pavel Srníček in goal certainly muddied the waters. The work permit snag certainly didn't help Keegan's case of building a squad to challenge Manchester United, who had three star foreigners of their own.

The players themselves enjoyed the Premiership. Wages were competitive and the standard of football was improving. It certainly did not have the weather of La Liga or the best talent money could buy in Serie A, but it was certainly a league on the up. To capture the voice of the players, *The Independent* rounded up some of the newest imports to the league and let them explain the effect the English game had on them two months into the season.

Unsurprisingly, Klinsmann was having a great time. He was scoring goals, playing in an attacking side and had won over the fans and media early on with his diving celebration. He picked out Teddy Sheringham and Ian Walker for being particularly good in welcoming him to the club. As you can imagine, someone who had already played in France and Italy in his career loved being in London. The football was to Klinsmann's liking, too, and he noted that: 'I enjoy the matches because it is a very offensive style: all the English teams like to attack.' Clearly, the Ardiles philosophy was fine by Jürgen.

The speed and intensity of the game was another trend mentioned by the players. Robbie Slater of Blackburn found that 'if you play in midfield on the continent, you get a few touches but here you really don't'. In the Midlands, Nii Lamptey was adjusting to life in a second European country after his move to Belgium from Ghana. The young starlet felt the pain of the endless five-a-side games and sprinting. Southampton's Ronnie Ekelund was surprised at just how quick the game was, mentioning that players lost the ball a lot and everything was played at high speed. Clearly, moving from Cruyff's 'Dream Team' to Alan Ball's Saints was a transition he may not have been prepared for. Another youngster, Daniel Amokachi, marked the pace of the game as something he was having to acclimatise to, but playing in Mike Walker's side was difficult for everyone.

The first games of October saw Blackburn's misery compounded after their European exit with the loss of their unbeaten record to Norwich at Carrow Road. It started well enough when the inevitable happened inside the first five minutes of the game and Chris Sutton scored. Modern footballers often refrain from celebrating against their old sides. Sutton was not so reserved. He wheeled away, mobbed by his team-mates. However, it didn't get any better for Blackburn after that, with goals from Mark Bowen and Jon Newsome earning Norwich victory. The winner saw Newsome make a mazy dribble like an uncoordinated Brazilian from the 70s before seeing his shot deflect up and over the helpless Tim Flowers. Not the start to the month Blackburn wanted.

Aston Villa and Arsenal were clearly hungover from their European exploits, because they both lost home games. Losing at home to Newcastle was certainly not an embarrassment for Villa, especially with Rob Lee and Andy Cole on form and firing. A 2-0 defeat in front of your own fans is never easy, but the league leaders were a different proposition. At Highbury, the Gunners' league form continued to baffle, with Crystal Palace 2-0 up at half-time despite not having a single win to their name. Both goals came from John Salako and direct, pacy counter attacks led by Chris Armstrong; the first was a tap-in from an Armstrong effort that came back off the post and the second another simple finish from a low cross. Ian Wright pulled one back, scoring his 100th goal for

Arsenal since his move from Palace in 1991. At the end of the game, Alan Smith was a relieved man. George Graham, not so much.

Everton were rooted to the bottom of the table. Manchester United were trying to keep pace with Newcastle. They faced each other at Old Trafford in what was far from a routine United win. Peter Schmeichel had to be at his best to repel Everton's free kicks but the man who put the game out of reach was Lee Sharpe. Making the first goal for Andrei Kanchelskis with an inch-perfect cross to the back post, a the versatile Sharpe then bobbled the ball over the helpless Neville Southall after a pass from Paul Ince that showcased the creative side of the tough-tackling midfielder.

Noel Whelan had an enjoyable Saturday afternoon at Elland Road with two goals to beat Manchester City. He was helped by Gary Kelly, who led a rapid counter-attack from Leeds to give Whelan a simple tap-in, before his second finished the game just before the 90th minute. Even after a win against the champions, Ipswich could not maintain their improved form and fell to a 3-1 defeat at The Dell. Saints moved up to eighth after the comprehensive win secured by a goal from Neil Maddison after a brilliant Le Tissier cross, a Ronnie Ekelund diving header after an outrageous long-range effort from Southampton's talisman had hit the bar and a fine finish from Iain Dowie. Saints had now won four of their last five.

After three league games without a win, Liverpool and Steve McManaman impressed the Anfield crowd with a 4-1 victory over Sheffield Wednesday. McManaman walked away with the matchball after what looked like a hat-trick, but it was not to be, with his second credited as an own goal by Des Walker. With dissent in the camp still rife, Trevor Francis's team were leading 1-0 at half-time, but an onslaught from Liverpool saw them cave in all too easily. At times,

Liverpool's football was scintillating, passing and moving with ease through their opponents to create multiple chances.

A run of three consecutive league defeats was not what Spurs expected after their summer transfer expenditure. They managed to pause the rot, rather than stop it, with victory over Wimbledon at Selhurst Park. Sheringham opened the scoring before Steve Talboys's quick response brought the game level. Then, two of Spurs' expensive foreign stars took centre stage. Klinsmann played a ball across the box to the onrushing Popescu, who fired his shot along the ground and past Hans Segers. A 2-1 victory and a good night's sleep for Ossie Ardiles.

Chelsea lost a second consecutive home game when West Ham visited Stamford Bridge. All of the goals were squeezed into a 12-minute spell in the second half after Martin Allen had opened the scoring on 53 minutes. Another side seemingly jet-lagged from European efforts, Chelsea's cause was not helped with the sending-off of Steve Clarke. They dropped two places to seventh.

A home fixture against QPR helped Nottingham Forest maintain their unbeaten record as they emerged with a 3-2 win. The sides exchanged goals in the second half before Stan Collymore scored Forest's third in the 88th minute to continue to push his side up the table. Second place in the league, only two points away from Newcastle. Frank Clark had made his side hard to beat and the impact his two strikers had in the early part of the season was instrumental in their success.

A draw between two sides at the wrong end of the table brought the weekend to a close when Leicester hosted Coventry. Another goal from Dion Dublin, Coventry's second, was cancelled out by a late Iwan Roberts equaliser, which was his second of the game. Roy Wegerle had put Coventry in front. However, goals were not the main talking point in the game. Referee Keith Cooper found himself in the spotlight when he enforced the new FA directive on the tackle from behind, all too strictly. Gary Gillespie was the unfortunate party when a clumsy tackle resulted in a straight red. Co-commentating with Ian Darke, Andy Gray confirmed what viewers thought; a yellow card. The referee disagreed and Gillespie was off inside half an hour. Jimmy Willis was the next man off and this was an even more controversial decision. Willis's crime seemed to be making an attempt to head the ball clear and making contact with an opponent. Gray was incredulous in the commentary box, while Willis struggled to keep his emotions in check, having to be shepherded off the pitch by one of the Leicester coaches. Ten men apiece and it was soon one goal apiece. By the end of the game it was 2-2, which was the result that neither team wanted.

After being refused the £1.5m he needed to sign Dion Dublin, Howard Kendall walked away from Goodison Park. Returning to the club where he made his name as a manager with two league titles and two cup wins, Kendall was replaced in January 1994 by Mike Walker, who had Norwich in the title race in the inaugural Premier League season and gave them a famous European victory over Bayern Munich. He quit the club due to perceived interference from above, claiming chairman Robert Chase sold key players without consulting the manager.

The first six months of Walker's tenure at Everton was certainly not successful as they tumbled down from 11th in the league and won only five games under him. Fortunately, the most important win, on the last day of the season against Wimbledon, meant they did not get relegated and finished 17th in a congested final table. Early transfers had not worked out but Vinny Samways and Daniel Amokachi had shown some promise. Failed attempts to sign a more experienced striker was frustrating.

Walker was an idealist and wedded to a passing game. He wanted players to be flexible in their approach, switching between different styles of play depending on the opposition, but always playing their game. Norwich under Walker had been a thrilling team to watch, not only for their own goalscoring exploits, but for the amount they conceded. Everton were different and did not have the same ability to find the back of the net. The defensive frailties still remained. To try and overcome these deficiencies, Walker looked north.

Everton chairman Peter Johnson brokered a deal with Glasgow Rangers to bring in Duncan Ferguson, Iain Durrant and ex-Evertonian Trevor Steven. The deal cost Everton £35,000 a week, a figure that did not include the players' wages. Immediately there were problems. Ferguson, who wore a bright red blazer for his press conference unveiling, had a 12-match ban imposed by the Scottish FA and a court appearance for a headbutting incident with John McStay. Durrant had had fitness issues for two years, so his loan deal was limited to a month to monitor his fitness. Then, to add to the misery, Steven did not agree personal terms with Everton and was also carrying an injury. Not what Walker and the winless Toffees needed to hear. Ferguson was thrust into action in the Coca-Cola League Cup. Everton had lost the home leg against Portsmouth 3-2 and the winless streak continued. A 1-1 draw meant that the pressure increased on Walker and Everton crashed out on aggregate. Not a great start for the Scot.

Everton were not the only Premiership side to go out; Ipswich, Leicester and Leeds could not overcome lower league opposition over two legs. The same outcome did not befall the likes of Aston Villa, who triumphed 8-0 on aggregate over Wigan, while Southampton, Liverpool and Arsenal also recorded emphatic victories. Bryan Robson's First Division promotion contenders Middlesbrough also managed a thumping win, with Scarborough beaten 8-2 on aggregate. Tottenham were the third team to hit eight goals over two legs, with their kamikaze 6-3 away win over Watford followed up with a 3-2 defeat at White Hart Lane. Not a positive result at home for Ardiles, but progression into the next round.

There was interest at both ends of the table as the next set of Premiership fixtures got under way. Another defeat for Everton rooted them to the foot of the table. This time, it was a Matt Le Tissier-inspired Southampton who beat them, with Ronnie Ekelund finding the net again. Leicester got a hammering from Chelsea at Stamford Bridge, with John Spencer adding two goals to his tally for the season. Aston Villa had been dragged towards the wrong of the table, too, and a 3-2 defeat at Anfield was their fourth in a row. Sheffield Wednesday moved in the right direction with a win against Manchester United, who had now lost three consecutive away games.

The papers reported the Manchester United defeat as a picture of a team in crisis. Swaggering football had been replaced with wastefulness in front of goal. *The Times* commented that 'they could have had the game won by the interval' with the *Daily Telegraph* adding: 'Brian McClair, in particular, Paul Ince and Lee Sharpe must have had their manager cringing at their profligacy in front of goal.' Alex Ferguson admitted in his season diary that he told his players: 'Enough is enough.' His frustration with their lack of energy at the start of games was in stark contrast to how rivals Newcastle played. One player who did stand out for Ferguson was Keith Gillespie who 'has good composure, good temperament, is a good crosser of the ball and is a really nice boy – no big ideas and no pretensions'. A win at Maine Road would have put Nottingham Forest top of the table. It looked like it could happen when Andy Dibble hooked

Stan Collymore's shot into the net. Manchester City got themselves back in the game and eventually into a 3-2 lead. With a few minutes left, Forest's unbeaten run was under threat. Up stepped Ian Woan with an unlikely finish. A lob, from outside of the box and with his weaker foot, found Andy Dibble scrambling back. The ball crossed the line and Forest's unbeaten run had been preserved.

At the end of such an incredible game, Frank Clark was the more relieved of the two managers and admitted that his side 'got out of jail.' His opposite number Brian Horton was less philosophical. He was proud of his side's performance and believed they 'served up some superb soccer,' but ultimately was disappointed with his result.

On *Super Sunday*, Newcastle put their own unbeaten record on the table. Blackburn visited St James' with the hope of making a dent in Newcastle's lead at the top of the table. Only an 88th-minute own goal by Tim Flowers preserved Newcastle's unbeaten record and rescued a point for Keegan's side. Alan Shearer had given the visitors the lead from the spot after Srníček recklessly felled Jason Wilcox. The other live game of the weekend was at Highfield Road and saw Coventry record their second win of the season, beating Ipswich 2-0.

England against Romania was the latest in Terry Venables's friendly preparation for Euro 96. In-form Rob Lee scored on his debut, cancelling out Ilie Dumitrescu's opener. Matt Le Tissier was given a full 90 minutes by Venables, but failed to impact a game that was dominated for the most part by Romania. After Romania's impressive showing at the World Cup, their precise passing and superior technical ability showed that England had a long way to go before they could be considered as a contender in Europe.

Newcastle had built their impressive start to the season on a ferocious desire to attack. Early in the season, they made a habit of scoring two or three goals before half-time. Keegan had built a side to overwhelm the opponent and make the second half a procession. The team was not the best defensively, but the attack was elite. In their three games before travelling to Crystal Palace, however, they hadn't scored a goal in the first half. In fact, the previous two games had given them goals in the final ten minutes of the game. Expending extra energy to win, or draw as in the case of the Blackburn game, was not what Newcastle usually experienced. The same happened again at Selhurst Park. A tough Crystal Palace side withstood the waves of attacks until Peter Beardsley scored the winner with only a minute left. Despite the difficulty in overcoming tough opponents, Keegan's side now had a five-point lead on Nottingham Forest, who were set to feature on *Monday Night Football*.

At Ewood Park, Blackburn and Liverpool met in a thrilling contest. In the first half, Robbie Fowler continued his goalscoring run in the league with his eighth Premiership goal. Blackburn fought back early in the second with two close-range finishes from Atkins and Sutton, with Shearer the provider for his strike partner. Liverpool's composed pass-and-move style was a contrast to Blackburn's direct wing play, which made for an intriguing match. Liverpool's equaliser showcased the quality in their build-up play, with John Barnes scoring an inventive scissors-meets-bicycle-kick finish that left Flowers helpless. Blackburn didn't settle for a draw and continued to press until Sutton managed to bundle his way through the Liverpool defence and hammer a low finish past David James for his ninth league goal of the season, two ahead of Shearer. For Kenny Dalglish, a win over his old side put Blackburn into second.

Seven goals went in at Filbert Street, with Leicester getting one more than Southampton. The Foxes looked comfortable with a 2-0 lead at half-time and that soon became three early in the second half. However, Iain Dowie's 79th-minute goal opened the floodgates, with Franz Carr hitting a fourth for the Foxes before a Le Tissier goal and a second for Dowie made things tense for the home fans. Brian Little was more than relieved to get three points. It was only a second win in ten games but maybe suggested there was light at the end of the tunnel.

The two Manchester sides recorded victories against London teams, United beating West Ham 1-0 at Old Trafford and City defeating QPR 2-1 despite having to play with ten men from the 71st minute and then nine men from the 78th.

Despite two goals for Ian Wright in a 3-1 win over Chelsea, Arsenal wanted to add further goals up front.

Les Ferdinand was a wanted man. Many teams had tried, and failed, to prise the prolific striker away from Loftus Road. QPR wanted value for their main asset and, with prices for players increasing, even more so for goalscorers, they did not budge on their valuation. George Graham decided that he wanted to get involved with the race for the striker and submitted an offer of £4m, which was quickly rejected. Wright was carrying the side as an attacking threat. His partners, Alan Smith and Kevin Campbell, did not provide enough to get the team results but Graham had to wait to find additional attacking options.

On the Sunday, Sheffield Wednesday recorded their second consecutive win live on Sky Sports at Portman Road and, the following evening, Nottingham Forest reduced the gap at the top with a 3-1 victory over Wimbledon. Forest's core of key players – Collymore, Roy, Stone, Woan and Bohinen – were the architects of the victory and continued to impress. A European place was certainly on the cards and maybe even a title challenge.

Back in the promised land of European football for another set of midweek fixtures, Manchester United faced

Barcelona in the Champions League group stage. Johan Cruyff's side were having a difficult start to the season, despite his star players' exploits at the World Cup. Romario turned up late for pre-season training, Gheorghe Hagi was struggling to adapt to life at the Nou Camp and Ronald Koeman and Hristo Stoichkov were not yet hitting the heights in the league. United were protecting a proud 38-year unbeaten record at Old Trafford and Barcelona certainly wanted to test that.

The game was a clash of two distinct styles of football. The blood and thunder of English football up against the continental quality in possession. United started quickly and used their width effectively to attack Barcelona's box. Penetration out wide led to chances and it was a brilliant cross from Lee Sharpe that Mark Hughes powered home with a trademark header. Romario, a constant thorn in Gary Pallister's side, got the equaliser with a precise finish that went through Schmeichel. The big defender told his manager after the game that the Brazilian was the best footballer he had ever played against because of his constant movement. Level at half-time was a fair reflection.

Barcelona's passing in the second half got much sharper and they repelled United's attacks. Cruyff's men got their second through Jose Maria Bakero, who fired in a powerful shot after Paul Parker, playing at centre-back, missed a header. More chances came for the home side with Andrei Kanchelskis and Mark Hughes, in an uncharacteristic miss from a relatively free header, failing to take advantage. It wasn't until the 80th minute that Lee Sharpe scored. Determined dribbling by Paul Ince released Roy Keane, who found himself as a right-winger, and he drove the ball into the six-yard box as Sharpe darted from the edge of the box. As the ball came across, Sharpe was not in a position to manufacture a shot. Instead, he flicked his right foot towards the ball and the impudent touch got the ball past Busquets in the Barcelona goal. All square.

After the game, Cruyff was clear that his side had had the best of the contest. His quote probably summed up his philosophy and how it compared to one of the strongest teams in England: 'Although United ran a lot, they couldn't get near the ball.' He felt the point put his side in pole position to progress from the group, especially with United visiting the Nou Camp in the next fixture. His opposite number was much more positive about his side. Ferguson said that he was more than happy with this result. He later wrote that he felt that United had 'the greater penetration, probably the better chances and produced the more exciting football'. The rematch in two weeks had the potential to be interesting.

In Europe's second competition, the UEFA Cup, Newcastle faced Athletic Bilbao at home and Aston Villa travelled to Turkey to take on Trabzonspor. Finally, in the Cup Winners' Cup, Arsenal went to Denmark to play Brøndby, with Chelsea at home to Austria Vienna.

For Newcastle, they found their attacking verve against Bilbao and were 3-0 up before the hour mark. Ruel Fox got the first inside ten minutes after his shot squirmed past the keeper. Beardsley dispatched a penalty won by Cole, who then scored the third with a sublime header from Fox's cross. Despite his goal, Cole looked somewhat off the pace and his ongoing issue with shin splints may have contributed to him not looking as alert and dynamic as usual. But, at 3-0, it looked like Newcastle would cruise to victory even without Cole at his electric best. The Basque side had other ideas. Two goals in eight second-half minutes gave them two crucial away goals.

In the other UEFA Cup game, Aston Villa were disappointed to lose 1-0 away from home. They hoped they could record an away goal to bring back to the Midlands. Arsenal and Chelsea completed the set of fixtures on the Thursday evening. After a quick start with goals from Ian Wright and Alan Smith, Arsenal conceded in the second half to record a 2-1 win. Two away goals would help in the second leg. Chelsea drew a blank at Stamford Bridge and hoped for better next time out.

Back in the world of domestic football, a quintessential English footballer was on the move: Julian Dicks. His move north just did not work out. After signing for Liverpool in a deal that sent Mike Marsh and David Burrows to Upton Park, Dicks was valued at more than £2m. Terms of this new transfer were much more favourable to the Hammers. *The Independent* reported a fee of £100,000 and a further £50,000 per 25 games played. After Burrows returned to Merseyside, Marsh was the last man standing in the deal.

Now the deal was complete, Dicks returned to the West Ham side immediately at home to Southampton. Despite a fallout with Roy Evans in pre-season meaning he had not played yet this season, he showed no signs of rust and even picked up a customary yellow card for his troubles. Martin Allen and Matthew Rush got the goals for West Ham, moving them towards mid-table mediocrity.

QPR, Wimbledon and Aston Villa continued their poor form and suffered defeats against Norwich, Liverpool and the still-unbeaten Nottingham Forest, who had now racked up 23 games since their last defeat. League Cup holders Villa were on an awful run of form. Despite success in cup games, Villa had now gone six games without a win in the league. On their own poor run, Wimbledon were possibly experiencing a hangover from their sixth-place finish the previous season. Selling John Fashanu and John Scales did not help and Joe Kinnear had enough credit at the club to fend off any doubters.

QPR had also declined from a solid finish in 1993/94. However, an alarming nine-game streak without a win did not put pressure on Gerry Francis in the dugout. He had proved himself as a good manager at the top level. The main pressure on the QPR manager was the constant refusal to sell the club's main asset, Les Ferdinand. QPR had been a selling club, which Francis attributed to the chairman Richard Thompson. Common for clubs without the financial weight of the big clubs, selling players was part and parcel of football and Francis had helped the club raise £10m with the sale of the likes of Paul Parker and Andy Sinton. For now, Francis was safe, but he had to address the downturn in form.

Mike Walker was not in such a strong position. His signings were expensive and not performing. The team were in freefall. Still winless, the losing streak had hit four games for a second time in the opening 12 games of the season. A desperate situation for the club who had barely recovered from the drama of the final-day survival victory over Wimbledon. Four games without a goal, despite investing heavily in Daniel Amokachi and Duncan Ferguson, did not help matters. Ferguson's looming court case and troubled reputation was not necessarily what they needed in what looked like an impending relegation battle. The defeat at Palace, despite creating decent chances, including one from inside the six-yard box for Amokachi that seemed harder to miss than score, rooted Everton to the bottom of the table with three points.

There was no hangover for Newcastle after their midweek exertions, the Magpies recording a home victory over Sheffield Wednesday. Goals from Andy Cole and Steve Watson in the first half gave Newcastle control of the game. A goal from Ian Taylor made a game of it in the second half, but the unbeaten run continued and the place at the top of the table was secure for another weekend.

Tottenham arrived at Maine Road without a clean sheet to their name but an improving defence. After 15 minutes, ex-Spurs striker Paul Walsh made sure his old side had no chance of getting a clean sheet this time. Spurs' attacking play was excellent but the finishing was poor. Instead of leading the game themselves, they were 3-1 behind at half-time. Goals from Niall Quinn and another for Walsh meant Ilie Dumitrescu's penalty barely registered. Even when the Romanian scored within a minute of the second-half restart, City continued to attack.

The home side did not stop. Barely six minutes after Spurs looked to have got back into the game, Steve Lomas headed in from three yards after more great play. It did not stop there. Another City goal, this time from young midfielder Garry Flitcroft, made it 5-2. A phenomenal result for Brian Horton and his players, but disaster for Ardiles. Whatever he was doing defensively with his team was not working.

Almost 30 years after the game, Brian Horton remembered how much he loved watching that City team play. He recalled the excellent performance of Paul Walsh and the striker's determination 'to prove a point' that day against his old club, who had let him go after an altercation with coach Ray Clemence. Horton called Walsh 'an outstanding footballer' and the display against Spurs proved the point.

City looked up the league table at possible European qualification. Horton had a side who knew exactly how to implement his system. City had tenacious midfielders with energy and good passing, with wingers either side of them who had the energy to attack full-backs mercilessly. Then, between Quinn, Rösler and Walsh, they had a blend of strength, height and speed. Turning draws into wins was the target for City if they were to stand a chance of European qualification.

Thanks to midweek fixtures, Chelsea and Arsenal had their games moved to Sunday afternoon. Ian Wright extended his brilliant scoring streak to ten consecutive games. He scored two first-half goals in a 2-1 win over Coventry and took his tally to nine in the league and 15 in total. Chelsea made harder work of a home game with Ipswich, but goals from Dennis Wise and Neil Shipperley gave them a 2-0 win in the end.

Manchester United versus Blackburn Rovers was the *Super Sunday* showpiece game – a clash of the title challengers from the previous season. United had come out on top, as they had in the title race of 1993 against Aston Villa and Norwich. Alex Ferguson was aiming for a third consecutive league title to emulate the great Liverpool side of the early 1980s. One of the Scottish manager's first ambitions was to win the league title with United; now European football was coming into his mind as one area in which his team could improve. Before that, he had to make sure their form continued in the domestic game.

Blackburn had two pre-war titles, but now the money invested by Jack Walker gave them a chance to compete again. Money had been spent, but Dalglish had been wise. The heavy investment had been in players who were young or coming into their prime. He had broken the transfer record twice to bring in quality strikers. The SAS scored goals with ease. Shearer and Sutton were the perfect partnership for Dalglish's team. The goals proved it; a combined total of 22 goals in all competitions. Their individual league tallies were equally impressive, with seven for Shearer and nine for Sutton.

Before the game, Ferguson had some selection issues. Paul Parker was nursing an injury and David May was out, so that left Ferguson with the decision of whether to blood a young Gary Neville at right-back. Neville had been mainly a central defender on his rise through the youth ranks but, due to his lack of height, Ferguson was starting to see him more as a right-back. Knowing that Blackburn created down the flanks, Ferguson chose to pick Roy Keane as a defender. Denis Irwin took up his usual position at left-back, with Bruce and Pallister in the centre. In his diary of the season, Ferguson explained Blackburn's tactical focus around playing 'balls through the channels [and] playing around from the back four to the wide players is to create space around the channels'.

The rivalry between the two sides had built into genuine competition. United hadn't found their feet in the season to this point and sat three points behind their opponents. Rovers had lost only one game so far, compared to three for United. Away form was an issue for Ferguson's men. Old Trafford was a fortress, but it had not worked for them away from there yet. With Eric Cantona, still suspended from European competition, back in attack alongside Mark Hughes, United had every chance to get a result.

Blackburn drew first blood with a goal in the 13th minute. Known for commanding his box, Peter Schmeichel reached close to the halfway line with a punch out from a Graeme Le Saux free kick. The ball fell to Paul Warhurst, who hit a first-time shot without thinking. It lobbed the United defenders and the backpedalling Schmeichel, and found its way into the back of the net. A roar spread through the stands at Ewood Park.

On the stroke of half-time, controversy struck.

Lee Sharpe broke behind the Blackburn defence, chased by Henning Berg. The Norwegian defender's touch knocked the ball into the United midfielder's path. As they crossed, Sharpe collided with Berg and hit the deck. A whistle from Gerald Ashby; penalty to Manchester United. The Blackburn players were incensed and surrounded the referee. On commentary for Sky Sports, Andy Gray did not believe what he had seen. In the melee, Ashby reached into his pocket and showed Berg the red card. Total disbelief on the pitch, in the stands and in the commentary box.

Boos and whistles echoed around the ground as Eric Cantona waited to take the penalty. Not feeling any pressure, the Frenchman slotted the ball into the net. Flowers dived the wrong way. All square and delight for United.

Even though they were known for spending big, Blackburn still did not have the mentality of a club that regularly challenged for honours but their team spirit and drive was epitomised by Colin Hendry. With some help from a rare error from Schmeichel, the Scottish defender got Blackburn level early in the second half. Barely a minute later, Andrei Kanchelskis collected a rebound from his own failed cross and fired past Tim Flowers. All square again, with United determined to get in front.

Goals from Mark Hughes and another for Kanchelskis earned United a win shrouded in controversy. There was some sympathy for Blackburn, who were hard done by with the penalty decision and the red card.

Kenny Dalglish did not hide his emotions after the game. 'We prefer to lose by the ability of the opposition, not the inability of the referee' was his furious statement after the game, reported by the *Daily Mirror*. With three points in the bag, Alex Ferguson admitted that, after watching a video of the incidents, he felt the decision was incorrect. There was no comment from referee Ashby. Berg, the man who had given away the penalty and been sent off, was devastated, and shared his feelings. He told the paper, 'This was the first red card of my career and I'm very disappointed.' In the first meeting of two sides tipped to be left standing at the end of the season, decisions had overshadowed the football.

Ex-Leicester City man and now Leeds captain Gary McAllister was instrumental in the victory over Leicester on

Monday Night Football. His first goal was equal parts positive midfield play and naive defending. He had the freedom of the box to curl the ball around Leicester keeper Gavin Ward. Mark Blake equalised for the Foxes and notched his third goal in two games. The midfielder showed a threat on the break, but he would not add to his tally for the rest of the season. Leeds continued to push and had the best chances. Noel Whelan got the winner midway through the second half to keep Leeds in ninth place and Leicester in 18th.

The third round of the League Cup brought a break in the league fixtures. Two-legged ties gave way to single knockout games, with a provision for replays if required.

The headline result was another defensive disaster from Spurs, who fell to Notts County, bottom of Division One, at Meadow Lane. Two goals down after 20 minutes and then a man down after 36, Spurs never looked like getting a result. Chants of 'We want Ossie out' reverberated around the stadium from the Spurs end and it looked like the end of the road for Ardiles. County caretaker manager Russell Slade had prepared his side well for the game and they fully deserved the victory. At St James' Park, Newcastle had yet to lose a game. They were not about to start when Manchester United arrived. Late goals from Philippe Albert and Paul Kitson gave the Geordies a well-deserved win. It set them up perfectly for another game against United three days later at Old Trafford. Ferguson was not too disappointed, as the game gave him the opportunity to use some of his young stars from the youth team. The likes of Gary Neville, Nicky Butt, Paul Scholes and David Beckham were given their chance and held their own until they tired towards the end of the game. Newcastle took full advantage and took the victory.

Elsewhere, Aston Villa, Blackburn, Liverpool and Manchester City earned good victories to take them into the next round. Nottingham Forest beat Division One title challengers Wolves 3-2 thanks to a brace from Stuart Pearce and another goal for Bryan Roy. Arsenal drew 0-0 at Oldham to add a replay to their congested fixture list and Norwich's draw at Prenton Park with promotion hopefuls Tranmere meant a replay was also added to their schedule.

Back in the league, the final fixtures of October brought another defeat for Leicester, but some positivity for their opponents Crystal Palace, who now had two 1-0 wins in a week, with goals in both games from Andy Preece. Aston Villa slid into the relegation zone with a 2-0 defeat at Loftus Road thanks to a goal from debutant Danny Dichio and a last-minute strike from Gary Penrice. Six defeats in seven now for Ron Atkinson. Things did not look good. For QPR, the end of a nine-game winless streak gave Gerry Francis a positive result before a home game against Liverpool in two days.

Everton stopped the rot with a 1-1 draw against Arsenal. A goal apiece for David Unsworth and Stefan Schwarz inside the first half an hour completed the scoring. A slight bit of breathing space for Mike Walker. A home game against West Ham was next, providing a chance to record a first win of the season. The Hammers' form was patchy at best, with a record of four wins, two draws and five defeats going into the game against Tottenham, who licked their wounds after the battering at Notts County and the mauling at Maine Road.

Ossie Ardiles's start to the season was not as disastrous as Mike Walker's at Everton, but he was certainly a manager in need of a win. He changed his line-up for the West Ham game, dropping Teddy Sheringham to the bench and using Gica Popescu as a sweeper. Jürgen Klinsmann opened the scoring to end his goal drought of five games before Matthew Rush equalised just before half-time. An injury to defender Justin Edinburgh meant that Sheringham had a reprieve and was on the pitch from the start of the second half. Obviously, he scored minutes later. He also laid on the third goal for Barmby. The win provided a slither of hope in a terrible week for Ardiles and Spurs.

Wimbledon were another team who had had a tricky start to the season. They welcomed Norwich to Selhurst Park, who had sold striker Efan Ekoku to the Dons two weeks earlier. Hollywood scriptwriters may not have indulged in such a cliche as scoring against your old club, but Premiership ones did. The only goal of the game came thanks to some tireless work from Ekoku to finish from a difficult angle. A single win in the month of October for Joe Kinnear's side and a first defeat of the month for Norwich. Add 'form guide goes out the window' to the list of cliches for this game.

Two unbeaten runs came to an end as the top four faced off against each other. The previous season's top two came out on top and Newcastle and Nottingham Forest surrendered their unbeaten starts to the season.

After the League Cup victory, Newcastle faced a very different Manchester United side. Coming off the back of the Blackburn victory, Ferguson was confident. He had rested his stars in the cup game, but Newcastle had fielded a full-strength side. It paid off for United with an early goal for Gary Pallister. Both teams attacked and provided great entertainment. Newcastle did not like to sit back and took the game to United.

Not until the 77th minute did United find the goal to seal the game. Keith Gillespie, off the bench to replace Ryan Giggs, who was nursing an ankle injury, found the net and made the game more comfortable for the home side.

Manchester United would face Barcelona next at the Nou Camp and the defeated Newcastle forward Peter Beardsley believed that forward Mark Hughes would give Dutch defender Ronald Koeman a tough game. The ex-Old Trafford player said, 'Sparky was vital to them – as usual.

You always get the goods with him.' Hughes's performance might not have contributed a goal, but his all-round play caused problems for Newcastle throughout the game. Rumours continued to circle the Welsh striker, with other Premiership clubs ready to pounce if his United future was not resolved.

Despite the looming trip to Spain, Steve Bruce maintained that the focus was on the league and Europe. Alex Ferguson's desire to win on the continent with domestic domination secured did not come at the cost of the league form. Bruce told the *Daily Mirror* that, 'All this talk that we prefer the European Cup to the League is absolute nonsense – and we've proved that once and for all now.' The prospect of falling ten points behind Newcastle may have been too much for Manchester United, but after a statement win, they looked at the league table positively. Newcastle stayed top but, with the unbeaten run gone, they wanted to bounce back as soon as possible.

Blackburn travelled to the City Ground to face Nottingham Forest and aimed to put their league defeat against Manchester United in the past. An early Chris Sutton goal laid the foundations for a hardworking performance that focused on stopping Bryan Roy causing damage to Blackburn's defence. They succeeded and when Sutton scored again, assisted by his strike partner, the win was sealed. A great response from the title hopefuls and the first blemish on the record of Frank Clark and his side on their return to the big time.

After a Robbie Fowler double secured Liverpool a victory at Portman Road on Saturday, 29 October, they were in action again at QPR. Trevor Sinclair opened the scoring with a brave diving header to give the home side the lead after 28 minutes. Liverpool's new system of three centre-backs was not as well oiled as Roy Evans hoped, but the relentless pressure from Les Ferdinand, Kevin Gallen, Andy Impey and Sinclair meant they had little time to rest.

An interesting point in the game was Sky Sports' frequent cutting to the directors' box at QPR. In there was Terry Venables, England manager and legendary ex-QPR player and manager. Next to him was Rodney Marsh, another Rangers old boy. Six months or so earlier, ambitious First Division side Wolves had made an approach for QPR boss Gerry Francis. Slightly unsettled that the chairman had given his blessing for conversations to begin, Francis turned down the offer. In the press, Marsh commented that Francis should have taken the role, eventually filled by Graham Taylor. Francis knew that something was amiss so told Marsh and chairman Richard Thompson exactly that. By the time of the Liverpool game, QPR were not showing the same form that had got them to fifth in the table the previous season. Stories swirled that Marsh would become the new director of football at QPR. A clear power play by Thompson to put pressure on Francis.

In *The Team That Dared to Do*, Francis details the feeling of Marsh being brought into the club and creating widespread confusion. He tells author Chris Slegg how he had tried to contact Thompson, but to no avail. The footage from Sky was another humiliating incident for Francis to take.

Les Ferdinand's goal at least gave Francis something positive to celebrate. The winner was an opportune finish made easier by David James's erratic positioning for a lofted through ball. The man Francis was being told he had to sell had done the business on the pitch again. Business off the pitch soon took centre stage.

Pos	Team	P	W	D	L	F	A	GD	Pts
1	Newcastle United	12	9	2	1	29	12	+17	29
2	Nottingham Forest	12	8	3	1	25	13	+12	27
3	Manchester United	12	8	1	3	21	9	+12	25
4	Blackburn Rovers	12	7	3	2	25	12	+13	24
5	Liverpool	12	7	2	3	28	13	+15	23
6	Leeds United	12	6	3	3	18	13	+5	21
7	Chelsea	11	6	1	4	21	14	+7	19
8	Norwich City	12	5	4	3	12	11	+1	19
9	Manchester City	12	5	3	4	21	17	+4	18
10	Arsenal	12	5	3	4	17	13	+4	18
11	Tottenham Hotspur	12	5	2	5	21	24	-3	17
12	Southampton	12	4	3	5	18	22	-4	15
13	Coventry City	12	4	3	5	14	20	-6	15
14	West Ham United	12	4	2	6	8	14	-6	14
15	Queens Park Rangers	13	3	4	6	19	23	-4	13
16	Sheffield Wednesday	12	3	4	5	15	21	-6	13
17	Crystal Palace	12	3	4	5	8	14	-6	13
18	Wimbledon	12	3	3	6	9	18	-9	12
19	Aston Villa	12	2	4	6	11	18	-7	10
20	Leicester City	12	2	3	7	14	24	-10	9
21	Ipswich Town	12	2	1	9	11	24	-13	7
22	Everton	12	0	4	8	8	24	-16	4

The Sackings (November)

KLINSMANN. SHERINGHAM. Barmby. Anderton. Dumitrescu. The Famous Five. The brainchild of one man. The thing that became his undoing. The adventure at White Hart Lane came to an end for Ossie Ardiles after turbulence on and off the pitch. Heavy investment in the playing side had boosted early results and stock values, but a points deduction and FA Cup ban hung over the club. Swashbuckling early-season football had quietened the white noise around Ardiles and his team. When results started to dip, the manager was first to go.

Fans turned on him after the embarrassing loss to Notts County. Ardiles was adamant that he would not resign and he kept his word. Instead, he was called to Alan Sugar's house and agreed a parting settlement of £500,000. A press conference was called for Tuesday, 1 November, with Sugar and Ardiles appearing side by side. Both men shared how difficult the parting was, but it was the end of the road. The search for a new manager began immediately, with Steve Perryman stepping into the breach as caretaker manager.

One man who was glad to see the spotlight on another manager was Mike Walker, who was under immense pressure of his own. The valve was loosened slightly as Everton finally recorded their first win of the season at home to West Ham. Gary Ablett scored the only goal of the game, which brought a wave of relief to the blue half of Merseyside.

With Everton still rooted to the bottom of the table, Ipswich secured a much-needed win at home to Leeds. Goals from Steve Sedgley and Geraint Williams pushed them to 20th in the table and stopped a five-game losing streak. John Lyall was another manager who was struggling to reverse the trend from a poor end to the previous season. Leeds remained in sixth place and recorded only their second blank of the season.

The league programme was combined with European fixtures for the first days of November, with Aston Villa and Newcastle in UEFA Cup action – two second legs that were finely balanced, both ending up with away goals defeats. Newcastle fell 1-0 to Athletic Bilbao, but Villa made much more of a mess of the return leg against Turkish side Trabzonspor.

Trailing 1-0 from the first leg, Villa had levelled on aggregate after a red card for Ogün Temizkanoğlu after his fantastic save on the goal line stopped Dalian Atkinson from equalising. The only problem was that Temizkanoğlu was not the Trabzonspor goalkeeper. Steve Staunton saw his penalty saved by goalkeeper Viktor Grishko. Then Ugo Ehiogu hit the follow-up. Saved again. Then Dalian Atkinson put in the rebound. The tie was level, but then, in two crazy injury-time minutes, Villa were out.

First, a corner in the 91st minute, with only four Trabzonspor players in the Villa box, resulted in a goal. The all-important away goal and now Villa had to score two goals to go through. With 93 minutes on the clock, Ehiogu scored after the ball was launched into the box. It was too late. Seven games without a win in the league and then knocked out of the UEFA Cup. Ron Atkinson was on borrowed time.

Crystal Palace finally hit a rich vein of form. A thumping win at Coventry gave them their third win in a row. It was the first time Palace had scored more than two goals in a game and a third consecutive league game with a goal for Andy Preece, who had four goals in total during that run. John Salako was the star of the show with both assists for Preece, a goal of his own and a deflected cross that set up a chance for Ricky Newman to arrow a shot past Steve Ogrizovic.

Blackburn and Manchester United also played on Wednesday, 2 November, but in two different competitions. Blackburn beat Sheffield Wednesday at Hillsborough thanks to a goal from Alan Shearer while their rivals stepped into the Nou Camp to face Barcelona in the Champions League.

Alex Ferguson had multiple selection issues. Still without Eric Cantona in Europe due to a four-match ban, David May and Lee Sharpe were also out injured. That meant grappling with restrictions of foreign players for the competition; teams were allowed to select three foreign players and two assimilated players who had played in the country for five uninterrupted years, including three as a junior. Paul Parker came back into the side in place of May but, with Sharpe missing, the left-hand side caused a problem.

No Sharpe meant Denis Irwin at left-back. Another foreign player. Mark Hughes and Andrei Kanchelskis picked themselves due to big-game experience and current form. That left one place and it was filled by Roy Keane, so no place for Peter Schmeichel. Ferguson recalls the conversation he had with his Danish keeper, who was shocked at missing one of the team's biggest games: 'Sit down and listen to me. You are playing your best football for us, the best form you've shown, but you have to pick a team.' Clear words from the manager, which meant Gary Walsh took the No.1 shirt in the biggest game of his career.

All of the selection headaches did not matter for much when playing against the best striker in the world in Romario. Johan Cruyff told the press how much his side had dominated the ball in the reverse game and they did the same again this time, but with devastating impact. Steve Bruce and Gary Pallister were led here, there and everywhere by the diminutive Brazilian. Four goals conceded, but not really due to Walsh's performance. Great goals by a great team. United could not stop the constant flow of Barcelona attacks and the game showed the chasm between domestic and European football.

Newman, Armstrong and Salako scored in another win for Crystal Palace as the Eagles soared to tenth place in the table. A huge turnaround for Alan Smith and hope that a relegation battle could be avoided. For Armstrong, it was a first league goal since the opening day of the season. Ipswich, their opponents, were back to losing games after the brief high of beating Leeds.

A defeat for Steve Perryman soured his only game in caretaker charge of Spurs, but Blackburn were hitting form and a goal from Jason Wilcox and the obligatory effort from Alan Shearer gave the title challengers a good win. The rumours swirled after the game about the next man through the door at White Hart Lane. From the favourite David Pleat to new contender Gerry Francis, newspapers linked a number of managers to the club; the list also included ex-England boss Bobby Robson and Leo Beenhakker of Club America in Mexico.

The brilliantly inconsistent Manchester City drew with the streaky Southampton in a pulsating 3-3 draw. After a single goal in the first half, Ronnie Ekelund bagged two for the Saints in the second half after a double from Paul Walsh had put City 2-1 up. Peter Beagrie equalised as the game approached the last ten minutes. Ekelund was proving to be a hit with the Southampton players and fans after his move from Barcelona. His brace against City took his total to five league goals for the season, not bad for a 21-year-old on loan from Barcelona as a favour from the legendary Johan Cruyff.

Victory for Newcastle came as Paul Kitson took the injured Andy Cole's place in the squad. The new signing did not miss a beat. His goal after 20 minutes set Newcastle on the path to victory, with another from Peter Beardsley putting the game out of reach for QPR. Youngster Danny Dichio hit his second in as many appearances, but Newcastle held out for the win. They continued to sit at the top of the table and, with European football no longer on the calendar, they could focus on the league and domestic cup competitions.

Chasing a European place was Nottingham Forest's ambition, but another defeat to a rival dented that slightly. Robbie Fowler got the only goal at Anfield, which meant Forest had lost two consecutive games for the first time. The loss also dropped them to third place, with Blackburn moving into second behind Newcastle.

Manchester United put the Barcelona blowout behind them and beat Aston Villa 2-1 at Villa Park. Paul Ince and Andrei Kanchelskis cancelled out the opener from Dalian Atkinson. Youngster Nicky Butt felt the full force of Premiership action with a nasty clash that saw him replaced after six minutes and resulted in him losing his front teeth. Gary Walsh had a much better experience after conceding four in midweek, giving a solid performance that showed he was a capable deputy for Schmeichel. A fourth league win in a row for the champions and third place in the table. In the other two Sunday games, Chelsea and Coventry drew 2-2 and Arsenal drew a blank at home to Sheffield Wednesday. Dion Dublin had now hit eight goals in his first ten league games for Coventry.

Goals had dried up for Nottingham Forest as they hosted Newcastle on *Monday Night Football*. Stan Collymore was in the midst of a mini goal drought and Newcastle missed Andy Cole. In a game without too many chances, Paul Kitson, Cole's replacement, and Collymore missed great chances.

The two high-fliers had to settle for a goalless draw. Forest slid down to fourth in the table, but Newcastle were able to hold on to top spot, with Blackburn not in action during the midweek fixtures and Manchester United looking on.

Before those fixtures took place on the Wednesday and Thursday night as the international break approached, Mike Walker lost his job as Everton manager. Poor form since the start of the season, as well as ineffective spending, meant that his position was untenable, despite the positive results of the last two games. Unbeaten in three games, it looked like Everton had stopped the rot. Despite that, Walker could not save his job.

Walker's tenure at Everton had been a disaster. He barely lasted a year at the club, oversaw a large turnover of players and was, at times, lambasted for the way he wanted his team to play. A passing game, focused on keeping the ball was not implemented effectively and results did not materialise. For Walker, the European adventures with Norwich were in the distant past. He now faced a long-running battle with Everton over compensation, arguing that he was owed for the remaining two years of his contract.

The chaotic start to the month continued with the news that Spurs would not, after all, face a sanction from the FA in the form of a points deduction. An arbitration panel also decided that Spurs should be reinstated into the FA Cup. An incredible turnaround for Spurs, who believed that they deserved this verdict from the start. The search for a manager continued.

With one case concluded, another one opened. Football was shocked when reports emerged alleging that Southampton goalkeeper Bruce Grobbelaar had taken a bung while playing for Liverpool to fix a match. *The Sun* reported that they had video evidence of the goalkeeper helping a Far East betting syndicate to pull off betting stings. All of the national papers ran with the story as one of the main features of the day. On Merseyside, the *Liverpool Echo* ran with 'Bruce dives for cover' and *The Mirror* with 'Accused: Grob faces world ban'. Immediately, the FA called for an investigation into the allegations, but Grobbelaar was not suspended from football and was allowed to carry on playing for Southampton.

The Sun's allegations centred around the alleged payment of £40,000 to throw a game between Liverpool and Newcastle. John Fashanu and Hans Segers were both named as the alleged middle men in the plot. Grobbelaar maintained that he was trying to entrap his business partner Christopher Vincent, having made bad investments in Zimbabwe. On the recordings obtained by the newspaper, Grobbelaar is heard saying that he had lost £125,000 accidentally after saves he made in the 3-3 draw between Liverpool and Manchester United at Anfield in January 1994. The game was a classic. United raced into a 3-0 lead before Liverpool pegged them back to draw the game 3-3. In the recording, Grobbelaar, this time as a Southampton player, was heard saying that if his side had lost to a single goal against Manchester City, he would have netted £50,000. That game also finished 3-3. It was a dark day for the Premiership, a league that was trying to build a reputation as a place for top players and the best football.

In his autobiography, Grobbelaar recalled the events that led to the story being published. He was at Gatwick Airport to take a flight back to Harare when he was approached by two journalists from *The Sun*. They told him of the allegations set to be published in the paper the following day. Grobbelaar recalls that he 'sat down bewildered, punch drunk, almost. The allegations were so incredible as to be incomprehensible.' The keeper protested his innocence to the editor of the paper, Stuart Higgins, and continued to deny any involvement in the scandal that had the potential to ruin his marriage and finish his career. He phoned his driver, Tony Milligan, and they made a plan. Milligan flew to Zimbabwe with Grobbelaar's personal kit and the accused keeper travelled to Heathrow and flew back to Manchester and met his lawyers in Liverpool.

The highly complex story that Grobbelaar retells in his book is one of being amazed that he had been asked to fix matches. He retells a story of the video recordings being made and discussion over payments. A story of entrapment on both sides is what he believed happened. Chris Vincent on one side trying to frame his business partner, Grobbelaar planning a sting to show he had done nothing wrong.

Working late on the night the story broke, Grobbelaar and his lawyers did everything they could to warn *The Sun* of their actions. It was too late, as the story had broken on the radio that night. Grobbelaar knew he had a long fight on his hands after these revelations were made public. For now, he was the Southampton goalkeeper and wanted to prove his innocence.

Events off the pitch upstaged the football on it, but Wimbledon and Aston Villa decided to do something about that. Three goals came in the first half at Selhurst Park. A Warren Barton penalty for Wimbledon and then one goal each for Garry Parker and Dean Saunders gave Villa a 2-1 lead at Selhurst Park. Even though Villa were reduced to ten men after Andy Townsend was sent off, another goal for Saunders, expertly rounding the keeper to finish, made it 3-1 to Villa and it looked like Ron Atkinson had motivated his side to finally end their barren run of eight games without a win. But then, disaster struck.

First, Neal Ardley finished off a well-worked move and gave Wimbledon hope after 65 minutes. Wimbledon continued to put the pressure on the Villa goal. The equaliser came from the boot of Vinnie Jones. A long-range effort deflected into the corner and past the helpless Bosnich. It was 3-3 with 83 minutes gone. Wimbledon did not stop there.

Another direct move down the right-hand side, with great one-touch passing, got the ball to Efan Ekoku in the box. Debutant Øyvind Leonhardsen, signed from Rosenborg and the Norwegian Footballer of the Year for 1994, reached the ball off Ekoku's touch and lashed it into the top of the net. Bosnich would never have stopped it. After an indifferent start, the Dons were in 16th place and looking back up the table again.

In the other game of the evening, it was the start of the game that brought chaos. John Spencer scored for the third consecutive game inside the first three minutes to put Chelsea in front. Shell-shocked, Liverpool fought back with two goals from Robbie Fowler, up to 16 for the season in all competitions, separated by only 50 seconds. The first came after a run and incisive pass from Jan Mølby and the second was a header from a great cross by Rob Jones. Liverpool finished the scoring after 25 minutes when Neil Ruddock's header found the back of the net. Liverpool were top scorers in the league with 32 goals and Roy Evans had a strong attacking line-up backed up with a good defence. Four points separated them and Newcastle. A title challenge was in their sights.

After poor results earlier in the season, and some tough matches in Europe, Manchester United hit their stride against Manchester City at Old Trafford. Derby games always stirred up performances from players. It was the chance to leave a lasting mark on fans and create iconic memories. Andrei Kanchelskis was the chosen one in this game.

Kanchelskis had become known for his pace on the right wing. He had added goals to his game, but put his passing range on show for United's first goal. A sublime ball from the halfway line, over the head of the City defenders and straight onto the Nike swoosh of Cantona's boots, provided the perfect assist for the first goal. Cantona's left-foot finish was emphatic and United were 1-0 up. Then Kanchelskis's goalscoring instincts took over and he notched a hat-trick with goals either side of half-time and the clincher to make it 5-0 just before the end of the game.

Local newspapers in Birmingham tried to work out what had gone wrong for Ron Atkinson's Aston Villa. After the calamitous 4-3 defeat at Wimbledon, various concerns were aired in the *Birmingham Mail* in a whole feature dedicated to fan letters. Poor signings were mentioned in almost all of the correspondence. The reliance on an ageing group of players also caused concern. For once, chairman Doug Ellis was not the man in the firing line; it was Atkinson who drew the fans' ire. The team had underperformed at this point in the season and the fans saw it.

A day later, the papers reported that Atkinson had departed Villa Park. This time, 'Deadly' Doug Ellis may not have acted too soon. Perceived loyalty to senior players was what probably cost Atkinson his job, as they did not perform on the pitch. Those rumoured to be the possible successor included Graeme Souness, a friend of Ellis, along with Bolton's Bruce Rioch, one of the best managers outside the Premiership, and ex-Villa man Brian Little, who was admired due to his impressive promotion record.

Another candidate added to Ellis's managerial shopping list was Gerry Francis. An overachiever on a small budget at QPR, Francis had just had his letter of resignation accepted by chairman Richard Thompson. Controversy surrounding an incident with Rodney Marsh and his possible return to the club as a director was enough for Francis to request to leave. A highly rated coach and manager, Francis had worked extremely hard to prevent the club from selling their best assets, but he could not take any more, so became the fourth manager in ten days to leave their position. Ardiles, Walker and Atkinson were pushed, but Francis was adamant he would walk.

Incredibly, the managerial merry-go-round continued at pace. The longest-serving manager in the Football League, Joe Royle, returned to Goodison Park 20 years after he left as a player. Everton was Royle's home and, after his exploits as Oldham manager, was the man chosen by chairman Peter Johnson to steady the ship and get Everton up the table again.

The *Liverpool Echo* had Bruce Grobbelaar on the front page with the news that the former Liverpool goalkeeper was to sue *The Sun* for libel after the previous days of match-fixing allegations, but Joe Royle was front and back page news. 'By ROYLE appointment' read the back page headline. The new manager could not turn down the opportunity to join his boyhood club. His fondness for Oldham was clear, but he said: 'It was always going to take a lot to make me consider another job. The one at Everton is one of the biggest.' A local hero immediately endeared himself to Evertonians across Merseyside. It was a huge challenge, with the club sitting at the foot of the table, but Royle was ready.

Royle's excitement to join Everton was reported by *The Mirror*. The new manager did not even discuss contract terms with chairman Johnson, he was desperate to get to Goodison and start work. In the same paper, it was reported that a £600,000 three-and-a-half-year deal had been agreed with Royle, who brought assistant Willie Donachie with him. Everton paid the £250,000 compensation required to release them from their contracts and they started work immediately. The first game of the new manager's reign was set for Monday, 21 November. At Goodison Park. Against Liverpool.

The managerial mayhem continued, with Ray Wilkins the next man to make the headlines. Having joined Crystal Palace as a player-coach in the summer, Wilkins had not played since the opening day of the season. Now 38, he was getting towards the age when management looked like the next step. Aston Villa chairman Ellis decided that Ray Wilkins was the man for him. He believed Wilkins could provide the Keegan-style boost Newcastle had experienced. It had paid dividends for John Hall, so Ellis decided to try it himself.

Ron Noades gave Villa permission to speak to Wilkins, but made it clear that compensation would be required from any club who appointed him as manager. To complicate matters for Villa, QPR had also requested to speak to their former player, which Noades granted.

Wilkins spoke to QPR at length, but there was seemingly no contact from Villa, despite Wilkins telling *The Mirror* that they had his number. Five years at QPR as a player had left a mark on him and he returned to Loftus Road as player-manager with a price of £100,000 in compensation. For the fans who were left bitterly disappointed at the exit of Gerry Francis over boardroom machinations rather than on-the-pitch performances, the appointment of Wilkins was a positive.

That left Villa without their top target so they turned to the man who was about to lose out to the ex-QPR manager for the Tottenham job. The managerial merry-go-round meant the lack of Premiership action was barely missed. With Wilkins in post at QPR, Gerry Francis was announced on the same day as the new Spurs manager. His rumoured £250,000-a-year contract had been agreed with Alan Sugar and he held a meeting with the players on his first day.

The new man at White Hart Lane spoke to *Mirror* journalist Harry Harris on the day he was appointed and declared that 'the game can seriously damage your health'. Francis's first task was to release Steve Perryman from his first-team role in order to bring in his own coaches. Improving the defence was next on the list; a repeat of Ardiles's all-out-attack approach was not on his mind. At 42, this was a step up in terms of club, but he had already shown at QPR that he did not need a huge budget to improve players and league position. Alan Sugar had already backed the previous manager with sufficient funds, so now it was time for Francis to work his magic on them. The target set by Sugar was simple: 'Win the Premier League this season, that's all.'

David Pleat had turned down the chance to join Francis at Spurs as a director of football, so returned to Luton amid speculation that Doug Ellis wanted him at Villa Park. Luton chairman David Kohler, frustrated with the rumours about his manager's future, warned Villa to back off. For Pleat, it was a chance to manage a club in the Premiership and have total control of the team on and off the pitch. Rumours that Villa offered to double his wages to tempt him to leave Kenilworth Road were not denied by Ellis, but he confirmed a manager would be announced whenever that happened.

Back at Loftus Road, Wilkins was straight into the throes of managerial life. He confirmed that Les Ferdinand and Trevor Sinclair, the club's prize assets, were not for sale. Ferdinand was coveted by numerous clubs, with Arsenal the most recent to have a bid rejected. With his two best players confirmed to remain at the club for the near future, Wilkins prepared for his first game as a manager, against Leeds.

While the managerial merry-go-round kept journalists busy, the FA was occupied with other matters. The Grobbelaar allegations meant that the national organisation in charge of the game had to take a stand. As with any high-profile case, there was not a lot that could be said in the press, so the FA announced an investigation, primarily into the accusations levelled at Grobbelaar, but also the allegations against Aston Villa striker John Fashanu and Wimbledon goalkeeper Hans Segers. None of the players were suspended from playing, but the investigation, announced by chief executive Graham Kelly, showed how seriously the FA viewed the matter.

Grobbelaar welcomed the decision not to suspend him from football and told the press that his lawyers in Liverpool would present his case in the 14-day window to answer the allegations. After representing his country, he planned to fly back to England and get back to action for his club side. Lawrie McMenemy, Southampton's director of football, was told about the investigation and prepared for the media circus to follow.

John Fashanu protested his innocence when the inquiry was announced. In an interview with *The Voice*, he said that, over the previous 18 months, there had been a conspiracy to implicate him in wrongdoing. He claimed that two men, prominent in football, bugged his house and plotted to ruin his career. Further accusations of selling fake passports and being part of money laundering schemes infuriated the Villa striker.

Football took a backseat in a crazy few days in the Premiership, but another England friendly meant that league action also took a backseat. Nigeria were the guests at Wembley to face an England side that featured six players from the pacesetters in the Premiership: Tim Flowers, Graeme Le Saux and Alan Shearer from Blackburn with Peter Beardsley, Rob Lee and Steve Howey representing the league leaders. Liverpool bettered that with Rob Jones, Neil Ruddock and John Barnes joined by the substitute Steve McManaman, who replaced the injured Lee inside half an hour. Ruddock won his only England cap alongside fellow debutant Steve Howey in central defence, but the Nigerian side, full of talent, gave them plenty to do.

Nigeria, decked out in an incredible green and black home shirt with eagle-like wings on the sleeves, had a talented squad. Daniel Amokachi, watched by his new manager, Joe Royle, featured in attack alongside Rashidi Yekini and the talented trio of Jay-Jay Okocha, Finidi George and

Emmanuel Amunike. Success at the 1994 World Cup had raised the expectations of a nation and Nigeria played well and challenged Venables's much-changed side.

Captain David Platt scored the winner for England, a typical Platt header from a brilliant free kick curled in by Dennis Wise. England were never comfortable during the game and Nigeria caused plenty of problems. Alan Hansen and Jimmy Hill summarised the action after the game. Hansen was impressed by Venables's organisation and Hill by Nigeria's skill on the ball. A confident, balanced performance by England, but another challenging game to continue the Euro 96 preparation.

After a nine-day break, the Premiership returned. Since the last games, Everton, QPR and Spurs had a new manager and Villa had sacked one. In classic football cliche fashion, managerless Villa faced Spurs at White Hart Lane. Unsurprisingly, the visitors also recorded a victory in thrilling fashion.

For Gerry Francis's new side, defence proved to be the issue. After 27 minutes they were 3-0 down. Despite a more solid 4-4-2 formation, Spurs struggled. The lack of confidence spread to the fans, who reacted to the Villa goals with silence. Teddy Sheringham gave the team some hope with a goal before half-time. But losing David Kerslake to injury just before half-time did not help Francis's ability to make changes. A team talk that was part rant and part constructive also resulted in new dad Nicky Barmby replacing Darren Caskey and taking up a role on the left wing. Tottenham, to their credit, improved dramatically and scored two goals in the second half to draw level. An injury-time winner from Dean Saunders meant that Francis rewrote his team talk as he walked back into the dressing room. The pain of Premiership football.

After the game, the papers talked about Francis's need to raise funds to sign new players. Alex Ferguson was on the lookout for a new striker, with the fraught discussion around Mark Hughes's contract making headlines, so, naturally, Teddy Sheringham was an obvious link. The £5m-rated striker was praised by Francis after the Villa defeat. The *Daily Mirror* reported Francis after the final whistle: 'Teddy had an excellent game. He's developing a marvellous partnership with Jürgen Klinsmann, and I wouldn't want to break that up.' Sheringham distanced himself from a move away from White Hart Lane despite their position in the league. Francis had to get things right on the pitch and get his side up the table.

On his managerial debut, Ray Wilkins had more to smile about. The hard work of youth-team prodigy Kevin Gallen created two goals for Les Ferdinand in the first half. A second-half own goal by Alan McDonald, who nutmegged the keeper Sieb Dijkstra, did not dampen the QPR spirit. Gallen got his goal with some predatory play in the box to put QPR 3-1 up. Five minutes later, Brian Deane scored with a fantastic header to put pressure on the home side, but Wilkins's first win was secured. After the game, the new manager looked calm and composed, his pre-match nerves a thing of the past.

Blackburn and Manchester United had winning runs coming into the weekend's fixtures. Title aspirations for both sides had been set before the start of the season. At this point, they had delivered on their ambition. At Portman Road, Blackburn comfortably beat Ipswich 3-1, with Shearer and Sutton both on the scoresheet. That meant four in a row for Rovers. United reached the top of the table with a 3-0 home win over Crystal Palace that ended their opponents' four game winning streak. Cantona and Kanchelskis scored again to take their combined league goal tally to 17. It was a welcome break for Ferguson, who was now preoccupied with contract talks with striker Mark Hughes.

The game also marked an important moment for Manchester United, with further evidence that the 'Class of 92' were becoming an integral part of the side. Kevin Pilkington, aged 20, took the place of the injured Peter Schmeichel after only seven minutes, joining fellow youngsters Gary Neville and Simon Davies on the pitch. Paul Scholes was another prodigy who Ferguson rated highly and he replaced Davies after 72 minutes. Keith Gillespie had already made an impact in games and the rapid winger replaced Kanchelskis once he had scored the third. The future was bright for Ferguson's team.

Defeat for Newcastle at Wimbledon knocked them off the top of the table. In an attacking assault from both sides, five goals hit the back of the net in the first half. Wimbledon raced into a lead after only two minutes, before four goals in nine minutes from Efan Ekoku, Peter Beardsley, Paul Kitson and Mick Harford left Wimbledon in a 3-2 lead at half-time. The glut of goals ended at the interval and Wimbledon held on to record the victory. Seven goals scored in the last two home games for the Dons lifted them to 14th in the table. A second defeat in four games dropped Newcastle to third place.

Nottingham Forest also stuttered. A 1-0 home defeat to Chelsea meant that Frank Clark's side had a single point and no goals from the last four games. A lack of form after an incredible start was understandable, but to maintain a European challenge they had to hold their nerve.

The battle at the top captured the headlines for footballing reasons, but down at The Dell, Bruce Grobbelaar captured the attention of the cameras and national newspapers. A flawless performance from the embattled keeper helped his team record their first win in five league games. Relief for manager Alan Ball and huge pressure lifted for Grobbelaar after fans welcomed him back to the club. A giant 'Bruce is innocent' banner was passed around between fans and showed the support he had from his club.

Memorable games at Goodison Park were commonplace in the mid-1980s. Competing with their Merseyside rivals for the title formed a glorious part of Everton's history but early years of the Premier League did not. Local lad Joe Royle was in the dugout for his first game as Everton boss. Roy Evans, another local lad, opposite him. Derby games between the two sides tended to favour the home team. A partisan crowd would power their side to victory, or, at worst, help them avoid defeat. Liverpool were not the same team as those of the 1970s and 1980s, but Evans had moulded a young squad into an attacking threat.

Royle wanted his side to 'go to war' with Liverpool. Evans's attacking unit purred in most games, scoring goals for fun. Robbie Fowler alone had scored more goals than Everton. Duncan Ferguson had a point to prove, as he was yet to find the net for his new side. Royle picked a side that battled for every ball, attacked every header and denied Liverpool space to create. That suited Ferguson perfectly. For 45 minutes, he pressed and closed down, a massive contribution to his team.

In the second half, he showed his goalscoring ability. Andy Hinchcliffe was the architect. A corner delivered right on to the edge of the six-yard box reached the Liverpool defenders and goalkeeper David James but they were beaten in the air by Ferguson, who headed into the net.

The second goal showed the best of Ferguson and the worst of James. Another Hinchcliffe cross was hung up in the box, Ferguson challenged the keeper, who flapped at the ball, the ball wriggled free and Paul Rideout, a half-time substitute who improved Everton's attack in the second half, poked the ball through Phil Babb's legs and in. Two goals, three points and a clean sheet for Everton. Everton were finally off the bottom of the table. The perfect start for the Royle reign.

But, while Royle celebrated Everton's famous derby victory, another manager took the headlines.

Leicester had just lost 1-0 to Manchester City, their third defeat in a row to a single goal and fourth in total since the thrilling 4-3 victory over Southampton. Manager Brian Little had worked wonders to get his side promoted, but the time had come to end his stay at Filbert Street. The official reason given for the manager's departure was 'personal reasons' but there were rumours linking him with the hot seat at Villa Park. All of the papers pointed to this as his next move, but the 40-year-old remained consistent; he had not made any plans yet. Whether this was a smokescreen for his actual intentions is unknown, but Leicester had rebuffed an approach from Villa to speak to their manager. The meeting ended with no resolution and a request to resign from Little. Leicester were managerless.

With the flurry of managerial movement, there were multiple links to every job. In normal circumstances, permission is requested by a club to speak to a manager, but there was concern that managers, and players, were being tapped up for new roles. So, considering the power they had, the Premier League drafted a code of conduct to put an end to the practice. Agents and buying clubs commonly pursued targets without the knowledge of the sellers. Tension created in these situations caused animosity between clubs and chairmen, so the league decided to step in. Manager movement in November caused plenty of discussion about the code and it continued into the public sphere.

Allan Evans led out Leicester for their midweek fixture at home to Arsenal. A gutsy and determined performance earned them a victory which took them to 20th in the table. Arsenal, although not at their best, lost to a side who worked for each other, backed by a group of fans who realised that Little left of his own accord. Even with the odds stacked against them, Leicester had shown that they could compete, especially at home.

Another unlikely midweek result was Manchester United's 3-1 loss to IFK Göteborg. Inspired by young winger Jesper Blomqvist, the Swedes took the lead in the tenth minute through their wing wizard, who was compared in the English press to Ryan Giggs, and scored a second within a minute of Mark Hughes's second-half equaliser. United could not cope with the passing of teams in Europe. Ferguson notes in his diary that losing the ball was like a death sentence: 'If you lost it, you have to wait a long time to get it back.' He also lamented the defending he had seen in the five group games. Poor performances at the back had cost them 11 goals, the worst in the Champions League. Selection issues had blighted the team, but the basics had not been done to the required standard. There was a slither of hope before the final group game in December; Galatasaray had beaten Barcelona 2-1 in Turkey, so United were in with a chance.

Managerial mayhem and shocking match-fixing allegations had hogged the headlines in November. Journalists did not expect to report on the revelation that a Premiership player and England international was an alcoholic and drug addict. The date 25 November 1994 was a monumental moment for the Premiership; the reputation of the league, built on television entertainment and flashy production values, had to cope with the admission of one of the league's star players. For Paul Merson, it was a defining moment in his life.

The face of Merson took centre stage on the front of the *Daily Mirror* with the headline: 'I'm hooked on cocaine.' Revelations inside the pages of the newspaper painted a picture of Merson as a binge drinker and drug addict. Depressed by large gambling debts, the Arsenal star turned to cocaine in January 1994 after a drinking session with friends.

A second try of the drug left Merson wanting more and the habit built to regular use alongside the drinking.

Footballers in this period were known to enjoy a drink. Midweek drinking before a Saturday game was commonplace and Arsenal were known for 'the Tuesday Club', a drinking culture built around a visit to the pub after training, with the likes of Tony Adams, Lee Dixon and Merson among the players who took part. It was the type of social, bonding event between players that managers thought brought team-mates closer together. If everyone was okay for training on a Thursday, there was no problem.

Merson's problem was that his drinking, and gambling, led him to take drugs at a difficult time in his career. He hid his problems from his wife and the club. His book *Hooked* tells the story of his addiction and how it blighted every minute of his life. Benders that lasted days kept him away from his family, but his wife put it down to his selfishness rather than anything more sinister. Merson said he would 'hang out in some dodgy places, kip round a mate's house or crash out in the spare room, hunkering down in front of the telly on my own in the middle of the night doing gram after gram'. The words in the world exclusive from *The Mirror* told his story in detail. Merson's admission kept him in the limelight, but football took a backseat.

On the same day, Aston Villa announced their new manager. There was a word of caution to others from chairman Doug Ellis, who said: 'Let me assure you that I have complied precisely with the code of conduct.' The new man had left Leicester days earlier for 'personal reasons' – Brian Little. Tongues wagged about how and when the deal was done. Ellis tried to be clear and upfront about how he had got his man.

Next to Little at the press conference was John Gregory, who had coached with him at Leicester. Both of them were

Villa old boys. As a player, Little was a one-club man who made his debut at 17. The club climbed from the Third to First Division with Little's goals and partnership with Andy Gray helping them to reach the top tier of English football. A career cut short at just 26, Little went into coaching and management. Gregory had been a versatile player, most at home in midfield, and played with Little at Villa, but ended up having the most success with Terry Venables at QPR. Now, Little and Gregory hoped to improve the fortunes of their old club.

Football returned on 26 November for the final set of fixtures in a month largely concerned with anything but football. Blackburn looked to take top spot from Manchester United and they faced QPR at Loftus Road. United had a visit to Arsenal to navigate and Newcastle faced struggling Ipswich at home.

Managerless Leicester, with Allan Evans on caretaker duty, did not follow up the positive result against Arsenal. Instead, Norwich earned a valuable three points with a 2-1 win and secured a place in the top half of the table. Daryl Sutch scored the last-minute winner and completed a Canaries comeback.

Joe Royle's side recorded a second consecutive victory, and another clean sheet, with a hard-earned victory at Stamford Bridge. Taking Daniel Amokachi's place up front, Paul Rideout scored the winner and closed the gap to the rest of the league. QPR were the team in Everton's sights and they succumbed to a rampant Blackburn Rovers, who took the lead early in the game through Chris Sutton. After that goal, it was all about Shearer. The striker recorded the third hat-trick of his league career and a first at Ewood Park. For his hat-trick goal, Shearer ignored the players around him to score an incredible 30-yard drive that ricocheted off the bar, the pitch and into the net. In his diary of the season, Shearer said it was probably 'the best goal of my career' and that it felt even better when he heard the Manchester United result.

The SAS had stamped their authority on the game – an emphatic 4-0 scoreline, underlined by their blossoming partnership. People were talking about the two leading the attack for Venables's England, too. One man that called for it to happen was the QPR goalkeeper Sieb Dykstra, who had watched goals fly past him all afternoon. He said, 'They are the best in Europe. If they were Dutch, they would be playing in the Holland team together. I am very surprised that they have not been picked for England.' It made sense that the players leading Blackburn's title challenge would be able to start for England. But Venables's task of selecting a strike force was not straightforward. Ian Wright, Andy Cole, Teddy Sheringham, Robbie Fowler and Matt Le Tissier all had claims to partner Shearer up front, but the man who played with him week in and week out might have had the best case.

Liverpool and Newcastle did not keep the pressure on Blackburn, held to home draws against Tottenham and Ipswich respectively. Gerry Francis was pleased with his side and the defensive effort they made against a creative and potent Liverpool attack. Robbie Fowler's penalty was cancelled out with a Neil Ruddock own goal. Newcastle had Andy Cole back in the starting line-up and his goal in the 86th minute of the game looked to have won it. The goal was a classic from Cole. Took the ball to his feet, bamboozled the defender, turned and fired into the net. Claus Thomsen, a summer signing from AGF Aarhus had been impressive for Ipswich. His goal matched Cole's for quality. Turning two Newcastle defenders, his finish beat Pavel Srníček and rescued a point for Ipswich.

Manchester United started the day a point ahead of Blackburn, but a draw at Arsenal was not what they needed after the disappointment in the Champions League. George Graham decided that defence was the best way to frustrate the attacking instincts of United, so he did just that. The Gunners never really looked like getting the victory, but United could not break them down. Numerous yellow cards in the game also resulted in Mark Hughes being sent off for two bookable offences. Ferguson commented in his diary that United 'got into good positions, but our finishing was poor'. From the Arsenal camp, Alan Smith was the first to talk about the revelations about Paul Merson's addictions.

Reported in the *Sunday Mirror*, Smith told of the team's surprise: 'All the lads on Friday morning were dumbstruck, really. There was no indication that this was coming.' He went on to say that the story came out so quickly that the players did not have the opportunity to speak to Merson about it. A long spell in rehab was required for Merson, so his team-mates had to wait. Smith spoke positively about Merson's decision and backed him to come out of it. He told the paper that it was an isolated incident and that 'Paul has been brave enough to own up to it'.

A draw was a fair result in a strange game that involved a crowd who could not seem to get behind their side, a Manchester United line-up bereft of the talents of Roy Keane, Ryan Giggs and Lee Sharpe and an altercation between United chairman Martin Edwards and referee Kelvin Morton after the game. A report was sent to the FA and action could have involved a hefty fine. The protests came after the Hughes's sending-off and the general performance of the referee that left United feeling like they were hard done by. Ferguson conceded that a draw was probably the right result. It was certainly the right result for Blackburn, who could celebrate draws by their three main rivals at the top of the table.

Brian Little sat in the Aston Villa dugout for his first game since taking over. Their *Super Sunday* opponents were

Sheffield Wednesday, stuck in the middle of the bottom half of the table. Ex-Owl Dalian Atkinson scored the first goal of the Little era with one that his manager would have been pleased with: a finish smashed into the net from inside the six-yard box.

Peter Atherton was not known for his goalscoring, but his equaliser was a mixture of quick thinking and pure quality. A clearance from Mark Bosnich, after a calm back pass from Phil King, found Atherton a good 30 yards away from goal. When he saw the Wednesday defender moving forwards with the ball, Bosnich scampered to get back into position. Atherton swung his right foot at the ball and it hurtled towards the goal. The Villa keeper struggled to organise his feet, the ball moved towards the top corner. There was no way Bosnich could stop the ball. It touched the underside of the bar and careered down the net. A worthy equaliser and the only way Wednesday could find the net, even though they created numerous chances. A point apiece was a fair result, but it left Villa in desperate need for more points; 19th place and 14 points was far from a good return.

After the torment of Paul Merson's drug confession being splashed across the papers, the last thing Arsenal needed was more press attention. More controversy hit the club as the back pages reported on a new book published in Denmark called *The Men Behind Brondby*. The author, Danish TV journalist Henrik Madsen, outlined that there had been inaccuracies in the reported transfer fee of John Jensen to Arsenal in the summer of 1992. The book stated that Brøndby received £900,000 from the transfer, despite Arsenal listing the price at £1.1m. Documents shown to the author stated that Arsenal actually paid close to £1.7m. Allegations outlined in the book claimed the extra money was given to someone at Arsenal by Scandinavian agent Rune Hauge.

Incredibly, the allegations were only revealed when Jensen's former club Hamburg, entitled to a 25 per cent sell-on fee, enquired about the cost of the transfer. Brøndby paid a quarter of the £900,000, but Hamburg had been told by someone at Arsenal that the fee was £1.7m, leaving Hamburg out of pocket. Arsenal gave an official 'no comment' statement to the press, but yet another story about the club, amidst a season of underperformance on the pitch, was not appreciated.

In a season in which a number of managers and players published diaries, George Graham did something similar. Detailing the highlights of his reign at Arsenal, the fallout was also described in detail, too. *The Glory and the Grief* took the reader from pre-season in August and created a timeline of the contentious events.

Graham needed advice at the start of August due to the investigation into Hauge's tax affairs by the Norwegian authorities. John Hazell, Graham's business manager, met with his client and the Arsenal boss explained that he had taken £425,000 from Hauge as a gift. Hazell recommended, for tax reasons, that Graham should seek advice and work out what to do next. A meeting with Arsenal chairman Peter Hill-Wood was organised and Graham disclosed the payments he had received. He maintained that the payments were a gift and nothing to do with the club. Hill-Wood had already signed an agreement with the Inland Revenue to say that there were no further issues with Arsenal's tax affairs.

In the book, Graham details various meetings with the board and vice-chairman David Dein. Even though Graham had succeeded at Arsenal and won trophies, the board were now sceptical that there may have been other payments in deals prior to the Jensen arrangement. Looking ahead, Graham stated that Dein asked him if there were future payments from transfers that he had not declared. Clearly, Graham was not happy and he suggested Dein deal with the transfer requests if he preferred.

By early November, various solutions were discussed by Graham and Danny Fiszman, one of Arsenal's directors, and Dein. Legal issues were mentioned in the meetings and the possibility of Graham being sacked or handing in his resignation; neither of which Graham entertained. Rune Hauge also emerged in London and confirmed to John Hazell that the gifts were, as Graham wrote, a thank you 'for opening up the British transfer market to him'.

After much negotiation, and advice from leading barristers, Arsenal and Graham came to an agreement about how to proceed. The manager submitted a letter to the club that outlined his intention to leave the club on 31 May 1995. He stood to receive a lump sum payment of £250,000, a further £250,000 produced from a testimonial match and a bonus of £250,000 if Arsenal qualified for Europe. The money earned, including a profit, would then be paid back to Arsenal in full, as this was classed as earnings from work completed as a club employee.

On the 17 November, George Graham handed in his resignation letter to chairman Peter Hill-Wood. It was just days before Arsenal faced Southampton at The Dell, which was Bruce Grobbelaar's return to league football after the bribery allegations. Graham had assurances from the board that information of his agreement would not be leaked or shared with anyone.

Just over a week later, Paul Merson's cocaine addiction was plastered all over the front of *The Mirror*. Arsenal were in turmoil behind the scenes. A victory over Sheffield Wednesday on Graham's 50th birthday was scant consolation for the chaos that had plagued November. Press stories about the money and resignation started to feature in the papers, too. 'No comment' was the response. It looked like the stories were not going away.

League Cup games seemed inconsequential in the timeline of the month but there were some great results for teams outside the Premiership. Bolton Wanderers recorded a brilliant 3-1 win at Upton Park to defeat West Ham and Millwall travelled to Nottingham Forest and won 2-0. Quarter-finals for those two. In the next round with them, Swindon Town and Norwich City, with Crystal Palace beating Villa 4-1 and Liverpool recording a 3-1 win at Blackburn Rovers. Ian Rush's hat-trick against the league leaders was overshadowed by a brawl between long-time friends Alan Shearer and Neil Ruddock.

Now that the football was over, Blackburn could look down from the top of the table at the rest of the league as genuine title challengers. In Europe, Manchester United struggled against all of their opponents, but their Premiership form saw them capture ten points out of a possible 12 and reach second place. Newcastle did not have such a good month. Andy Cole's absence meant that one win in four games was the best they could do but their imperious start to the season meant they were third, only a point behind Manchester United and two behind Blackburn. Nottingham Forest did not win a game and only registered a single point to leave them in fifth place, two behind Liverpool, who were also inconsistent. December featured a packed fixture list for the Premiership, with drugs, bribes and bungs still high on the agenda.

Pos	Team	P	W	D	L	F	A	GD	Pts
1	Blackburn Rovers	16	11	3	2	35	13	+22	36
2	Manchester United	16	11	2	3	31	10	+21	35
3	Newcastle United	16	10	4	2	34	17	+17	34
4	Liverpool	16	9	3	4	33	17	+16	30
5	Nottingham Forest	16	8	4	4	25	16	+9	28
6	Leeds United	16	8	3	5	24	19	+5	27
7	Manchester City	16	7	4	5	27	25	+2	25
8	Chelsea	16	7	3	6	25	20	+5	24
9	Norwich City	16	6	6	4	15	14	+1	24
10	Coventry City	16	6	4	6	19	26	-7	22
11	Southampton	16	5	6	5	23	26	-3	21
12	Arsenal	16	5	5	6	18	16	+2	20
13	Crystal Palace	16	5	5	6	15	18	-3	20
14	Tottenham Hotspur	16	5	4	7	25	31	-6	19
15	Sheffield Wednesday	16	4	6	6	17	23	-6	18
16	Wimbledon	16	5	3	8	17	28	-11	18
17	West Ham United	16	5	2	9	9	17	-8	17
18	Queens Park Rangers	16	4	4	8	23	31	-8	16
19	Aston Villa	16	3	5	8	20	28	-8	14
20	Everton	16	3	5	8	12	24	-12	14
21	Leicester City	16	3	3	10	17	29	-12	12
22	Ipswich Town	16	3	2	11	15	31	-16	11

The Fixers (December)

THE MONTH of November had been hellish for the Premiership. Eyes turned away from the players on the pitch to the scandals off it.

English football was not the only scandal-hit sport in 1994. Diego Maradona's drug-fuelled cries directly into a camera at the World Cup brought shame to the name of a great man. The tragic death of Colombian player Andrés Escobar, after an own goal contributed to his nation being knocked out of the same competition, was an awful event that rocked the game. Problems in English football paled into insignificance when the game had become a matter of life and death.

Further sporting scandals involved Michael Atherton's ball tampering, Diane Modahl's drugs test and accusations that Michael Schumacher deliberately crashed into F1 rival Damon Hill to secure the world title. Even ice skating found time to shock the world, with the case of Tonya Harding and the attack on Nancy Kerrigan. Torvill and Dean's illegal lift that cost them a gold medal at the Winter Olympics in Lillehammer may have been controversial, but nowhere near the same level of Harding's criminal enterprise.

O.J. Simpson and the white Ford Bronco became national news in the summer of 1994 amidst the investigation into the murder of Nicole Brown. An elite athlete in his prime, Simpson was a fugitive and the police chase he led was broadcast around the world. Sport, and the view of sports stars, had changed and 1994 had a large part to play.

Television coverage of sports increased over the course of the 1990s and English football benefitted from the huge interest. Money flowed into the game and clubs had more to spend on players and wages. Serie A had always been the place to look for the most expensive talent, but the Premiership was beginning to see the fruits of the 1992 television deal. Clubs in the First Division also increased their spending to try and reach the promised land. Increased revenue gave teams a chance to build more competitive squads and clubs were no longer frightened to spend.

Alex Ferguson decided he needed to spend money on a new striker. He had two main targets: Les Ferdinand and Stan Collymore. Even though Mark Hughes led the line effectively, he was not able to compete with the goals of Shearer, Sutton or Cole at Manchester United's title rivals. Ferguson enquired about Stan Collymore, but was quickly rebuffed by Frank Clark. After Gerry Francis's departure from QPR, new boss Ray Wilkins had managed to get the club to shun any offers for Ferdinand. The final target, a striker more suited to the withdrawn role Eric Cantona played, was Teddy Sheringham, but that became a non-starter when Spurs quoted Ferguson a fee of £5m. The search for a striker continued.

Another Scot who did not want to hand over money was George Graham, who paid £465,500 to Arsenal for his role in the John Jensen transfer. The final amount was higher, once the final interest payments had been calculated. In his book, he said that he was a 'stubborn Scot' and believed the money was 'rightfully mine', which was certainly not what Arsenal thought. With the money paid back and Graham's resignation letter submitted, attention turned back to Paul Merson.

Before the story broke, Merson had brokered a deal with *The Mirror* to explain how he had become addicted to gambling, which had led to drug use. He hoped to avoid the sharks of the press by coming clean with one paper. Even though he wrote a column in newspapers, it did not stop the press from writing about his antics. Undeterred by what could happen next, Merson's story was published, and generated enough income to pay off gambling debts and fund a six-week stay in rehab over Christmas. But, after meeting the FA to agree his next steps, he had to face the press.

Flanked by Graham Kelly of the FA, Gordon Taylor of the PFA and his manager, Merson looked lost. His pale, washed-out features told the story of a whirlwind period in his life. Life in the public eye is difficult, but public shame is worse. Merson was grilled by the press, who did not always take his side, but he had to face up to the life he lived.

In a statement, the FA explained what happened next. First came a four to six-week programme of rehabilitation on the south coast at a cost of £2,000 a week. At the time, Merson was a well-paid Premiership star on £6,000 a week and he was responsible for funding the treatment. Obviously, Merson was not eligible to play for Arsenal during this period and his progress was monitored by doctors and FA medical staff. Once the treatment was completed, Merson would then face 18 months of random drug tests. His return to football was in the hands of the FA and Arsenal.

Merson noted what a support George Graham was at the press conference. He wrote about his manager in his book on addiction, *Hooked*, saying that he 'knew what I'd been through and how hard I was finding it to read the prepared statement'. Graham had worked with Merson for eight years and was not about to let the situation stop his support. Both of them wanted to get back to football; for Graham, that was two days later at Nottingham Forest but, for Merson, the timeline was unknown.

White Hart Lane was the venue for an entertaining, attacking game of football between two teams desperate for a win. Gerry Francis was the happiest of the two managers thanks to a Teddy Sheringham hat-trick, which gave Francis his first win as Spurs manager. Four goals by half-time was typical of a game involving Newcastle and 2-2 was a fair scoreline at the break. Ruel Fox tormented Tottenham and his two goals had pegged back Spurs each time Sheringham scored. Spurs' quality shone through in the second half, with Sheringham's hat-trick goal and one for Gica Popescu taking the game away from Newcastle. Four without a win for Newcastle. The title challenge hung in the balance.

In the dressing room after the game, Francis applauded his players efforts after a well-deserved win. The catalyst for the win, Teddy Sheringham, was praised in the national and local papers, but the *Newcastle Evening Chronicle*'s Alan Oliver singled out Klinsmann for praise too. The striker 'cut deep into the United defence with his rapier thrusts' .His class had been apparent to anyone that watched him live, but Oliver picked out the way the German played the percentage game: 'He is prepared to be caught offside several times in a game. But he knows he isn't going to be caught every time. And that's when he cashes in.' The partnership had blossomed throughout the season and with the two performing so well in tandem, more wins for Francis would not be far away.

Wins for Blackburn and Manchester United capitalised on Newcastle's defeat, and draws by Liverpool and Nottingham Forest. Eric Cantona scored the only goal of the game in United's win, but Norwich performed admirably; John Deehan had continued the passing football that his predecessor had started and the performance at Old Trafford impressed Alex Ferguson. Blackburn made lighter work of Wimbledon thanks to goals from Mark Atkins, Jason Wilcox and Alan Shearer, who had waited by the phone all day to check his wife had not gone into labour.

Football has a way of bringing former players and managers up against their old clubs after they leave under a cloud; add Brian Little's visit to Filbert Street to that list. Leicester fans shared their feelings, loudly, with their old boss. A game that was not filled with quality ended in a draw, which did not suit either side in their battle to avoid the drop. Martin O'Neill turned down Leicester's offer and decided to stay at Wycombe Wanderers, which led to rumours that Sheffield United boss Dave Bassett could be the next Foxes manager.

Every point is important when you struggle at the bottom of the league, something Ipswich knew all too well. Another defeat, this time at home to Manchester City, was their 12th loss of the season and the end of John Lyall's reign. He left on good terms, but could not take the team any further. No sooner had the reports appeared in the press, Mike Walker, an East Anglian resident, was linked to the job, along with Steve Coppell and Mick Mills.

Two managers who enjoyed positive starts to new jobs featured in the live games on Sky Sports which completed the weekend fixtures. Ray Wilkins continued his win-then-lose streak with a victory at home to West Ham, which took his side up to 16th place. Les Ferdinand and Trevor Sinclair proved their worth again with a goal apiece to secure the three points. A late West Ham consolation goal did not dampen the mood at Loftus Road. Another new manager who enjoyed early success was Joe Royle. Everton had yet to concede a goal under his leadership and had won both games. A third win followed against Leeds, with Duncan Ferguson proving that the huge loan fee and looming criminal charges might be worth ignoring for now. Six unbeaten for Everton and the climb up the table continued.

Attention turned away from football again when the *Mail On Sunday* exposed the details of the alleged payments taken by George Graham. Months of negotiations behind the scenes had created a resolution for Graham and Arsenal, but the press was another matter entirely. Incredibly, considering what was happening, *The Mirror* ran with a transfer story that suggested Arsenal were about to bid a British record-equalling £5m for Manchester United's Champions League tormentor Jesper Blomqvist. Another Scandinavian transfer link was probably not what Graham needed at the time.

Once the papers got hold of the information around the payments from Hauge, accusations and speculation increased. Ex-professionals shared their views with the press and other papers scrambled to write their own version of the story. The *Mail On Sunday* had information about the £425,000 payment, which was more than Graham's annual £300,000 salary, and linked it to a Norwegian agent. Journalist Simon Greenberg, working alongside finance editor Lawrence Lever, was the first to name Graham as the recipient. Agents were not widely used by the Premiership, or in the other domestic leagues, but a few had infiltrated transfer deals as clubs opened their eyes, and wallets, to talent from abroad.

Writing for the *News of the World*, Paul McCarthy tried to contact Graham multiple times as the story broke. The Arsenal manager had a column in the same paper and McCarthy wanted to make sure he spoke to Graham about the details of the story. In *Fever Pitch: The Rise of the Premier League*, McCarthy recalls how Graham seemed calm and clear-headed when he spoke to him about the story and agreed to meet the journalist at Arsenal's training ground. Explaining that he had already paid back the money, Graham told him that giving the money back to Arsenal instead of Hauge was 'the right thing to do'. McCarthy published his exclusive interview in the paper, but the football world did not take kindly to Graham's explanations.

The final round of group games in the Champions League saw Manchester United defeat Galatasaray at home by 4-0. It was an emphatic victory in a campaign that United had stuttered through. Ferguson's faith in youth paid off with excellent performances from David Beckham, Simon Davies, Nicky Butt and Gary Neville. Two first-half goals, from Davies and Beckham, set United on their way to victory. The win came in vain, as Barcelona recorded the point they needed in a home draw against Gothenburg to go through to the next round and eliminate United.

Defeat in the Nou Camp had embarrassed United and proved that they were not quite ready for an assault on winning the European Cup. Ferguson was reflective in his diary and pondered which tactical set-up would work best in Europe. He thought the best way was to 'definitely play man-for-man in Europe. I think you've definitely got to get against opponents individually.' He analysed Ajax and Milan, the difference in their systems and how they structured the midfield when without the ball. Clearly, he had learned from the experience of going out at the group stage for the last two years. Ultimately, Ferguson admitted that conceding poor goals cost them in important games, a mistake he did not want to repeat.

Before the next round of fixtures, there was positive news for Spurs. After the wrangling with the FA over the points deduction and expulsion from the FA Cup, the club were reinstated in the cup competition, just in time for the third round in January. Spurs were able to celebrate the news in front of their home fans against Sheffield Wednesday.

Goals from Barmby, Klinsmann and Calderwood cancelled out Ian Nolan's opener. Since the defeat in his opening game, Francis had organised the side into a much more functional team that still used their attacking talents effectively. Wednesday could not put together a consistent run of form and saw themselves edging closer to the wrong end of the table.

Leicester and Ipswich looked destined for relegation. Both under caretaker managers and facing early-season title challengers, things did not get any better. Two goals from Philippe Albert and another from Steve Howey earned Newcastle a 3-1 victory over Leicester. It put an end to a four-game winless streak for the Geordies, who had fallen behind Blackburn and Manchester United. For Forest, it was a first league win in six games at home to Ipswich.

Stan Collymore had not scored in seven games, but four minutes into the game he had his goal and set Forest up for a routine victory. Then he turned creator. Forest's striker, wanted by Manchester United to partner Eric Cantona, set up goals for Scot Gemmill and Alf-Inge Haaland to put the game to bed after 27 minutes. Managerless Ipswich were shell-shocked. The final nail in the coffin for Ipswich was an incredible free kick from Stuart Pearce that blew Craig Forrest away.

Blackburn and Manchester United had turned the screw on the pretenders to the throne over the past few weeks. United had seven wins out of eight and Rovers had won six in a row, Ferguson's team the last to beat them in the controversial clash at Ewood Park.

Like Forest, Blackburn raced into a 2-0 lead inside the first 15 minutes. Alan Shearer got the second, which was his sixth goal in six consecutive games. He might have been outscored earlier in the season by his expensive new strike partner, but he was finding his rhythm and form at the right time. After Matt Le Tissier pulled one back, Shearer hit another, his 14th league goal of the season, to make it 3-1. His former team-mate Le Tissier found the net for the eighth time in the league.

Le Tissier's goal was one of his best. It had all the hallmarks of a classic goal. The time within the game was important; just over ten minutes left. The opposition had just scored from a counter-attack. And the fact he picked the ball up just inside the Blackburn half makes the goal even more unlikely. But when Le Tissier started to twist and turn past Mark Atkins, who was on ice in the middle of the pitch, the path to goal was still blocked. Berg and Hendry stood between him and the box, never mind the goal. So, instead of laying it off, or sliding in a team-mate, Le Tissier hit it. The power and accuracy from what seemed like an idle swing of the boot was magnificent. Flowers capitulated under the flight of the ball and crashed into the back of the net. Stunned Rovers fans behind the goal did nothing but clap. Le Tissier's reaction was simple; he pointed towards the goal to beckon his team-mates to recover the ball and start again. An iconic moment lost in defeat.

At Loftus Road, Manchester United were not prepared for the onslaught that QPR brought in the opening 30 minutes. Les Ferdinand, another wanted striker amongst the top clubs, scored an extraordinary goal for Ray Wilkins's side. With Ince tight on his back, and very little backlift on the strike, the ball rocketed past Gary Walsh. Ferguson feared the worst. He wrote in his diary after the game that without Cantona, Hughes and Kanchelskis, he was concerned his side might not have enough to win. Peter Schmeichel was a continued absence in goal, but Walsh more than ably deputised for the Dane. He had no chance with the goals, but Ferguson saw that his goalkeeper was 'looking stronger and he's got confidence and he looks formidable now'.

United's injury problems robbed them of their best players at various times during the season, but Ferguson blooded youth players throughout the season and they did not let him down. Paul Scholes took the limelight in London with two headed goals. First, he met Denis Irwin's inviting cross from past the penalty spot. Almost a flick of the head took the ball far into the bottom corner and away from Dykstra's glove. A powerful run and finish from Roy Keane came in between the youngster's goals. His second header was from a corner that evaded everyone but Scholes the poacher. A towering header from Les Ferdinand completed the scoring, but United ended up deserving 3-2 winners.

More revelations in the Sunday papers about George Graham took the attention away from Liverpool's goalless draw with Crystal Palace. The beleaguered Arsenal manager was now accused of taking a payment of £285,000 linked to the John Jensen deal. Arsenal quickly denied knowledge of these additional payments and Rick Parry, chief executive of the Premier League, gave notice that the inquiry commission which had been dealing with the issues at Spurs would turn its attention to another North London club. Football's reputation had taken a seismic hit in the previous two months and, with inquiries and investigations looking at alleged match-fixing and possible illegal payments, the game was tarnished.

Duncan Ferguson had rebuilt his reputation at Everton. A £4m signing for Rangers from Dundee United just 18 months earlier, he had scored twice in three games since Joe Royle took over from Mike Walker. As the striker's loan deal came to an end, personal terms were quickly agreed, with the transfer fee the next point of negotiations. Ferguson, at 22, was a good prospect and had shown glimpses of why Rangers shelled out such a large sum of money on a young player. His ban from the Scottish FA, which he had appealed, and his January court case did not deter Everton. Royle and Everton matched the fee Rangers had paid for the striker and a four-and-a-half-year deal for the player was his reward for a positive start at the club. He had to miss Everton's next game against Spurs, however, due to his international recall by Scotland boss Craig Brown.

Despite the controversy surrounding allegations of brown paper bags full of money and wire transfers from foreign shores, George Graham was still the Arsenal manager. On the morning of the Monday night game on Sky Sports, *The Mirror* ran a sensational story with the headline: 'Graham quit three weeks ago.' All the details behind the resignation letter had been revealed. Harry Harris's story outlined how it was planned for Graham to depart at the end of the season, when his resignation letter would be made public. That was out of the window. Events moved faster than he could imagine. He prepared for the evening game at Maine Road, which Arsenal won 3-1, and a visit to the Premier League inquiry team in a matter of days.

Being a Premiership manager was not easy, but that did not put off Mark McGhee. He accepted Leicester's offer to take over a team one place off the bottom of the league and seemingly destined for the drop. McGhee had made an impressive start to his managerial career with Reading, winning the Second Division title and creating a title challenger with an eye on promotion by December 1994. The new manager's ambitious plan, fuelled by a rumoured £200,000 bonus for keeping the Foxes in the league, was communicated in his first press conference. Talk of a 44-point target to reach safety, an improved passing game and a team that played without fear formed the core of his rallying call. Chairman Martin George also stated that funds were available to sign new players. The appointment was bold. Joe Royle, Ray Wilkins and Gerry Francis had already made immediate impacts in their new jobs; McGhee had to do the same.

Real-life football on a Friday night was unusual for the Premiership, but Ipswich earned a vital point at home to

Wimbledon. *Fantasy Football,* on the other hand, had become a fixture of Friday-night viewing for armchair football fans. Riding the wave of the endless fantasy football games that emerged in newspapers and weekly football magazines, David Baddiel and Frank Skinner, with the help of the immortal 'Statto', took an irreverent look, in keeping with the 1990s approach to pop culture, at the process of creating a side to earn points each week from the real game of football when spending a cool £20m budget. Managers in the fantasy league table included the likes of Delia Smith, Jo Brand and Jimmy Tarbuck. The show featured celebrity guests and iconic goals recreated in a local park or back garden. Sketches and skits poked fun at the serious world of football and *Fantasy Football* proved to be perfect post-pub programming.

In a relatively quiet weekend for goals, with the eight games including three 0-0 draws and a 1-0 win, Manchester United lost their long unbeaten home record to Nottingham Forest. The away side frustrated United with two deep central midfielders, Haaland and Gemmill, protecting the back four. Stan Collymore and Bryan Roy had caused defences problems all season and they did the same to United with the opening goal. The Dutchman played a simple pass into Collymore, who had defenders around him and stood a fair distance from goal. Collymore's hard running had been a feature of his performances, occupying defenders with his strength and then beating them with pace off the dribble. This time, he decided a shot was the best action. Close to 25 yards out, and under the challenge of two United defenders, Collymore protected the ball and sent a thunderous strike past Gary Walsh. It was the first league goal United had conceded at Old Trafford all season.

A hammer blow was struck by Stuart Pearce just after the hour mark, when his deflected shot careered past a helpless Walsh to give Forest a two-goal cushion. That didn't last long. Eric Cantona returned and showed the home side what they had missed. A headed goal flicked on from a Ryan Giggs corner gave United some hope, but Forest dug in and, with excellent work by Steve Stone and Ian Woan to frustrate, deserved the win. Importantly, Blackburn had dropped points at Leicester, with Mark McGhee, Alex Ferguson's first major signing at Aberdeen in 1979, celebrating one point closer to his target of 44 points (and £200,000).

Newcastle also missed the chance to close the gap to the top two even further when they could not find the net at Coventry in a 0-0 draw. Andy Cole missed a penalty to leave Newcastle goalless for only the third time in the league campaign so far. Another game without any goals featured managers in the infancy of their reign. Joe Royle met Gerry Francis at Goodison Park and, despite the attacking players on display, neither team found the net. Everton were on an incredible run without conceding that reached seven consecutive league games. Spurs were five unbeaten and Francis was more than happy with his team's application and defensive qualities to repel Everton's attacks.

Tony Cottee recorded a hat-trick in West Ham's 3-0 win at home to Manchester City. Across London, Arsenal suffered a disappointing defeat to Leeds. Howard Wilkinson had developed a strong side that bounced back after the disappointing title defence in 1992/93. Fifth place in 1993/94 gave fans hope that Europe could be achieved. A run of three successive away defeats ended with the victory and, by the end of the day, they had reached sixth in the table. For Arsenal and George Graham, stories in the Sunday papers waited for them.

A fourth consecutive draw for Liverpool killed any momentum that their early-season form had created. Another game without a goal on a second consecutive *Super Sunday* was not the advert the Premiership or Sky Sports wanted. For

Roy Evans, the injuries to Rob Jones, Jan Mølby and, most importantly, Steve McManaman had stifled the creativity and supply to Robbie Fowler and Ian Rush. The blame from Glenn Hoddle fell on the size of the pitch. Disappointed with the decision to shrink the pitch as Stamford Bridge was redeveloped, the Chelsea player-manager said in the press after the game: 'It has made it more difficult for us with a smaller pitch. The players have been saying it all season.' Both managers were frustrated, but a point was a fair result.

For the first time in the Brian Little era, Aston Villa were on the losing side. Three consecutive draws might not have taken Villa any closer to safety, but it stopped the rot. Southampton were not on a great run, but they had Matthew Le Tissier, who popped up in the last minute to win the game at The Dell with a brilliant free kick. Mid-table for the Saints and the promise of more if Le Tissier kept up his goalscoring feats.

The Coca-Cola Cup quarter-finals were to be played in January, but Newcastle and Manchester City had to replay their fourth-round fixture after a draw at Maine Road. Inconsistent form had plagued Newcastle for the last month and a half and that did not change when Brian Horton's men came to visit. The local press highlighted issues that had plagued Newcastle on the run that saw them start to fall out of the title race: poor defending, lack of bite in midfield and wastefulness in front of goal. Three things that could not have been said at the start of the season. Chances missed and poor goals conceded, the *Newcastle Evening Chronicle* gave fans their voice. When fans are given that chance, they do not mince their words. Comments ranged from 'Get out the cheque book Kevin' to 'Lacked the passion of Manchester City' and 'We seemed to be playing long balls instead of our usual passing game, which we are so good at'. In response to the result and the performance,

Keegan was not as kind. The key line pulled out by the *Newcastle Journal* from the manager's comments was that his side were 'brain dead' and that 'mentally, we are just a bit dead at the minute'. Keegan knew his side were in a tough spot – it was only two wins in 11 at this point – but he felt there was enough quality to keep going. They needed something to change quickly before the challenge for European places passed them by.

Football provided the papers with plenty of stories to sell copies as 1994 came towards a decidedly murky end. With the furore surrounding the investigation into George Graham, further stories began to emerge about other managers. Brian Clough, now retired, was brought in front of the Premier League inquiry. Rumours had circled around Clough taking money in the Teddy Sheringham deal when he left Forest for Spurs in 1992.

Ex-Liverpool manager Graeme Souness offered a furious threat of libel to papers that accused the Scot of taking payments from the agent Pini Zahavi. Souness denied allegations he had benefitted in deals he had made while manager at Rangers. Added to that, the Premier League inquiry announced it had plans to look into the 23 transfers involving Scandinavian players, which included players Souness had bought at Liverpool. Manchester City were also added to this list when a former director of Rosenborg stated that the club had only received £400,000 of the £550,000 transfer fee for Kare Ingebrigtsen. City, and the player, both refuted the allegations and stated that everything had been declared correctly to the Inland Revenue.

Amidst the accusations of transfer illegalities, Brian Little decided to spend some of Doug Ellis's money as he tried to find a way to reshape his Aston Villa squad. His first signing was Ian Taylor from Sheffield Wednesday in a deal worth around £1m. Guy Whittingham, who was not able to recreate the goalscoring exploits that brought him to national attention at Portsmouth, moved the other way to bolster Wednesday's attacking options. The Villa midfield was ageing and bringing in a player of Taylor's quality, and age, helped Little with his bid to improve his side.

Fixtures at Christmas have always been an integral part of the football calendar but in 1994 the schedule was particularly demanding for some clubs. After a full round of fixtures on Boxing Day, four teams played again the next day, with the remaining games completed on 28 December. Pressure for points and pressure to play in such a short space of time produced some interesting results.

Not a single home side won their Boxing Day match. Coventry, Crystal Palace and Leeds did not even find the net in front of their own crowds, with their opponents – Nottingham Forest, QPR and Newcastle respectively – drawing blanks, too. Nothing like a 0-0 draw in the depths of December to entertain fans. For Forest and Newcastle, it provided more evidence that they would not be able to sustain a title challenge after the promise of their early-season results. To make matters worse, all their rivals recorded Boxing Day victories.

Arsenal's form was barely in the news. The scandal surrounding the various transfer deals filled far more column inches than the struggles of the Arsenal attack. A fourth home game without a goal did not please the Highbury faithful. They made their feelings known, which was not lost on George Graham. A 0-0 draw was not the result the fans wanted. Brian Little was much happier that he could add another point to Aston Villa's total.

League leaders Blackburn recorded a 3-1 victory at Maine Road with early goals from Alan Shearer and Mark Atkins putting them into a two-goal lead. Niall Quinn promised to get City back in the game, but Graeme Le Saux's second-half strike secured the three points. It was some positive news for Blackburn, whose manager, Kenny Dalglish, had had to have his appendix removed. Alan Shearer wrote in his diary of the season that he did not think they would miss Dalglish too much. Not a criticism; he elaborated: 'The boss has got such a well-drilled routine and Ray Harford is such a capable No.2 that we just get on with things normally.' The victory proved that it took more than surgery to their manager to stop Blackburn.

Manchester United made difficult work of their visit to Stamford Bridge. Having sailed into a two-goal lead thanks to Mark Hughes and an Eric Cantona penalty, Chelsea came back strongly with two goals of their own. It was left to Ferguson's veteran forward Brian McClair to get the winner and give United the perfect result after the defeat at home to Forest. Although missing first-choice keeper Peter Schmeichel for the next six games with a back injury, United were back to a strong squad of outfield players and the quality told over the course of the game.

Four consecutive draws in the league for Liverpool did not look like the form of title contenders. A visit to Mark McGhee's Leicester provided them with a victory. In an eventful game, Leicester had a penalty saved while the game was 0-0 and went 2-0 down in the next 15 minutes with a goal from the spot from Fowler and another from Rush, before Simon Grayson was sent off for a second bookable offence in the last ten minutes of the game. A consolation from Iwan Roberts made the last few minutes uncomfortable for the Reds but they escaped with their first win since early November.

A story of strikers emerged at Goodison Park in the first defeat of Joe Royle's reign as Everton boss. Duncan Ferguson opened the scoring for Everton, starting to pay off that £4m fee, with a trademark powerful header but his joy was short-lived when Mark Bright equalised for Sheffield Wednesday. A clever free kick evaded the offside trap and Peter Atherton's cross was met by Bright. Trevor Francis had a striker signing of his own, Guy Whittingham, who quickly showed why he was a shrewd capture. Again, beating the Everton offside trap, Whittingham danced around the onrushing Neville Southall and scored into the empty net. An early second-half goal from Klas Ingesson and a late tap-in from Whittingham secured an emphatic 4-1 win for the visitors. Everton's superb defensive record, an impressive seven consecutive league clean sheets, had ended.

Just a day later, Spurs faced Crystal Palace and continued to show their kamikaze attacking was a thing of the past. A third clean sheet in a row earned them a point at White Hart Lane, making it four in total over the Christmas period after the 2-0 Boxing Day victory over Norwich. Another festive defeat for Norwich at the City Ground against Nottingham Forest hampered any European ambitions the Canaries still held.

Everton, Leicester and Villa had already secured new managers to help them beat the drop and now it was Ipswich's turn. Old boy and club legend George Burley arrived at Portman Road from Colchester. Like Little and Royle, he was a manager who had an instant connection with the fans. An important element of any relegation battle is the continued support and engagement from the home crowd. Ipswich did not have the pulling power in the transfer market, but they hoped Burley could do something to help the side. His departure from Colchester was acrimonious, with allegations of tapping up. Ipswich compensated Burley's old club, but it was clear the Premier League's idea for a code of conduct may need to be implemented sooner rather than later.

One of the new managers who had not tasted victory was Little. He was relieved to record his first win in the Villa dugout with a home victory over Chelsea. Glenn Hoddle's side conceded three goals again thanks to a Frank Sinclair own goal, Dwight Yorke and new boy Ian Taylor. Villa were headed in the right direction and had West Ham and Crystal Palace, thanks to a narrow defeat at Wimbledon, in their sights. Fellow strugglers Ipswich brought Arsenal boss George Graham some brief relief from getting pasted by the press. Ian Wright and Kevin Campbell scored for the goal-shy Gunners in a vital victory.

Leicester managed a draw at Manchester United thanks to a battling display that did not help either side's challenges at either end of the table. In his diary, Alex Ferguson gave credit to new manager Mark McGhee for a 'resurgence in spirit and determination'. He was more concerned with the performance of striker Mark Hughes. Ferguson thought that his striker seemed to be troubled by his ongoing contract situation at Old Trafford. He wanted to find a resolution as the papers had already started to speculate that Stan Collymore was the man to replace Hughes in the United attack.

The story of the night was Sheffield Wednesday's demolition of Coventry at Hillsborough. After hitting four at Goodison Park two days earlier, the Owls strikers clearly got goals for Christmas. Mark Bright had been a reliable goalscorer in the two full seasons since he signed from Crystal Palace. He got two first-half goals either side of a Chris Waddle effort to put his side 3-1 up. Peter Ndlovu's penalty did not deter Wednesday's attacking instincts and they continued to push in the second half. Guy Whittingham was having a brilliant time in Wednesday colours, with two goals on his home debut. Goals flowed for Francis's side and the early-season talk of mutiny in the camp had dulled. While they did not scale the heights of the previous two campaigns, nine goals in two games over Christmas was a gift to the fans.

There was a full slate of games on New Year's Eve and results affected teams at both ends. Defeats for Crystal Palace, Ipswich and Leicester added to their woes, but victories for Everton, Liverpool, Blackburn and Spurs kept them moving in the right direction. Pressure mounted on Coventry manager Phil Neal after the defeat to Tottenham, with another four goals conceded. Gerry Francis was a happy man, with his side ruthless in front of goal. Eight games unbeaten for Spurs who had recorded four wins and four draws in that run. Importantly, five clean sheets in a row showed how different the side was set up compared to the early-season carnage. Francis was awarded the Manager of the Month award for December as his side sat sixth in the table.

Another draw for Manchester United did not help their pursuit of Blackburn, who had beaten Crystal Palace. Goals from unlikely scorers, Nicky Butt and Gary Pallister, brought United back into the game twice. News of Alex Ferguson's CBE was released on the eve of the game and provided a nice birthday present. In his diary, Ferguson wrote that the award was for 'everyone at Manchester United and for my family, who have to put up with so much because of the demands of the job'. A victory at The Dell certainly would have been welcomed alongside his birthday presents. The game itself highlighted the main issue for United in close games: not being able to finish their chances.

Newcastle had not scored a goal in their previous two games. So, when Norwich went 2-0 up at Carrow Road, the writing was on the wall. The fearsome attacking unit was human. Cole and Kitson were not the same as Cole and Beardsley. They tried to develop a relationship, but the skill of Beardsley and intelligent running from Cole was not easy to replicate with another striker in the mix. Ruel Fox, against his old side, did benefit from the new strike partnership when a defence-splitting pass found Kitson in the box. Once the striker was bundled over, a penalty was given and Fox scored from the spot. Keegan's side couldn't find a way through and finished 1994 in fourth place and ten points behind the leaders.

Arsenal had crept into the top half of the table after their win at Ipswich, but were brought back down to earth by QPR, who had put a tough start behind them and found form. Up front, Les Ferdinand and Kevin Gallen had formed a great partnership. They showcased their excellent understanding with the first goal at Highbury after just three minutes. A great near-post cross from Ferdinand found Gallen on the edge of the six-yard box and the 19-year-old showed his predatory instincts to lash the ball past Vince Bartram.

QPR held on to their lead until just after the hour mark when a rare goal, a first for Arsenal, from John Jensen, who had a couple of long-range efforts that went close in the first half, got Arsenal back into the game. The Dane's shot curled around QPR keeper Tony Roberts and into the back of the net. The lead lasted ten minutes until Arsenal capitulated and conceded two goals in a minute from Bradley Allen and Andy Impey, who capitalised on Bartram's error at the back post. A huge win for QPR, who sat one place behind Arsenal in 14th.

Gallen was the name on everyone's lips after the game, but it was the plight of George Graham that made the headlines. After the allegations around illegal payments and the insipid performances on the pitch, Graham was under pressure. He told the team that there should be 'no New Year celebrations … I don't want any more problems'. About the game, he did not pull his punches either: 'This is the worst league form I can remember. I just hope the Tottenham match can motivate us again.' A derby might not have been the best thing his team needed. He admitted that the pressure was on and he desperately needed a result next time out.

Manchester United started 1994 12 points clear of Blackburn at the top of the table and ended with the positions reversed and a three-point gap. Alan Shearer and Andy Cole were still scoring goals and Roy Evans had transformed Liverpool after the departure of Graeme Souness.

It had been a turbulent end to the year with numerous managerial changes and accusations of match-fixing, bribes, bungs and fan brutality making the headlines. Everyone hoped 1995 would be different.

Pos	Team	P	W	D	L	F	A	GD	Pts
1	Blackburn Rovers	21	15	4	2	45	16	+29	49
2	Manchester United	22	14	4	4	42	19	+23	46
3	Liverpool	22	12	6	4	40	19	+21	42
4	Newcastle United	21	11	6	4	40	24	+16	39
5	Nottingham Forest	22	11	6	5	35	23	+12	39
6	Tottenham Hotspur	22	9	6	7	38	34	+4	33
7	Norwich City	22	9	6	7	21	19	+2	33
8	Leeds United	21	9	5	7	29	27	+2	32
9	Sheffield Wednesday	22	8	6	8	29	30	-1	30
10	Chelsea	22	8	5	9	29	30	-1	29
11	Manchester City	22	8	5	9	33	38	-5	29
12	Wimbledon	22	8	5	9	26	36	-10	29
13	Arsenal	22	7	7	8	26	25	+1	28
14	Queens Park Rangers	22	7	6	9	34	38	-4	27
15	Southampton	22	6	8	8	33	38	-5	26
16	West Ham United	22	7	4	11	19	24	-5	25
17	Coventry City	22	6	7	9	21	38	-17	25
18	Crystal Palace	22	5	8	9	15	21	-6	23
19	Everton	21	5	7	9	20	29	-9	22
20	Aston Villa	22	4	9	9	27	33	-6	21
21	Leicester City	22	3	6	13	21	37	-16	15
22	Ipswich Town	22	3	4	15	21	46	-25	13

The Kick (January)

NEW YEAR, same old Alan Shearer. A hat-trick at home to West Ham started the year off in the perfect way for Blackburn. His form since early November was imperious. Those goals at West Ham took his tally over those ten games to 13. An incredible return that coincided with a barren spell for his strike partner, Chris Sutton. Only one half of the fabled SAS was finding the net, but Sutton was still an integral part of the team. Sutton wrote in his autobiography, *Paradise and Beyond,* that Shearer was 'a machine. When he got half a chance he buried it. He had a low backlift and such power in his shooting.' The Geordie's goals had powered Blackburn into a six-point lead before Manchester United hosted Coventry the following day.

After the dismal cup exit to Manchester City in December, Newcastle hosted Brian Horton's side again. They could not find a way past a well-organised City side. A goalless draw was not what Keegan wanted from his side. City goalkeeper Andy Dibble repelled the Newcastle attacks and saved a Ruel Fox penalty to keep the scores level. Nottingham Forest took advantage of Newcastle's inability to find the net with a narrow win at home to Crystal Palace. Missing Stan Collymore, Forest got the win thanks to a goal from Steve Bull's cousin, Gary. Bryan Roy got his fifth assist of the season to create the goal for Bull, but Collymore's return to the side couldn't come soon enough.

Liverpool had a much more straightforward afternoon as they held on to third place. A brace from Robbie Fowler, sandwiched between goals from John Scales and Ian Rush, gave Liverpool their fourth win in a row and a third consecutive clean sheet. With his two goals, Fowler brought his tally for the season to 20, level with the metronomic Shearer. An assist for Rush topped off a brilliant performance and showed not only the development of the striker but the improvements in Liverpool since Roy Evans took over. Tragically, after the game, Fowler was told that a Liverpool YTS player named Ian Frodsham had sadly passed away from cancer. Frodsham had been a promising young player that had already played for England Under-18s. Fowler paid tribute to Frodsham in the *Liverpool Echo,* saying: 'It is unfair that this should happen to someone who had such a lot to offer the sport.'

In the battle at the bottom, Ipswich scored more than two goals for only the second time all season. The visitors, Leicester, had a day to forget. Chris Kiwomya was the star of the show. His two goals and an assist for Frank Yallop hauled Ipswich off the bottom of the table for the first time since the end of November. George Burley had his first victory, but there was a long way to go. Seven points and a hugely inferior goal difference stood between Ipswich and overtaking Crystal Palace. A mountain to climb, but, for a night, Ipswich celebrated a vital victory.

George Graham did not have a good Christmas. Continued bung allegations littered the back pages and his team's patchy form could not paper over the cracks. New players were needed to freshen up the squad, but transfers must have been the furthest thing from his mind. In the opposite dugout, Gerry Francis could do no wrong. A North London derby at home in the new year came at the perfect time. Gheorghe Popescu's goal midway through the first half gave Spurs another win and a solid rearguard action meant a fifth successive clean sheet and nine games unbeaten. The turnaround was incredible. At the end of the day, Spurs sat sixth in the league and were delivering on the promise of their summer investment.

Still in a job, but on borrowed time, George Graham had to go into the transfer market to try and bolster his team. Paul Merson was still in rehab and Graham's attack was firing blanks. The fact that John Jensen, who had never scored for Arsenal, was the only thing to celebrate in the last gameshowed how far the team had fallen. Graham needed to do something to arrest the alarming slide. Games were coming thick and fast. With an FA Cup third-round tie against former club Millwall and a Coca-Cola Cup quarter-final against Liverpool on the horizon, the pressure was mounting.

Amidst the bung allegations, transfers should have been a taboo subject, but English clubs were not put off. The news that Ghanaian striker Tony Yeboah had walked out on Eintracht Frankfurt piqued the interest of Arsenal and Newcastle, but it was Leeds who agreed a deal for the Ghanaian for a fee of £3.4m. Yeboah had what Leeds missed: an eye for goal and the physical attributes to succeed in the English game. The battle for a work permit under strict new rules began immediately.

There were more strikers on the move as Neil Shipperley left Chelsea for Southampton for £1.2m, a club record, to replace Iain Dowie, who joined Crystal Palace a week later. Aston Villa bolstered their squad with a double signing from Derby County. Having already lost Paul Kitson to Newcastle, it was Tommy Johnson and Gary Charles who now exited the Baseball Ground. Aston Villa was their new home as Brian Little parted with a combined fee of £2.9m to inject some life into his squad. After only a few months in England, Ilie Dumitrescu was on the move again as he left Spurs for La Liga and Sevilla.

Manchester United completed the fixtures with a home victory over Coventry. Goals from Paul Scholes and Eric Cantona defeated a poor Coventry side, who could not find the quality to compete, despite the best efforts of Dion Dublin on his return to Old Trafford. Mark Hughes did not feature in the matchday squad, but the youth products impressed with notable performances from Gary Neville, now at right-back, Paul Scholes, who enjoyed his role as a striker, Keith Gillespie, the pacy winger, and Nicky Butt, the combative midfielder. United still needed to be more ruthless in front of goal but their attacking had improved.

All season, Alex Ferguson had toyed with the idea of buying a new striker. Since the sale of Dion Dublin, meaning Ferguson lacked an English striker to help overcome the foreign player rule in Europe, he had discussed a range of strikers: Les Ferdinand, Teddy Sheringham, Andy Cole and Stan Collymore. It seemed that Collymore was the top target. The dynamic Forest striker was 23 and fitted the profile of what Ferguson needed.

Before the FA Cup tie with Sheffield United, scheduled for the evening of Monday, 9 January, Ferguson discussed signing a new striker with Bryan Kidd, his assistant. Manchester United had been quiet in the transfer market since winning a second consecutive Premier League title; David May, at £1.2m, had been the only addition to the squad. Ferguson was ready to spend and looked to his first target, Les Ferdinand. The news from Loftus Road was that Ferdinand was not for sale until the end of the season. Exactly what Ray Wilkins had said when he took over from Gerry Francis.

Ferguson took another phone call while his own transfer search moved on. Kevin Keegan called and asked if Keith Gillespie was available. A quick 'no' from Ferguson ended that conversation. But, knowing that he had been knocked back earlier in the season, Andy Cole's name came into the conversation. Ferguson wrote that he 'detected just a little uncertainty about Cole, so I told Kiddo and we agreed we should target him'.

The relationship between Cole and Keegan had soured. Keegan later wrote that Cole's attitude had changed. His effort on the training pitch was different. A side built around the dynamic No.9 did not work without him at maximum capacity. Newcastle's form had deteriorated, as had Cole's fitness due to a nagging shin splints injury. It seemed that Keegan, wanted to cash in on his striker and negotiated a deal with one of his biggest rivals to sell his star.

Cole had moved into Newcastle city centre after living in Crook when he first moved north. He had signed a new contract, he followed the advice of his manager to buy a place in the North East and that helped him settle. Cole scored goals and enjoyed playing for Newcastle. Even though the team had exceeded expectations in their first season in the Premier League, the blistering start to 1994/95 was unexpected. Before the season, Spurs had tried to sign the striker with a £5m bid that was quickly rebuffed. Cole scored freely but, as autumn turned to winter, the goals dried up, injuries recurred and Keegan even dropped Cole from the side.

Cole answered Keegan's comments about being 'tapped up' by United with a categorical denial that anything like that happened. He admitted that he was not close to Keegan any more. A training ground incident had been a problem between the two men, but Cole and Keegan got on as much as they needed to in order to help the team. There was no thought that Cole would leave Newcastle at that time. He was settled, scoring and the team were moving in the right direction.

Collymore was before Cole on Ferguson's hit list, so the call was made to the City Ground. But after three calls to Frank Clark, there was no answer. Finally, the call was returned and

Ferguson was told that Clark was not well enough to talk. Speculation had surrounded Collymore all season. It seemed that a move to Manchester United was inevitable. Collymore's agent, Paul Stretford, who also looked after Andy Cole, reassured the striker that the move to United would happen, that it was a case of sitting tight and waiting for Ferguson to make the bid. Now that Frank Clark had declined to speak to Ferguson, the prospect of Collymore leaving the City Ground looked unlikely. The weekend papers were full of speculation about Collymore's departure from the City Ground after missing the game against Crystal Palace. Fans pressured Collymore and the club with constant chants on the terraces that questioned the star striker and his commitment to the side.

Ferguson, frustrated by the antics of Frank Clark, and encouraged by a chat with Joe Royle, which started about the transfer of Mark Hughes before turning to talk of unrest with Andy Cole at Newcastle, gave Kevin Keegan a call. In his diary of the season, Ferguson outlines the conversation he had with Keegan about Cole and the inclusion of Keith Gillespie in any deal for the striker. In his autobiography, Keegan writes that it was Stretford, Cole's agent, who mentioned United were interested in buying the striker. Keegan concluded that he needed to sell Cole. Negotiations began with an opening offer of £5m plus Gillespie, who was valued at £1m.

A speedy winger, Gillespie was an exciting prospect who had played a number of games that season. He was Irish, which made it difficult to select him for European competitions. On the right-hand side, Kanchelskis was first choice, David Beckham was understudy and Terry Cooke was the next to emerge from the youth-team production line.

Ferguson and Keegan continued to haggle, with a fee of £6m plus Gillespie the final offer, which Keegan accepted. The decision was not made just yet. Keegan needed time to find a replacement. He would get back to Ferguson.

Back on the pitch, Premier League teams navigated the notoriously difficult FA Cup third round with relative success. Almost all teams progressed to the next round and only one was knocked out – Ipswich lost to mid-table Endsleigh Division Two side Wrexham. Additional fixtures were a pain for managers and replays for Arsenal, Coventry, Leeds, Liverpool and Manchester City congested the fixture list. The only all-Premiership tie also ended in a draw. Again, Newcastle, with Andy Cole in the starting line-up and cup-tied if he left, could not find a winner at home, drawing 1-1 with Blackburn. News cameras, journalists and Newcastle fans should have stayed at St James' Park for the next 48 hours when the season-altering transfer would become public.

Finding a replacement for a player like Andy Cole was not going to be easy. Keegan made Chris Armstrong his top target. The Palace striker was not as prolific as Cole, but showed promise. With £6m about to burn a hole in his pocket, Keegan offered £4.7m for the young striker, which was rejected by Palace. Alan Smith was furious and told the papers on the morning of the FA Cup ties: 'If Chris goes, so do I. I can't make the position any clearer.' Smith had just signed Iain Dowie from Southampton for £400,000 to support Armstrong in the search for goals. Terry McDermott, Keegan's assistant, admitted that there were two or three players that Newcastle were looking to sign, which was confirmed by Keegan, who admitted: 'I am looking to buy a player.' No reports of selling Cole had leaked into the papers and there were no questions about why Newcastle needed to sign another striker after the Kitson saga.

Ferguson prepared for United's FA Cup game at Sheffield United a day after Newcastle's game, which he had watched from the stands, by trying to find out which of his players had been struck down by flu. Amidst the selection headaches, he waited by the phone for Kevin Keegan to call back. Once the United squad had arrived at the hotel, Ferguson's phone rang. It was Keegan. The deal was agreed and Andy Cole was about to become a Manchester United player. Ferguson paid £6m and Keith Gillespie for one of the best strikers in England. Late goals in the game at Bramall Lane made it a perfect day for the Manchester United manager, who decided not to join the players on the way home, but to meet his new striker to begin contract negotiations. Brian Kidd arrived on the bus after the game without the manager, much to the confusion of the players. Detectives Bruce and McClair, who had an impromptu meeting with Gillespie and Ferguson in the toilets after the game to explain the Irishman's departure, speculated that it was Andy Cole that the manager was going to sign. Kidd's response to Bruce was: 'Well, Steve Howey's playing well. It might be him, you never know.'

The issue for Ferguson was not in the negotiations with Cole, which passed without any issues, but the feelings of Mark Hughes. The Welshman had been a mainstay of the side during Ferguson's reign, but he now had a player that was certain to take his place. Transfer rumours had appeared in the press and Ferguson fielded calls from Joe Royle, who was looking to partner Hughes with Duncan Ferguson.

Andy Cole was unveiled as a Manchester United player on Tuesday, 10 January. In a press conference at Old Trafford, Martin Edwards chaired the announcement, with Ferguson and Cole on either side of him. A massive transfer like this had somehow been kept away from the press, so the small room was packed. Ferguson was pleased to have a new striker and admired Cole's ability around the box, which he believed would be especially valuable in Europe when teams tended to deny United space. Breaking the transfer record was also another clear indication that United wanted to push Blackburn as far as possible.

For Cole, he admitted his surprise at the move. As far as he was concerned, there was no issue with Newcastle and he certainly had not expected to find himself at a rival club. Paul Stretford had broken the news to Cole as the two managers agreed the deal and he was driven down to Manchester immediately. Cole wrote that, on the drive he 'sat quietly, uncomfortable with what had just happened'. There were a lot of unanswered questions for Cole, even 25 years later, but the Andy Cole of 1995 felt the same. He told reporters in the press conference that the move was 'a big shock. And I bet it was a big shock for you boys [journalists] as well.' Cole reiterated the fact he never wanted to leave Newcastle. At St James' Park, meanwhile, Newcastle fans arrived to make their feelings clear.

Kevin Keegan was adored on Tyneside. The decision to sell Cole was not welcomed by the fans. In classic Keegan fashion, he emerged to speak to fans and tried to justify his decision to sell the team's star player. He pleaded with them to allow him to run the club as he needed to. He alluded to the sales of Gavin Peacock and David Kelly, a fan favourite who had won Player of the Year in the promotion season before being sold to make way for Peter Beardsley. Keegan did not think the sale of Cole was a gamble; he believed that he had maximised the value of a player who had 'lost a bit of his spark'. With no replacement lined up, Keegan had to work out who could lead the line in the next game – at home to Manchester United.

The quarter-finals of the Coca-Cola Cup took centre stage amidst the transfer drama. Four home wins saw Bolton, Crystal Palace, Liverpool and Swindon progress to the semi-finals. For Bolton and Swindon, it was a tremendous achievement as Division One teams. Even Crystal Palace, who were too close to the relegation zone for comfort, at least got a break from the gruelling league schedule to dream of cup glory. Liverpool's narrow victory over Arsenal potentially cleared the way for Roy Evans's side to lift the first trophy of his reign. The semi-finals, to be played over two legs, drew both Premiership sides against each other to leave a path for Bolton and Swindon to represent Division One in the final.

In the build-up to the Manchester United-Newcastle game, Alex Ferguson sat down with Mark Hughes to discuss the striker's future. After the papers released details about the impasse in contract negotiations a few months earlier, Ferguson felt it was his duty to let Hughes find first-team football. Joe Royle was persistent. There was no way he would let a deal die, so when Ferguson met Hughes, a meeting explained in his diary, he laid out the terms of what United would accept. If a club paid £2.5m, then Hughes could leave. The striker, as Ferguson told it, was concerned that Everton were not able to offer a deal with such a large fee involved. United still had a number of high-profile cup games ahead, which Cole was cup-tied for, and France had games that clashed with the league programme, so Hughes had a chance to be part of the first team in a reduced role.

George Graham, still Arsenal manager and still under investigation, dipped his toe into the transfer market again with a double signing. The Gunners needed help for Ian Wright. His record-breaking goalscoring run propped up what was a poor season in the league. An operation put Alan Smith out for a month, so reinforcements were needed. Off-the-field issues aside, Graham had work to do.

John Hartson and Chris Kiwomya were the two players the Arsenal manager hoped would turn around the team's fortunes. Hartson was only 19 but already a Welsh international and the £2.5m price tag was a British record for a teenager. Graham was pleased to have strengthened the squad but admitted in *The Independent* that: 'They are not the big-name players everybody hoped and expected I would get, but the big names I want are not available.' Kiwomya had not fulfilled his potential at Ipswich, but the hope was that he had a chance to do that at Arsenal. A tribunal had been assigned to set the fee.

Leeds were having issues of their own with the delay in signing Tony Yeboah. The Department of Employment had yet to ratify the paperwork for the striker's work permit. A cautious PFA, who advised the department, decided that his goalscoring exploits in Germany were not enough to waive him straight into the league. In one of the busiest weeks in Premier League football, Paul Merson emerged from rehab and faced the flash of the television cameras. The press conference announced his return to the Arsenal set-up but the emotional toil of the past couple of months showed. Merson held back tears as he described his treatment as 'the hardest six weeks I've ever done'. A question fired back from a reporter seemed simple: 'What did you have to do?' Merson's hand itched his neck; it stopped as his head dropped. Tears started and David Davies stepped in. Recovery continued out of rehab and Merson ended his association with the Tuesday Club and stepped back into football a different person.

Back to the actual Premier League, Blackburn's good form showed no signs of stopping, with a 3-0 home win over Nottingham Forest. Four wins in a row for Rovers, who had Kenny Dalglish back at the training ground post-operation. The win took them three points ahead of Manchester United for at least a day. Forest's Bryan Roy was not convinced by the way Blackburn played the game. He was reported in the press as saying that 'they play to score goals and not entertain'. Alan Shearer was not impressed. He wrote in response to Roy that: 'I always thought the finest form of entertainment was to put the ball in the back of the net as often as possible.' Shearer was not far wrong – Blackburn were top scorers in the league and top of the table.

Aston Villa and Crystal Palace recorded home victories and hauled themselves up the table. John Fashanu scored only his second goal for Villa since his move from Wimbledon in the 2-1 victory. Palace, who had not scored for nine games, fought off attention from clubs to keep hold of Chris Armstrong, but it was Ricky Newman and George Ndah who gave them a 2-0 win over Leicester, who were now four points behind Ipswich and rock bottom. The arrival of Mark Robins for £1m from Norwich was completed in the next few days and could not come soon enough.

The reason Ipswich had created separation from Leicester was an improbable win at Anfield. Liverpool's four-game winning streak and eight-game unbeaten run in the league did not matter to George Burley and his players. Adam Tanner's stunning goal on half an hour was all the visitors needed to record a victory. Ipswich had not won back-to-back games all season; it was a good time to start.

Gerry Francis, Manager of the Month for December, did not fall to any curse, recording another win. Ten games unbeaten was a remarkable feat for the new manager. The defence, after five consecutive clean sheets, buckled when Jeroen Boere gave West Ham the lead after ten minutes. Undeterred, Spurs attacked and, after a half-time dressing-down from the manager, emerged winners thanks to goals from Teddy Sheringham and a first in six league games from Jürgen Klinsmann.

Wimbledon marched up the table over the Christmas period with a strong set of results. Wins over Southampton, West Ham and Everton, and a New Year's Eve draw with Chelsea, put them ninth in the table. An away win at Norwich improved the position even further. Goals from Alan Reeves and Efan Ekoku cancelled out the opener from Jeremy Goss and meant the Dons leapfrogged their opponents and Leeds, who drew a blank in a draw at home to Southampton. Despite their modest budget and chaotic reputation, Wimbledon were performing better than their peers and the sixth-place finish in 1993/94 showed that investing in the right players pays off.

St James' Park walked in a 'Keegan Wonderland' against Manchester United in the first game since the sale of Andy Cole. There were no protests, no banners and no calls for the manager's head. The Toon Army got behind their manager and his players in a crucial home game against Manchester United. Football scriptwriters, those fabled creatures who seem to design every moment that matters, pitted two teams together who had made the headlines all week. Keegan's decision to sell his star player came under daily scrutiny. All he asked for was time.

One player who did not have time on his side was Mark Hughes. A glittering career at Manchester United seemed to be ending. Contract negotiations stalled and even though interest from Everton was concrete, the clubs did not agree on the valuation. It seemed like Hughes was on his way out and it would be more 'when' than 'if'.

Hughes started up front alongside Eric Cantona, as he had done for most of the season. With the scriptwriters hard at work, of course it was Hughes who opened the scoring. Roy Keane played the ball over the top of the Newcastle defence towards Cantona, who glanced the ball forward. Hughes was in behind and in on goal. He got to the ball first as Srníček raced out of his goal. United's No.10 lifted it over the keeper and into the net. One-nil. But there was no celebration from the goalscorer. The camera panned in on the Welshman. He had barely moved. His head dropped and he untangled his legs from the Newcastle goalkeeper and flopped to the ground. Strewn on his side, Hughes's team-mates surrounded him. Manchester United fans chanted his name as the medical staff arrived on the pitch. It was the end of the game for the striker.

Life without Cole did not phase Newcastle in the early stages of the game. They created chances, but it was not until the second half when they put together their best move of the match. Having been criticised for not playing their usual attacking game, focused on quick passing, Newcastle put together a passing move that started at the feet of Srníček and ended up with Paul Kitson getting the bounce of the ball off Gary Pallister in the box and firing his shot through the legs of Peter Schmeichel. The young striker spurned further opportunities, but United had the better chances as the game progressed. Keane evaded the Newcastle offside trap, only to slot his finish into the body of the Newcastle keeper. United continued to press and Ryan Giggs's jet-heeled break in the last minute involved a slalom around hapless Newcastle defenders before he picked out Eric Cantona at the back post. The Frenchman soared. He met the cross with both feet off the ground, made contact with the ball and it passed underneath Srníček, across the goal line and wide. Cantona dropped to his knees, anguished, as he watched the shot drift past the post. His manager had his hands on his head in disbelief. A point shared, with better finishing needed from both teams.

After the game, reports emerged that Hughes may have injured his cruciate ligaments, which would mean at least six weeks on the sidelines, maybe longer. Fortunately, the result of the collision was actually a large gash on his leg. Painful, but treatable, so a return to action was not far away. Alex Ferguson, helped out by the football gods, could pick Andy Cole and Eric Cantona without having to leave out the talismanic Hughes.

A slew of FA Cup replays filled the midweek fixture list and the shock of the round came at Highbury. Millwall had earned a goalless draw at home and piled the pressure on George Graham with a 2-0 victory. Both sides had opportunities to win the game. Ian Wright and Kevin

Campbell missed chances they were expected to score. Millwall had their own, too, and they had to wait until the last minute before starlet Mark Kennedy rounded off the win with a thunderous strike into the roof of the net past David Seaman to see Mick McCarthy's men into the next round.

The rest of the Premiership teams still in the competition progressed, with Liverpool needing penalties to get past Birmingham. In a replay at Ewood Park, Newcastle recorded a 2-1 win thanks to a long-range strike from defender Marc Hottiger and the winner from Lee Clark. After a barren spell, Chris Sutton had equalised for Blackburn with a cool finish in the box. Keegan was pleased to progress, but Blackburn had a clear focus on the league title now.

Postponements hampered the fixture list on 21 January with games between Leicester and Leeds, QPR and Ipswich, Wimbledon and Liverpool, Tottenham and Manchester City, and Southampton and West Ham all cancelled due to adverse weather conditions. The league programme across the country was affected, with more than 20 games called off.

Arsenal, who wished the rain had fallen on them, dusted themselves down and recorded a narrow victory at Coventry with the only goal of the game coming from John Hartson, his first for the club. Phil Neal felt the pressure in the Coventry hot seat. His team had tumbled from a relatively safe mid-table position into a relegation battle.

The relegation battle was fierce. Everton looked the most likely to get out of it, since the arrival of Joe Royle. Hosting Crystal Palace at Goodison Park, Duncan Ferguson scored twice, with another from his strike partner Paul Rideout. Not a vintage game of football by any stretch, but Everton worked hard and earned their three points. A goal from Chris Coleman threatened to get Palace back into the game, but Ferguson's second in the final minutes made sure they didn't. After his sending-off against Arsenal the previous week, the giant Scot showed the other side of his game. During his loan, and permanent signing, he proved why he was such a valuable asset. His manager loved what he saw and said as much after the game: 'He has a charisma which the fans have latched on to, but he's proving he can play a bit as well, with a deft touch and turn of pace.' The signing of Ferguson, completed by the chairman Peter Johnson, and the appointment of Joe Royle looked inspired. But Palace were in trouble.

At Portman Road, Ipswich looked to have secured three points until Craig Burley, the nephew of Ipswich boss George, equalised for Chelsea to make it 2-2. It was not what the home side needed in their fight to stay up. For Aston Villa, Brian Little proved to be fully in control of his side with an excellent victory against Nottingham Forest. The City Ground was never an easy place to visit, but Villa, in good form over the Christmas period and into the new year, got goals from their experienced strikers, Fashanu and Saunders, to earn the win. Stan Collymore netted a penalty for Forest, but back-to-back defeats frustrated Frank Clark.

Super Sunday might as well have been titled *The Big Match* as it featured the two sides at the top of the table who, after Newcastle's third consecutive draw and fourth blank in six games, could create distance between themselves and the chasing pack. Ewood Park had hosted the first meeting between the sides, also live on television, and it had been full of controversy and refereeing chaos. Manchester United had come out on top in that game, but the form of both sides since then was incredible.

Blackburn had won 11 of their last 12 league games, scoring 29 and conceding six. A remarkable 33 points from a possible 36 was title-winning form. It was almost impossible to match. Manchester United had won eight of the 13 league games they had played in the same period. Goals flowed, with 25 scored, despite Ferguson's desire to sign a new striker and the defence held firm, with 11 conceded. Clearly the two sides were the best in the league and by some distance. Consistency was key for both and United needed to convert draws into wins to keep up with their rivals. A game at Old Trafford was an opportunity to close the gap.

Five points ahead at the start of the game, Blackburn still had Stuart Ripley missing from the side, which cut off the supply line to Shearer and Sutton on one side of the pitch. Shearer's performances dominated the back pages and his goal tally was phenomenal. Rumours circulated in the papers that the striker was a target for Kevin Keegan. Flush with the Cole money, he was reportedly ready to spend £10m to bring Geordie Shearer home. The player's focus was on Blackburn; he did want to play for his hometown club at some point in his career, but just not yet.

Andy Cole, after his British record transfer, was joined on the pitch by three previous record holders in Shearer, Roy Keane and Chris Sutton. When the Premier League was formed in 1992, not many fans or commentators on the game believed that the £3.6m record fee Blackburn paid for Alan Shearer would be almost doubled within two and a half years into the price paid for Cole. A seismic shift in the money flowing through the top of the English game.

Ferguson had put out an attacking line-up, with Keane at right-back, McClair as the partner for Ince in central midfield, Giggs and Sharpe out wide and the newly formed duo of debutant Cole alongside the Gallic flair of Cantona. The game was tight, but United dictated the first half and had chances to take the lead.

Cole had the first opportunity of the game with his first touch as a Manchester United player. With the No.17 on his back, he burst through the defence from a ball over the top, but he skewed his shot wide of the post. Further chances were spurned as United exerted their dominance. Blackburn barely made a dent in the United defence and had to thank their own rearguard to go in level at half-time.

In the second half, the pattern of the game was similar, but Blackburn found a way to repel United attacks. There was no way they would give up the top spot without a fight. The home side played much more football than the league leaders, who did not offer much in the form of a cohesive attack. With a defender like Colin Hendry marshalling the back line, Blackburn were able to fight off the onslaught.

Finally, in the 80th minute, United hit the back of the net. The talismanic Cantona powered a header past Tim Flowers, who had a good game, after some grafting from Giggs out wide saw him rob Henning Berg of the ball and the resulting cross was curled perfectly on to the head of the Frenchman. One-nil to United. It was fully deserved and it looked to be the winner.

Then, Paul Durkin joined Gerald Ashby in Blackburn's refereeing hall of shame when he disallowed a goal from Tim Sherwood. A ball angled to the back post found Shearer up against Keane. He towered over the makeshift right-back and directed a header across the box. Brave as ever, Blackburn captain Sherwood threw himself between Bruce and Pallister and powered a header past Schmeichel, who was in starfish mode. Sherwood turned away in delight, until he saw Durkin. His arms, raised above his head to celebrate, quickly dropped down on to his head. Disbelief washed over him. Shearer was livid and roared at Durkin. Undeterred, the referee kept his arm aloft to signal the free kick to United. He had judged Shearer to have pushed Keane as they jumped together at the back post. Andy Gray, on co-commentary for Sky, was not convinced. 'Well, I tell you, there's no more than an arm up there … I certainly thought that Shearer didn't do a lot wrong.' None of the United players appealed for a decision or surrounded the referee, which added to Blackburn's case.

The goal was chalked off and United, despite missing chances after the incident, were victorious and closed the gap to two points, albeit having played one game more. Controversy reigned again in the Premiership.

In the press before the game, Dalglish had predicted that the atmosphere may be too much for the referee. Ferguson was not happy that his opposite number was trying to play mind games with the officials. He stated: 'I just hope the officials will be able to handle the atmosphere and the pressure.' In the cauldron of Old Trafford, Dalglish had a point. The Monday-morning papers looked back at a weekend of football, with the focus on one game only.

'Vintage whine' read the headline on the back of the *Daily Mirror,* with a photograph of Eric Cantona wheeling away in celebration emblazoned between the two words. Dalglish was furious and branded Durkin 'a disgrace', accusing the official of costing his side the title. He reiterated the point that if Keane had been fouled, he would have appealed immediately. Ferguson had his say and disagreed with Dalglish, obviously. Somewhat revelling in the Blackburn manager's pre-match words, Ferguson replied with a sly dig, saying: 'Kenny wanted a perfect referee, a strong official and he got one. He got his wish.' The rest of the back pages were dedicated to Andy Cole's debut, including a minute-by-minute breakdown of his performance,h and columns that laid out all the things he did not do. Time to settle seemed to be against him already.

Monday Night Football saw West Ham lose at home again, this time to Sheffield Wednesday, who had Chris Waddle and Mark Bright to thank for their two goals. Two red cards for the Hammers did not help their cause and Wednesday happily took advantage. The Owls rose to seventh in the table, with West Ham 20th and in the relegation zone.

There was also good news for Leeds as they finally confirmed the signing of Tony Yeboah. For £3.4m, Howard

Wilkinson added a prolific striker to his squad. The search for the elusive No.9 had spanned many leagues across Europe, with targets including Duncan Ferguson, Karl-Heinz Riedle, Tomas Skuhravy and Ruben Sosa. Top scorer in the Bundesliga for two consecutive seasons, Yeboah was a quality addition at a competitive price. Arguably fitting Wilkinson's style better than the other targets, he was in line to be in the squad for the game against QPR.

It was Phil Masinga who was the star of the show for Leeds at home to QPR in a 4-0 victory. Yeboah watched from the bench before coming on in the last ten minutes. Masinga clearly needed to prove his worth and he did just that. On Merseyside, Everton travelled to Anfield for the derby, which ended goalless and meant Everton were unbeaten against their rivals for the season. Another new striker, John Hartson, hit his second in as many games to give Arsenal an early lead at home to Southampton, only to see Jim Magilton rescue a point for the Saints.

There were six Premiership games scheduled for Wednesday, 25 January, but only one of them is still remembered today. Wins for Newcastle and Nottingham Forest did nothing to improve their title chances. A first goal for Mark Robins in his new colours was not enough to haul Leicester off the bottom of the table.

At Villa Park, Mark Bosnich recreated Harald Schumacher's aerial assault on Patrick Battiston at the 1982 World Cup when he almost decapitated Jürgen Klinsmann in a hideous incident which made headlines, but not the national news. It would be overshadowed by an event that involved another international star.

Eric Cantona did not have the career path expected of a talismanic, inspirational figure. Various incidents during his career in French football had made the headlines and had fans, journalists and the football world questioning whether he deserved the time and patience afforded to him. When he made his move to Leeds, after an infamous aborted trial at Sheffield Wednesday which featured Cantona donning the blue and white stripes of the Owls in a six-a-side game, his temperament and ability were questioned, especially when playing for a club with a manager nicknamed 'Sergeant Wilko'.

Mainly used as a late substitute against tiring defences during Leeds' run to the title, Cantona signed permanently for Leeds after his initial loan spell, but history soon repeated itself when he fell out with Wilkinson after being dropped from the Leeds side. That led to a transfer that changed the history of the Premier League, signing for Manchester United for £1.2m after Alex Ferguson rebuffed Wilkinson's attempts to sign Denis Irwin. An incredible turn of events and one that charged Manchester United's title challenge in 1992/93, ultimately leading to back-to-back championships with Cantona as the star and team leader. His place in the side was reflected by the protection given to him by his manager. Ferguson made sure that Cantona knew the rules, but he also knew how to handle a star who had such vital importance to the side. Cantona's disciplinary record was one that regularly had to be defended by Ferguson; spitting at a fan on his return to Elland Road, sent off in the ferocious atmosphere of the Ali Sami Yen, two red cards in the league with a stamp on John Moncur and then against Arsenal, and a red card in a friendly against Rangers that delayed the start of his league campaign.

Up to this point in the season, Cantona had scored 12 goals and created six more in 21 starts. He was a core part of the United attack, his withdrawn role key in the tactical set-up. In *The Mixer*, Michael Cox notes that Cantona 'was capable of playing either as a traditional centre-forward or as a playmaker'. His goal and assist numbers told the same story, with the Ferguson 4-4-2 becoming more of a 4-4-1-1 with Cantona almost functioning as a No.10 behind a more direct striker. Having partnered Mark Hughes, Andy Cole was now the Frenchman's foil in the United attack.

Crystal Palace had been on an atrocious run of form. After they reached tenth position off the back of four consecutive wins, the decline had been steep. A nine-game winless run was ended with a home win against Leicester but that was followed with a 3-1 defeat at Everton a week later. Hosting Manchester United was never an easy task and Ferguson's team arrived full of confidence after the home win against Blackburn. They wanted to regain top spot.

The two teams met at Selhurst Park on that cold Wednesday night in January.

The first half of the game passed by without too much incident, barring persistent fouling from the Crystal Palace team that broke the flow of the game. It was a tactic that was used often to stop the United attacking juggernaut. Playing against that style of football did not make things easy. Few chances were created and the pitch did not help United play any sort of passing game to threaten Palace.

United started the second half positively. Then, three minutes into the second half, after a long kick upfield from Peter Schmeichel, Cantona was sent off. Pulled and dragged by Richard Shaw as the ball was in the air, the Frenchman kicked out at the Palace No.14 and the linesman spotted it. The Palace players swarmed around Cantona. The referee showed the red card to a roar of approval from the home fans. Paul Ince and Andy Cole were at the heart of the melee and tried to protect their team-mate. Clive Tyldesley, on commentary duties for *Match of the Day*, commented that the sending-off had written the morning headlines; prophetic for the wrong reasons. Cantona turned his collar down and headed off the pitch.

Shaking his head and booed off the pitch, Cantona was shepherded towards the tunnel in the corner of the ground at

Selhurst Park, making the exit all the more painful. Norman Davies, the Manchester United kit man, was tasked with getting the striker safely back to the changing room. Referee Alan Wilkie looked on as he waited for Cantona to leave the pitch before he could restart the game. Alex Ferguson paid no attention to what was happening as he tried to reorganise his players.

The next thing the television cameras showed was Cantona slipping out of Davies's grip and towards the crowd. The name and number were central in the shot: Cantona 7. It was an iconic image of Cantona, off the ground, studs first, tangled in the crowd. 'Cantona is getting involved with some supporters; well, this is outrageous' were the words of Tyldesley in utter disbelief. Davies managed to get Cantona by the arm, as the players ran to the chaos. Schmeichel grabbed Cantona as the rest of the United players descended into the crowd. Again, the yellow Umbro numbers on the back of the black United shirts stood out. Ince 8, Sharpe 5, Cole 17. A stand-off between the fans and players ensued as Cantona was dragged out of sight.

Peter Schmeichel wrote in his autobiography *ONE* that he didn't hear anything that a fan shouted at Cantona, but he saw the one who sprinted down towards the United player. The goalkeeper was also hit by hot tea as he tried to get Cantona safely off the pitch.

At the same time, the police had got involved. Stewards and players were entangled as fans made their feelings known to the Manchester United players. The scenes were chaotic and the controversial Frenchman had whipped up a storm again. The rest of the game paled into insignificance, with David May's goal and Andy Cole's goal drought forgotten forever. Cantona had written so many headlines as United's saviour, but the devil in him had taken over and created a saga that dragged on.

After the game, Ferguson was still oblivious to what had happened and did not understand the seriousness of the incident. There was talk of beer being thrown down at Cantona and an allegation against Paul Ince, but most striking was the lack of knowledge that all parties shared. Until he arrived home and his son Jake told him that Cantona had karate-kicked a fan, Ferguson had only parts of the story from meeting with the referee, the United directors and officers who had told him of the Ince allegation. He refused to watch the video until he was ready. That came at 5.25am on Thursday, 26 January, but it was too late; the inquest had already started.

After the game, *Sportsnight*, the BBC's midweek highlights show, featured an interview with Palace manager Alan Smith, who predictably focused on the game, and Palace fan David Haddock, who offered his view on what unfolded. He described a scene of Palace fans booing Cantona and throwing abuse at him as he passed the rows of fans. One particular fan was highlighted as the target of Cantona's fury with a kick and punch landed over the advertising hoardings.

Des Lynam, presenting *Sportsnight*, read a statement from Chief Superintendent Terry Collins that explained two Crystal Palace fans had made allegations against Eric Cantona and Paul Ince of assault. The two players were allowed to go home and be interviewed at a later date. Gary Lineker was in the expert's seat and suggested a long ban and possibly even the end of Cantona's career. Both men agreed that the action Cantona had taken was unprecedented. The incident was shown again and again. The black Cantona 7 shirt was about to become iconic. Less iconic was the poor joke made by Lineker that Cantona had lost 'les marbles'. Ill-timed and ill-judged considering the fallout that was to come. His parting comment, in response to Lynam, highlighted that it was the incident we would hear most about after the game.

The next day, football dominated the papers. Cantona's actions, illustrated by the iconic image taken by photographer Steve Lindsell, took up column inches from every journalist in the land. Football had become national interest again and Cantona was the main protagonist.

On the front cover of the *Daily Mirror*, the image of the flashpoint was emblazoned with the words 'Cantona to be charged'. The back page of the same paper featured another evocative headline: 'Is this the end for the MADMAN?' Cantona's temper was well known, but his actions had taken opinion to another level. After that first day of reporting, the papers did not let up. Article after article on the incident, about Cantona's past and particularly Manchester United's handling of the affair. There were no winners in this situation.

One thing that could not be denied was that this was a true turning point in the history of the Premier League. There was wall-to-wall coverage of arguably its biggest star. Cantona fulfilled the star role perfectly; his style of play was mysterious and alluring, while his persona exuded enough mean and moody to make him look like a film star. Courting controversy was par for the course for 'King Eric' and, as many have said before, this was akin to a JFK moment for Cantona and the league. The column inches devoted to talk of Cantona, Manchester United and the sport in general were priceless; any press is good press, as they say. It did not feel like that for Alex Ferguson, though.

Telling the story of the season, Ferguson's diary was mainly focused on difficulties managing injuries in the squad, battling against Blackburn and reaction to matches. After the Cantona incident, the sole focus was meetings with the club, lawyers and trying to do the right thing for all parties. The gates to The Cliff were closed and Ferguson battened down the hatches. He knew he needed to make the right decisions as soon as he could. Every journalist and editor wanted Cantona punished.

An initial meeting between Ferguson, chairman Sir Roland Smith and chairman of the plc, Maurice Watkins, resulted in the general thought that no player was bigger than the club and that Cantona should be released from his contract. All of the men exercised caution about what they could do, while trying to maintain balance. Eventually, a decision was reached to suspend Cantona, which the player and the PFA agreed to. While the meeting was in progress, the BBC *News at Ten* programme led with Cantona's actions as one of the main stories.

Matthew Simmons was the victim of Cantona's attack. Most of the papers had focused on the footballer, but now a picture was painted of the victim in the whole affair. Just 20 years old, Simmons's murky past was national news. Reports of his attendance at British National Party and National Front rallies in 1992 came to light, as well as a violent assault on a petrol station attendant at the age of 17. Lewis Rajanayagam, the victim of that assault, shared his side of the story with the papers and told of his terror at being attacked by Simmons. It became clear that this was not necessarily a simple case of a volatile footballer attacking an innocent fan.

The papers had a field day. Even more stories for the daily need to fill column inches. Cantona was single-handedly helping sell copies of the papers. Days and days of coverage took their toll on the player and club. Ferguson, who had started the week talking to Cantona's agents about a new contract, was inundated with phone calls about Manchester United's conduct. He felt his club had acted as fast as they could in the circumstances. If the papers had their way, Cantona would have received his P45 in the dressing room at Selhurst Park.

Maurice Watkins, Manchester United solicitor, presented the punishment for Cantona to the press. Amidst a great deal of second-guessing, the club had to outline the consequences of their star player's actions before the FA could complete its investigation. The result of the discussions and meetings was that Cantona was banned from playing in league and cup games for the remainder of the season. Added to that, a fine of two weeks' wages – £10,800, not the widely reported £20,000 – was issued to the Frenchman. For United, the punishment fitted the crime, but there was no precedent set; they had to wait for the FA's verdict to find out if things would get worse.

Any ban from the FA was enforceable in England, but not elsewhere. There was a chance that Cantona would not have to sit out the rest of the season. Even before the incident, Inter Milan showed interest in Cantona and Massimo Moratti, the soon-to-be Inter chairman, was in attendance at Selhurst Park to watch Cantona and Paul Ince. United, though, were unmoved. Cantona had played the best football of his career in England and it was unlikely that a move to Serie A would be sanctioned by the club. Rumours circled as they do but, for now, Cantona waited for the outcome of the FA investigation.

While the constant scrutiny of Cantona continued, Blackburn were back in action with a Premiership game, a fact that had slipped into the background, in the only league fixture of the weekend. They beat Ipswich 4-1 at home thanks to a hat-trick from Alan Shearer. It put Rovers four points clear at the top of the table with a game in hand on Manchester United. With Cantona suspended by United for the rest of the season, the stakes in every game had risen.

Manchester United were in FA Cup action and brushed aside Wrexham 5-2 with one goal each for Ryan Giggs and Brian McClair, a brace for Denis Irwin and an own goal by Tony Humes. Thoughts of Cantona hung around Old Trafford as fans bellowed his name. The fact the game passed without too much incident was a welcome reprieve from the press battering of the preceding few days.

In the rest of the fourth-round games, Crystal Palace reversed their league form and beat Nottingham Forest. Spurs, Wimbledon and Newcastle eased to victories against Football League teams while Everton, Manchester City, QPR and Leeds narrowly got past their opponents and made it into the next round. Adding to their fixture lists were Liverpool, Sheffield Wednesday, Southampton and Chelsea, who all drew. Norwich and Coventry were in an all-Premiership tie, which ended in a goalless draw to force a replay that neither team needed.

Pos	Team	P	W	D	L	F	A	GD	Pts
1	Blackburn Rovers	25	18	4	3	56	20	+36	58
2	Manchester United	26	16	6	4	47	21	+26	54
3	Liverpool	25	13	7	5	44	20	+24	46
4	Newcastle United	25	12	9	4	43	26	+17	45
5	Nottingham Forest	26	13	6	7	39	28	+11	45
6	Tottenham Hotspur	25	11	6	8	41	36	+5	39
7	Leeds United	24	10	7	7	33	27	+6	37
8	Sheffield Wednesday	26	9	9	8	33	32	+1	36
9	Wimbledon	25	10	5	10	31	40	-9	35
10	Norwich City	25	9	7	9	24	27	-3	34
11	Arsenal	26	8	9	9	29	28	+1	33
12	Aston Villa	26	7	10	9	32	35	-3	31
13	Chelsea	25	8	7	10	32	35	-3	31
14	Manchester City	25	8	7	10	33	39	-6	31
15	Southampton	25	6	11	8	35	40	-5	29
16	Crystal Palace	26	6	9	11	19	26	-7	27
17	Everton	25	6	9	10	25	33	-8	27
18	Queens Park Rangers	24	7	6	11	35	44	-9	27
19	Coventry City	26	6	9	11	23	43	-20	27
20	West Ham United	25	7	4	14	22	32	-10	25
21	Ipswich Town	26	5	5	16	29	53	-24	20
22	Leicester City	25	4	6	15	23	43	-20	18

The Bung (February)

FEBRUARY STARTED with football, two games on the first day of the month. Newcastle enjoyed a 2-0 victory over Everton at home with goals from Ruel Fox and Peter Beardsley. A second win in a row at home provided some relief for Kevin Keegan, who was still reeling from the decision to sell Andy Cole. The game was marred by two red cards for Everton, which gave them little chance of getting any sort of result.

In the night's other game, Blackburn and Leeds faced off at Ewood Park. The game typified the season. Alan Shearer was thwarted by John Lukic before Gary Speed set Brian Deane free and in on the Blackburn goal.

Acres of grass stood between Deane and Tim Flowers. The Blackburn and England goalkeeper came haring out of his goal and slid towards Deane. The goal was gaping, but the Leeds striker was strewn on the floor with no chance of getting anywhere near the ball. Referee Rodger Gifford had no choice but to show a red card. Half-hearted appeals from the Blackburn players, led by Ian Pearce, but Flowers had no complaints.

Only a few minutes later, Blackburn won a penalty after Chris Sutton was bundled down in the box. Some might say it was soft, but the referee pointed to the spot. Shearer dispatched the penalty, obviously. The controversy continued in the second half when Gary McAllister's long-range effort looked to have crossed the line. Gifford, at close quarters, and his linesman said no.

Then, five minutes before the end, McAllister was bundled over in the box for a penalty. Blackburn's players were incensed and charged towards the linesman. Gifford rushed over to support his fellow official and shepherd the players away. Leeds' Gary Kelly ensured he wasn't far away and told the officials he approved of the decision. McAllister made no mistake from the spot with a powerful strike down the middle and past substitute goalkeeper Bobby Mimms.

A 1-1 draw was not the result Blackburn needed and neither were the actions of a fan who tried to attack referee Gifford. Luckily, Mimms was able to intervene and prevent any harm coming to the referee. Kenny Dalglish condemned the fan after the game.

A day later, the back pages, still dominated by the Cantona affair, were awash with more shame for football. Robbie Fowler, Joe Kinnear and Vinnie Jones had added to the FA's workload with charges of their own, all accused of bringing the game into disrepute. The sheen from the Premiership was wearing off fast.

In the first weekend fixtures of the month, Andy Cole netted his first for Manchester United in a victory over Aston Villa that featured another striker, John Fashanu, being carried off with a knee injury. Alex Ferguson's preparation for the game was mainly taken up with the Cantona affair and the protracted contract and transfer negotiations with Mark Hughes and his agent. Despite sometimes difficult discussions, Ferguson managed to agree a new two-year deal for his striker, which at least meant the manager had a partner for Cole.

Newcastle and Arsenal had games to forget, both suffering away defeats. Keegan's Newcastle had been on a decent run, five unbeaten, but it came to an end with a crushing loss at Loftus Road. Les Ferdinand, who continued to impress home fans and opposing managers, scored twice in the first seven minutes. Both goals were assisted by Kevin Gallen. The youth-team prodigy made his mark in the first team. Three days earlier, Arsenal had held AC Milan to a 0-0 draw at Highbury in the first leg of the European Super Cup, a match that saw the return of Paul Merson after his spell in rehab, but Sheffield Wednesday proved too much for the Gunners. Going behind in the first minute to an Andy Linighan goal did not deter Trevor Francis's team who equalised within five minutes thanks to Dan Petrescu. A Klas Ingesson goal and a last-minute Mark Bright effort added more misery to George Graham's season.

Everton under Joe Royle were a team transformed. In his first 12 games, the Toffees had picked up 19 points. Although not clear of the relegation scrap, which arguably included teams as far up the table as Norwich in tenth place, Everton's 2-1 victory over the Canaries in Royle's 13th game was important after two difficult games against Liverpool and Newcastle. Norwich still had not recorded a victory in their four games of 1995. John Deehan was beginning to look over his shoulder. Luckily for both teams, defeats for Leicester and Ipswich, to West Ham and Crystal Palace respectively, meant that two of the relegation places looked set, even with 15 games remaining.

Blackburn visited White Hart Lane and hoped to restore their five-point lead at the top of the table. Spurs had other ideas. Aston Villa might have ended their excellent unbeaten run, but the league leaders had no such luck. A superb performance and 3-1 victory summed up Gerry Francis's tenure to date, with a solid defensive unit that started with the first line of defence in Klinsmann and Sheringham, and the counter-attacking punch of Barmby and Anderton. Blackburn had an off-day. Probably one too many after a return of four points from the last 12, but the dressing-room tension Alan Shearer wrote about in his diary was dismissed as heat-of-the-moment tension. Blackburn remained top. The lead was now two points, with Manchester United playing before Blackburn in the next round of fixtures.

Before the evening's FA Cup replays took place, the daily papers confirmed another black mark on the season with the conviction of Dennis Wise for assault. He had been charged with common assault and criminal damage after he attacked a taxi driver and broke a window of the cab. Wise had been selected by Terry Venables for the upcoming friendly with the Republic of Ireland and had continued to train and perform as usual throughout the proceedings. The Chelsea midfielder was ordered to pay costs and damages before being sentenced in March.

Replays are never a welcome addition to the fixture list for any football team and this was certainly true of Sheffield Wednesday, who followed up their victory over Arsenal with a 4-3 penalty shoot-out defeat to Graham Taylor's Wolves. All the more incredible was that goalkeeper Kevin Pressman had helped Wednesday into a seemingly unassailable 3-0 lead in the shoot-out. Nothing was unusual during the 1994/95 season and when Wolves roared back to win 4-3, there was little surprise that something so unusual had happened.

Liverpool, Southampton and Norwich progressed to the fifth round while Arsenal's conquerors, Millwall, knocked out another London side with a shoot-out victory over Chelsea.

The victory for Millwall caused headlines for all the wrong reasons. Football violence became the focus of press attention yet again. First a fan managed to get on to the pitch and headed straight for the referee, only to be dragged away by stewards. Millwall's fans had also entered the pitch when they scored, to the fury of manager Mick McCarthy, who ran towards the jubilant fans as they got on to the pitch. When

Kasey Keller saved John Spencer's penalty to win the shoot-out in dramatic fashion, the Millwall players wheeled away in celebration. Chelsea fans were not happy and the riotous behaviour started.

On the final whistle, the Chelsea fans charged towards the massed Millwall fans behind the goal. Fights broke out and objects were thrown before mounted police entered the pitch. A line of horses and officers pushed the Chelsea fans back to their own end and away from the Millwall supporters. In the centre of the pitch, a line of police was a stark sight for the television cameras and fans in the ground. This did not feel like football. For Chelsea, some serious thought had to be given to the behaviour of their fans, as well as their players.

The game of the weekend was Aston Villa's record-equalling 7-1 victory over Wimbledon at Villa Park. Recent signing Tommy Johnson had yet to find the net for Villa, but he managed to score a 16-minute hat-trick to immediately endear himself to the home fans. His third goal put Villa up 4-1 up at half-time after they had gone behind in the 11th minute to Warren Barton's opener. Wimbledon were shell-shocked. Joe Kinnear had moulded his players into a top-ten side and the result was a real disappointment. He said after the game: 'Villa outplayed us all over the park and the more we chased, the more we got punished.' Their position in the league table was also conceded to Villa, who climbed to ninth after sitting in 18th just seven games earlier.

Nottingham Forest had rivalled Newcastle in the top three of the league at the start of the season, but when they met each other on Saturday, 11 February, Newcastle were in control of third place. Goals from Ruel Fox and Rob Lee put the home side 2-1 up before Jason Lee got one back almost immediately after the restart. There were now five points between the sides and the defeat at Loftus Road was left behind. Keegan and Newcastle thought less about Andy Cole and more about the push for Europe.

Cole's new team concentrated on the league. United's European campaign was a distant, painful memory. A solid unbeaten run continued with victory in the Manchester derby at Maine Road. Torrential rain was not unusual in the North West and, despite the concerns of club officials about the looming threat of the weather turning the pitch into a swamp, the game was played without a problem.

Making his Premiership debut for Manchester United was another outstanding prospect from the production line – Phil Neville. Like his brother, he played in defence, but City's wingers did not give the youngster an easy ride. The home side attacked with pace and controlled much of the game for the first half. Manager Brian Horton said after the game that he wished the game had finished at half-time. If only. Instead, Alex Ferguson swapped the younger Neville for another protege, Paul Scholes. With the introduction of the young attacker, Andy Cole was unleashed on City. He made the first and scored the third, with an Andrei Kanchelskis goal sandwiched in between. Another victory for United. An 8-0 aggregate score against their local rivals and top spot secured in the Premiership table for the next 24 hours.

The only problem for Ferguson came after the game. Breaking news reached him that his suspended star striker, sunning himself in the West Indies, had allegedly attacked an ITN reporter. Coverage of the incident was wall-to-wall and reporters were not about to let Cantona out of their sights. For Ferguson, it meant more attention away from football.

Cantona's holiday was supposed to remove him from the glare of the press. Despite the added miles, the press decided to go to him. Terry Lloyd, ITN reporter, along with cameraman Mike Ingram and soundman Mark Lyons were on a public beach filming Cantona, who was on a private beach next door. Lloyd claimed that the irate Frenchman came over to the public beach, got him in a headlock and then recreated his Selhurst Park kung-fu kick on him. Cantona had apparently been upset because photographers had been taking pictures of his wife, who was six months pregnant, while they were using the private beach. Despite the column inches devoted to the latest indiscretion from Cantona, there was some sympathy with the star over what was deemed an invasion of privacy by many, including his manager. Ferguson wrote that the newspapers' use of images of Cantona's pregnant wife, on holiday, was 'absolutely disgusting'. ITN's two-line statement in response to Ferguson's opinion condemned the manager's stance in siding with violence. Cantona's response to the whole issue was to threaten to sue the news network.

Compounding the anger Ferguson felt over the treatment of his star player, he had to watch Blackburn make easy work of Sheffield Wednesday. In a game that was not much more than a procession for the home side, goals from Tim Sherwood, Mark Atkins and Alan Shearer were too much for the visitors. Chris Waddle's equaliser had briefly given the chasing pack hope that the game would be competitive, but Atkins's goal had quickly restored Blackburn's lead. After the game, Shearer, Sherwood and the suspended Graeme Le Saux boarded a private jet at Blackpool Airport and headed for Heathrow to join up with the rest of the England squad.

Before Terry Venables took charge of another friendly, Tony Cottee scored twice against his old club Everton at Upton Park. It was a welcome point for Harry Redknapp. West Ham had fallen down the table after a poor run of results. For Redknapp, it was his first season in the top flight and he wanted to ensure his side stayed in the league.

The life of a manager is determined by his ability to get results. Redknapp had secured a win and a draw in his last two games. Not brilliant, but it was a start. For Phil Neal, one win since the end of November was more than enough for the Coventry board to say enough is enough. He was relieved of his duties on Valentine's Day, with Ron Atkinson quickly installed as his successor. Neal's statement on his removal from the job targeted 'all those whingers who seem to enjoy continually sniping at the club and certain players'. The Sky Blues were not far off mid-table, but Atkinson was rumoured to have been promised a bumper £100,000 bonus to keep them in the Premiership. He set about spending some of the club's money straight away, signing Kevin Richardson from his old club, Aston Villa, for £300,000.

Another man dipping into the transfer market was George Graham. Despite the poor form and allegations of bungs hanging over him, he spent £2m on Dutch winger Glenn Helder from Vitesse Arnhem. Graham appeared confident about his prospects at the club, saying: 'You don't give £6m to a manager if you are going to sack them.' He had a point. Arsenal also had ten days off, which gave the manager plenty of time to get on to the training ground with his new signing.

In a break from league action, Liverpool faced Crystal Palace in the League Cup semi-final first leg. A few hours earlier, England had taken the field at Lansdowne Road to face the Republic of Ireland. Robbie Fowler's 92nd-minute winner gave Liverpool the upper hand in the tie, but the game was forgotten in the swarm of violence and horrific images from across the Irish Sea.

Terry Venables's first away match in charge of the England team was called off after 27 minutes. Violence in the game between Millwall and Chelsea, the incident with the fan on the pitch at Blackburn, plus Eric Cantona's violent excursion into the crowd at Selhurst Park added to an air of aggressive tension that still reared its ugly head in the national game. The days of hooliganism may have faded, but the game in Dublin showed that they still existed, and they were organised.

A day of violence between English and Irish fans (and within the English groups) plagued the build-up to the match. Warring fan groups fought in pubs and the city centre after there had been reports of stabbings in the days previous.

The stream of ferries across the sea brought known hooligans, and larger groups of violent supporters travelled over. They were known to the National Crime Intelligence Service's Football Unit, who had compiled information in the month leading up to the game. Throughout the day, violence marred the preparations for the game. Fights lasted all day and, as the 6.15pm kick-off approached, tensions escalated.

England fans stormed the turnstiles to get into the ground without tickets, which caused further issues, as did the placing of the majority of fans in the upper tier, above Irish supporters. On that lower tier, there was a mix of fans due to the English FA returning them to the FAI, only for them to be resold to Irish fans. As the national anthems were played, the Irish booed 'God Save the Queen' before some English fans retaliated with Nazi salutes and a chorus of 'No surrender to the IRA' throughout the Irish anthem 'Amhrán na bhFiann'. During the verbal carnage, English fans began to rip up the wooden seats around them.

After a goal from Ireland's David Kelly, and one disallowed for England, the fans turned. A group littered with National Front members began to rain down wooden missiles on the fans below. Some landed on the pitch and, after 27 minutes, referee Dick Jol took the players off the pitch. Fans on the top tier continued their assault from their higher vantage point.

Sky Sports' coverage of the game showed images of fans goading the Irish supporters and the Gardai. Martin Tyler, disgust in his voice, told viewers how hooligan fans had been identified before travelling, had been seen in the city during the day and continued to bring shame on the country. In the studio, Alan Ball and Gerry Francis condemned the violence, but made the point that it would be unfair on the well-behaved majority of English fans if the upcoming European Championship were taken away from England.

Once the game was abandoned, fans from the lower tiers spilled on to the pitch to avoid the violence from above. Missiles continued to rain down and caused injury and harm to many. Almost two hours after the game had started, English fans were still in the stadium. Then, the Gardai took action to remove the fans with force. Batons in hand, the Irish police turned to the massed ranks of England fans left in the stadium. Blows rained down and blood was shed. They used the full force of their power to round up the England fans and get them on to trains and the waiting ferries. Despite the awful weather conditions, which meant a number of boats did not sail, some supporters left on the Holyhead ferry to be removed from the country.

On media duty after the game, managers Terry Venables and Jack Charlton reflected in disbelief on what they had witnessed; the two experienced men commented that they had not seen anything like this in their long careers. England captain David Platt knew that the fans' actions meant the conversation would not be focused on football, as had been the story of the season. News reporters and commentators condemned yet another black mark on the English game.

The press reflected the scenes with headlines on the front and back pages the next day. 'Sick scum', 'Lepers of world football' and 'Sabotage' were added to the long list of shameful headlines written during the season. Football was again in the national firing line.

After the events in midweek, a weekend mixed with league and cup action at least made sure there was something other than violence and controversy to talk about in football. Only four Premiership teams were in action and three of them had been managed by Ron Atkinson.

In his first game in the dugout for Coventry, his ninth club, Peter Ndlovu scored the first and created the second for Mike Marsh to make sure that 'Big Ron' had the perfect start to his time at Highfield Road. A first home win since November and a second consecutive victory gave the fans and the new manager hope. That one victory meant Coventry shot up four places to 13th – a clear indication of how tight it was in the bottom half of the table.

After a 7-1 win away from home, Aston Villa earned another victory, this time against Sheffield Wednesday, that took them to ninth in the table. Dean Saunders hit another two goals and the striker played a key role in the improvements the team had made under Little. The dramatic and brilliant turnaround overseen by the new manager had restored belief in the Villa players and put them on a run of five wins in the last six games. If not for the awful start to the season, this version of Aston Villa may have been in the conversation for European qualification. As it was, staying safe in the league and achieving a respectable position was key.

In the FA Cup fifth round, the two Football League teams left in the competition had mixed results. Watford earned a 0-0 draw at home to Crystal Palace, but Millwall lost 1-0 at another London club, QPR. Liverpool and Wimbledon plus Spurs and Southampton played out draws, which gave them replays in an already busy fixture list.

The big winners of the weekend were Everton, who put five past Norwich, whose form continued to decline. Five different scorers hit the back of the net for Joe Royle's side, who had not conceded a goal in the competition. Their victory set up a quarter-final with Newcastle, who beat Manchester City 3-1, at Goodison Park.

Manchester United welcomed Mark Hughes back to the side like a new signing after his return from injury and freshly signed new contract. Without Cole and Cantona, the goals came from the core players Ferguson had relied on for years: Steve Bruce, Brian McClair and Hughes. Two goals in the first five minutes certainly helped his side to control the game and, despite Tony Yeboah scoring in the second half, Hughes's 72nd-minute goal made sure there was no late drama.

There may not have been any Hollywood-worthy drama in football over the weekend, but it quickly emerged that it was not just Arsenal's poor form that could see George Graham lose his job. The Premier League inquiry findings about the payments he took for the signing of John Jensen had leaked. Reports suggested that Graham was guilty. It was clear that the inquiry did not think the payments were a gift and amounted to corruption.

On the afternoon of 21 February, one of Arsenal's most successful managers was relieved of his duties by the board. The statement said: 'Arsenal Football Club have now been informed by the FA Premier League inquiry of the results of their investigations into alleged irregularities concerning certain transfers and the board have concluded that Mr Graham did not act in the best interests of the club.' After two league titles, three cups and a European trophy, Graham's managerial career at Arsenal was over. His reputation in tatters, he went on the offensive.

In his diary, Graham had written of his part in the inquiry. He had decided against giving evidence, as he had lost confidence in the process. This was just three days before he was sacked. Now that the Premier League findings had emerged in the media, he doubled down and released a statement that condemned the process. After outlining his commitment to Arsenal over a 15-year period, he made his feelings on the inquiry known: 'I deeply regret that this kangaroo court judgment should have been reached in such a hole-in-the-corner way. My record of loyalty and service demanded better treatment. I believe this matter should be fully investigated by the Football Association. What is the future for football if standards of justice inside the game can be ignored in this way?'

Released from his contract without compensation, Graham vowed to take the club to a tribunal. His £300,000-a-year salary was one of the highest in the league and reflected the years of success he had brought to Arsenal. That original compensation package of close to £1m seemed a long way off. For the Gunners, they had to move on quickly and appointed Graham's assistant, Stewart Houston, as manager until the end of the season.

The new man had to lead the team out that evening after all the dramatic events of the day. A classic '1-0 to the Arsenal' victory, a first at home since October, followed, the goal coming from one of Graham's most recent signings, Chris Kiwomya. Paul Merson got the assist, a player Graham had developed and stood by despite his public battle with his demons. A day of turmoil for Arsenal, but winning a football match made things more bearable.

Fixtures continued a day later, with both title challengers in action. Blackburn raced into an early lead against Wimbledon with goals from Shearer and Mark Atkins, his second in as many games. Efan Ekoku pulled one back before half-time and the Dons made the game difficult for Blackburn on a pitch that showed the wear of the winter and an intense period of fixtures.

At Carrow Road, Manchester United made a similarly fast start with two goals in the first 15 minutes from Paul Ince and Andrei Kanchelskis. Those early goals meant United dominated the ball and, without creating too many chances, they came away with a straightforward victory.

The game of the night came at Villa Park. Brian Little, who faced a chorus of 'Judas' from the travelling fans, took on his old club with his new one in good form. Villa had turned the corner and moved up the league table with impressive victories. Little had added players to freshen up the side and it worked. When Leicester arrived, another victory seemed inevitable.

When Dwight Yorke scored at the hour mark, Villa were 3-0 up. Leicester looked dead and buried. A minute later, Mark Robins found the net. Still, not much hope when you are 3-1 down away from home and have only won one game in the last 12. When Tommy Johnson nonchalantly lobbed Kevin Poole from outside the box just five minutes after that to make it 4-1, the chances of any kind of result seemed to disappear.

Football never works out the way you think. In another mad three minutes, Leicester found another two goals, from Iwan Roberts and David Lowe. So now, after 80 minutes, it was 4-3 to Villa and their defence was under constant attack from crosses into the box. As the game ticked into the last minute, another corner was lifted into the penalty area and the poaching instincts of Lowe took over again. His goal, Leicester's fourth, rescued a point for the Foxes and lifted them off the bottom of the table. Manager Mark McGhee said after the comeback that if the team got any higher in the table, he would get a nosebleed.

Attention turned back to Eric Cantona on Friday, 24 February when the FA announced their punishment for the Frenchman. The police had already charged Cantona and team-mate Paul Ince with common assault for their part in the fracas. Now, rather than facing Scotland Yard, Cantona was put in front of Geoffrey Thompson, Ian Stott and Gordon McKeag. Men with experience at varying levels of the game, they listened to the voice of the player and his regret over the situation, before taking three hours to deliberate.

Ferguson wrote that Cantona conducted himself really well during the whole event. His striker was 'so placid' throughout the lengthy discussions, possibly due to the fact that Ferguson had told him: 'No matter what the verdict is, you say nothing. If anyone says anything, it'll be me.' That warning was enough to make anyone keep their mouth closed and arms folded.

After everything had been said and done, the Manchester United contingent in the room could not believe the verdict. The ban imposed by the club was doubled. Instead of a suspension until the end of the season, Cantona was not allowed to play first-team football until 1 October. Ferguson was furious. The club had acted promptly to suspend the player, only for the FA to deem it insufficient. Not content with the ban, the punishment also included a £10,000 fine and an extension of the ban from England to around the world.

The sentence was described as 'savage' by Ferguson, who despaired at being without his talisman not only for the rest of the season but for a large chunk of the next. At that point, the vultures began to circle, with São Paulo of Brazil apparently ready to make an offer. Serious interest came from the irrepressible Massimo Moratti, who wanted to make Cantona a star in Serie A with Internazionale. United and Cantona were unmoved and focused on his upcoming court appearance in March.

Back in the somewhat serene world of actual football, Ipswich recorded a rare win that lifted them off the bottom of the table. Coming from behind at home to Southampton, Alex Mathie and Lee Chapman scored to cancel out Neil Maddison's opener for the away side. Alan Ball's Saints had not been in the best form in recent games and dropped to 18th and one place outside the relegation zone. Four teams had to go down and a team with a player as talented as Matt

Le Tissier were desperate to avoid the drop. Despite the win, Ipswich still needed a miracle, as they were eight points away from their opponents.

Leicester were involved in another high-scoring game, but this time they were on the wrong side of the result. Coventry carried on their good form with four goals at home to beat the Foxes 4-2. David Lowe and Iwan Roberts got on the scoresheet again to bring the scores level at 2-2, but the quality of Coventry showed. A goal from Sean Flynn and a late Peter Ndlovu effort put the game out of reach to make it two out of two for Ron Atkinson. Three wins in a row and the heady heights of 12th for the Sky Blues. Leicester sat rock bottom.

Management looked easy for Stewart Houston. Two wins and no goals conceded. Arsenal's first back-to-back victories since October. Somehow, Arsenal had reached eighth in the table. Chris Kiwomya's two goals in a 3-0 victory against Crystal Palace at Selhurst Park were exactly what the new boss needed, especially with European fixtures on the horizon.

Another team preparing to travel abroad were Glenn Hoddle's Chelsea. Mired in mid-table for most of the season, they turned up at Upton Park and won 2-1 thanks to second-half goals from Craig Burley and Mark Stein.

Although Newcastle's title challenge had subsided, they were still playing good football. A brace from Peter Beardsley gave the Geordies a 3-1 victory at home to Aston Villa. Keith Gillespie was starting to show what he could do, making a great run to set up the first goal for Barry Venison, a rare goalscorer, who rifled a shot into the top corner. Villa's Andy Townsend matched that strike with an Exocet of his own from outside the box to draw the sides level. Beardsley's two goals showed that he had lost none of the skill he could execute in close situations. The footwork was intricate and quick, with the second goal the pick of the two. Aston Villa's defenders didn't know how to deal with him. Newcastle's No.8 knew exactly what he wanted to do and his goals were well deserved.

At the top of the table, it was a rare weekend without a win for Blackburn or Manchester United. For the league leaders, a 0-0 draw at Carrow Road and for the reigning champions, a 1-0 loss at Goodison Park thanks to a Duncan Ferguson header from a perfect Andy Hinchcliffe corner. Three points separated Blackburn and United at the top of the table after 30 games.

Nottingham Forest were unable to close the gap on Newcastle and Liverpool above them as an 87th-minute Simon Barker goal rescued a point for QPR at Loftus Road after Steve Stone scored for Forest just before the hour mark. A few days later, Newcastle extended the gap between themselves and Forest to ten points with a 2-0 victory at Ipswich with goals from Ruel Fox and Paul Kitson. They were not mathematically out of the title race, as they sat nine points behind Blackburn, but results in the last three months of the season had to go their way.

On the same night, Chelsea returned to Cup Winners' Cup action with a visit to Belgium to face Club Brugge. They were challenging for the title and featured some of Belgium's top talent. It was a close contest that was decided by a single goal from Gert Verheyen in the 82nd minute. That was not the story of the night.

Once news emerged that a 14-year-old Belgian had been stabbed and a Chelsea fan had been arrested, it seemed like the authorities had their work cut out. But, after the violence at Lansdowne Road, the Belgian police were prepared. The main tactic was to remove any Chelsea fan who carried a forged ticket or had travelled without a ticket at all. At this point, they would be herded into a huge, empty bus warehouse with water cannons trained in their direction.

Arrests started quickly and kept pace throughout the build-up to the game. According to varying reports, the number of arrests was between 250 and 400. From the point of view of many Chelsea fans, their valid tickets had been ignored and instead they were lumped into the warehouse in the cold and missed the match. They were unable to collect any belongings, despite showing officers their hotel keys.

More than 500 officers on the streets of Bruges had every intent in keeping the peace. Mirroring the use of batons to beat England fans in Dublin, the liberal use of force was defended due to the potential violence that could occur. In news reports, many Chelsea fans described how they were treated like animals by the aggressive officers. Confident that they had got their tactics right, a police spokesman said that calling cards bearing slogans such as 'Chelsea Headhunters: No Surrender' had been confiscated.

The main issue for Chelsea fans and Steve Beauchamp of the National Football Supporters' Association was the lack of effort by the Belgian police to distinguish between the average match-goer and the football hooligan. Although it may have seemed the heavy-handed tactics had worked and kept problems down to a minimum, there was little consideration for whether arresting a man in his 70s was an effective use of police effort.

Reputations of supporters certainly followed clubs around and Chelsea were known for having a formidable group of fans who regularly incited violence at football matches. The fact that there were only two arrests during the evening was a win for the authorities at a cost to the match-going fan. Football clearly had a long way to go.

For England, as host of the upcoming European Championships, cleaning up its reputation as a nation of football hooligans was paramount. The events in these early months of 1995 did not help the situation.

Pos	Team	P	W	D	L	F	A	GD	Pts
1	Blackburn Rovers	30	20	6	4	63	26	+37	66
2	Manchester United	30	19	6	5	53	22	+31	63
3	Newcastle United	30	16	9	5	52	31	+21	57
4	Liverpool	28	14	9	5	48	23	+25	51
5	Nottingham Forest	30	13	8	9	42	33	+9	47
6	Leeds United	28	11	10	7	35	28	+7	43
7	Tottenham Hotspur	28	12	7	9	46	40	+6	43
8	Arsenal	30	10	10	10	35	32	+3	40
9	Sheffield Wednesday	30	10	9	11	39	40	-1	39
10	Wimbledon	29	11	6	12	35	50	-15	39
11	Aston Villa	31	9	11	11	46	45	+1	38
12	Coventry City	30	9	10	11	33	47	-14	37
13	Chelsea	28	9	9	10	37	39	-2	36
14	Norwich City	29	9	9	11	27	33	-6	36
15	Manchester City	29	9	9	11	37	44	-7	36
16	Everton	30	8	10	12	30	39	-9	34
17	Queens Park Rangers	27	8	8	11	40	46	-6	32
18	Southampton	28	6	13	9	40	46	-6	31
19	Crystal Palace	29	7	9	13	21	31	-10	30
20	West Ham United	29	8	5	16	29	39	-12	29
21	Ipswich Town	30	6	5	19	31	60	-29	23
22	Leicester City	29	4	8	17	31	54	-23	20

June '94: England did not qualify for the World Cup in the USA, but all eyes were focused on the pitch, especially from Premier League clubs.

July '94: On a boat in Monaco, Alan Sugar secured the £2m signing of Jürgen Klinsmann in a summer defined by transfers.

August '94: Robbie Fowler soaked in the adulation of the crowd after he scored against Arsenal and recorded a quick-fire hat-trick.

September '94: Bryan Roy of Nottingham Forest featured in USA '94 and impressed after making the move to the Premier League.

October '94: The title-challengers faced off in a match full of controversy as Manchester United left Ewood Park with a 4-2 win.

November '94: A clean sweep for Blackburn Rovers with Kenny Dalglish manager of the month and 'The SAS' splitting the player of the month award.

December '94: Stan Collymore was a striker in demand as he scored the goals that had Nottingham Forest competing at the top end of the table.

January '95: In a move that shocked English football, Manchester United signed Andy Cole from Newcastle United for £6m and £1m-rated winger Keith Gillespie moved the other way.

February '95: King Eric held court with the assembled media after his kung-fu exploits in the crowd at Selhurst Park.

March '95: Manchester United recorded a 9-0 victory over hapless Ipswich at Old Trafford, with Andy Cole scoring five times.

April '95: Steve McManaman had a breakout season for Liverpool and shone in the Coca-Cola Cup victory against Bolton.

May '95: Blackburn Rovers are crowned champions at Anfield after a dramatic final day.

The Massacre (March)

IN THE FA Cup fifth-round replays, Liverpool overcame Wimbledon in the final game of February, Crystal Palace narrowly defeated Watford and Spurs went goal crazy in extra time with a fantastic 6-2 win at Southampton. Tottenham's early-season ban from the competition was a long way away now.

A surprising omission from the Palace side was star striker Chris Armstrong. There had been speculation all season that he wanted to move to a bigger club, but his absence had nothing to do with his transfer wishes. After Paul Merson came clean about his drug struggles, the FA started to send their drug squad out to training grounds on a regular, but random, basis. Crystal Palace had been visited and Armstrong had tested positive for cannabis. A four-match ban was issued for the striker, who was integral to Palace's chances of maintaining their Premiership status. Whatever was happening in what was a thrilling race for the title, a close relegation battle and excitement in the cup was continually pushed to the back of the public's mind as the continued stream of revelations about off-the-pitch activities painted a picture of a season of sleaze.

There was only one game that everyone talked about on Saturday, 4 March. Manchester United versus Ipswich at Old Trafford. One team was desperate to win a third consecutive Premiership title and the other hoped they would be in the same league next season. Hope for both teams, at either end of the table. The only emotion felt by Ipswich after being mauled by United was embarrassment.

The home side were in the mood. Chances came within the first few minutes, which gave an indication of the afternoon Ipswich were about to have. After 15 minutes, Roy Keane got the first with a strike from outside the box. Then Andy Cole took over. His first came minutes after Keane's goal and he made it 3-0 to United with his second before half-time. Blackburn, who had a better goal difference than their challengers at this point, were 1-0 ahead at Villa Park. Alex Ferguson told his players that the key focus was to 'make sure we get the goals today. The one thing we take out of today is the goal difference.' It is fair to say that the second half was a riot for United. Constant carnage in the Ipswich box with poor decision-making and a stream of attacks making it impossible to defend. Cole's hat-trick goal felt like a classic Manchester United attack and finish. Ball out wide at the feet of Denis Irwin. Cross whipped into the box and a striker, Cole, on the end of it. From the other wing, Ryan Giggs taunted and teased the Ipswich defenders, who hacked at him to make it stop. His cross sped across the six-yard box for Mark Hughes to strike the ball as he slid. It ricocheted between post, ground and the net to make it 5-0.

Hughes's second goal capped a six-minute run of three United goals. At 6-0 there was no sign of an end to the pain for Ipswich. It was Cole's turn to take the limelight again with a neat finish after a well-worked move that included neat interplay between Hughes and McClair. Ferguson's words must have been ringing in the players' ears because that was four goals in the second half and 65 minutes played.

Any game that has such a high number of goals borders on the ridiculous, but the eighth goal featured Craig Forrest handling the ball in no man's land outside his box. A quick yellow card from the referee. An even quicker short free kick that found Paul Ince with the goal to aim at and a bunch of Ipswich defenders who scrambled in vain to get back. Add to that that Forrest had barely reached his box, never mind found his way back to the goal line. The misery ended for George Burley's broken team with an 87th-minute Cole goal. That allowed the classic brackets to be used in papers, on the vidiprinter and anywhere else that showed football results: Manchester United 9 (nine) Ipswich Town 0.

A record-breaking day for Manchester United and a display of supreme attacking pressure against a side who capitulated. Blackburn's goal difference was wiped out. The title race was tight. Three points separated the two sides with midweek fixtures coming up.

Not to say that a match that features nine goals is not full of drama, but the game at Filbert Street between Leicester and Everton featured yet more late Leicester goals after inexplicably giving the opposition a head start. For Everton, it looked like a well-earned away victory was in their grasp as Anders Limpar's long-range effort and Vinny Samways's tap-in, from a brilliant counter-attack that featured some outrageous one-touch passing and off-the-ball movement, made it 2-0 at half-time. Things were never that simple for the Toffees. A red card for goalscorer Samways after his wild swipe at Mike Galloway under the nose of the referee sent him down the tunnel. Minutes had passed in the second half and Everton were up against it.

Mark Draper got one back for the home side on the hour mark before red-card magnet Duncan Ferguson used an elbow to a defender's face to add to his collection straight after the goal. Seven games he had managed without getting sent off. The inevitable happened once Royle's men only had nine men to repel the Leicester attacks. David Lowe, Mark Robins and then Iwan Roberts were involved in the equaliser that earned them a point, when what they needed was three. Everton, on the other hand, threw away the chance to increase the gap from the dreaded drop zone.

Goals at Anfield from the master, Rush, and the apprentice, Fowler, gave Liverpool an important 2-0 victory against Newcastle. The battle for third place was getting to be as close as the title race. Liverpool's games in hand from their cup run meant that the gap was artificially inflated. Keegan had managed to turn around the poor form from Christmas and New Year. Draws turned into wins, with five victories from the previous six games before defeat at his old club.

Norwich's race to the bottom continued with a draw at home to Manchester City, who had suffered themselves since hitting sixth in early December. One win since then did not help the league position. Still, 14th place was far enough away from danger to get too worried. For John Deehan and Norwich, panic had set in. A dramatic downturn in form meant a drop from the European places and seventh on New Year's Eve to a place above City after the 1-1 draw that featured two goals in the last ten minutes of the game. Both sides needed a reaction to avoid dropping any further down the league.

Four goals in the last 11 minutes created an incredible end to the Nottingham Forest-Tottenham game at the City Ground. Teddy Sheringham gave Spurs the lead in the 79th minute, Forest scored two in a minute with five minutes left in the game before well-known goal machine Colin Calderwood popped up in the 87th minute to rescue a draw for Gerry Francis. Spurs had dominated much of the game, but it was Forest who scored the pick of the goals with Lars Bohinen's rocket screaming past Ian Walker.

Coming into the away game with Wimbledon, QPR had beaten Newcastle 3-0, claimed a draw at Anfield and held Nottingham Forest at Loftus Road. Despite Dean

Holdsworth getting the first goal, a double from Les Ferdinand and one from Ian Holloway proved that life after Gerry Francis was similar to life under the current Spurs manager. Ferdinand's goals summed up his performances over the course of the season. A short lay-off from a free kick gave him space to hammer the ball into the net from range and the second, from another ball into feet from Holloway, who got two of the most generous assists, saw him score after a powerful run from just inside Wimbledon's half. Pace to get away from his defender, control to protect the ball and a strong finish across the mangled pitch past Hans Segers. A man in form and in demand.

Chelsea's European hangover meant they were only able to record a goalless draw at home to Crystal Palace and, in another London-based fixture, West Ham got the better of Arsenal and gave Stewart Houston his first taste of defeat.

Ron Atkinson faced his former employers Aston Villa on Monday night. A goalless draw was not a great result for either side, but clean sheets normally keep managers happy. It was a fourth game without a victory for Brian Little, who had seen an upturn in fortunes until this point. Two wins and two draws from Atkinson's first four games meant that Coventry had found a way out of the relegation danger zone. Eleventh place felt like paradise for the Sky Blues.

By the time Manchester United travelled to London, it was clear that they did not bring enough goals with them. After the attacking exertions against Ipswich, a late Steve Bruce goal was all the champions could muster against Wimbledon. For 24 hours at least, United would be top of the table – a psychological bonus before Blackburn faced Arsenal at home the following evening.

Wednesday, 8 March was a busy evening in the calendar. Seven games were played, with wins for Nottingham Forest, Newcastle, QPR and Tottenham. On the receiving end of those defeats were Everton, West Ham, Leicester and Ipswich. Sometimes, when all of the teams in the relegation fight lose, nothing is gained or lost. More than ever, it looked like the bottom two sides, Leicester and Ipswich, were doomed. Far from marooned at the bottom, the issue was more their consistently poor form than distance from safety.

Four minutes was all it took for Blackburn to respond to United's win a night earlier. Hold-up play by Sutton, ball into Shearer, touch and turn, goal. A simple pattern executed perfectly all season. Graeme Le Saux's high finish past David Seaman was the product of some quick passing on the left-hand side. Blackburn had a reputation for being direct, but their play was more nuanced than that. Short, quick passes to release the wide players on either flank, facilitated by Shearer and Sutton, both adept at dropping deep to bring the wide men into play, formed the core part of the attacking play. It was used perfectly to free Shearer, who passed quickly out wide to Sutton, and his lofted cross found Le Saux on the edge of the box. Not an easy finish, but Le Saux dispatched it brilliantly.

Shearer's tenth penalty of the season was put away confidently and Blackburn led 3-0. A minute after the penalty, Tim Flowers, who produced save after save in a man-of-the-match performance, palmed a shot into the path of Steve Morrow, who tapped in. A 3-1 win for Blackburn. Two goals added to the goal difference, one behind Manchester United, and the three-point lead restored at the top of the table.

Coca-Cola Cup semi-finals took centre stage on the 8 March, with Liverpool beating Crystal Palace 1-0 at Selhurst Park thanks to a goal from Robbie Fowler. A 2-0 aggregate victory was well deserved for Roy Evans and his team, with a trip to Wembley set for early April.

In the other semi-final, an incredible comeback from Bolton Wanderers at home to Swindon made the headlines.

Once Jan Åge Fjørtoft had scored in the 57th minute, Swindon were 3-1 ahead on aggregate, but Bruce Rioch's side did not lie down. Highly rated youngster Jason McAteer pulled one back to level on the night. Then, substitute Mixu Paatelainen levelled the aggregate scores before talisman John McGinlay found the net with two minutes left in normal time. It was 4-3 on aggregate and Bolton were in the final.

Before the next round of league fixtures, Blackburn sold the man who had started Kenny Dalglish's spending spree. Alan Wright, who had been the most expensive transfer from a Fourth Division club at £500,000, signed for Aston Villa for £1m. Graeme Le Saux had established himself as the first-choice left-back and Wright wanted first-team football. The move made sense for all parties.

Five Premiership games produced three away wins and two score draws. Nottingham Forest drew level on points with Liverpool after a fantastic second-half performance at Filbert Street earned them a 4-2 win over Leicester. The home side were now 12 points away with only ten games to go.

For Forest, the talk focused on Stan Collymore's future rather than a push for a European place. The back pages of the Sunday papers suggested that Everton were in pole position to sign Collymore for a record-breaking £7.5m. With the transfer deadline approaching, Joe Royle wanted to push the deal through before then, rather than waiting until the summer. It was clear that Collymore's relationship with Frank Clark had fractured, similar to Cole and Keegan's breakdown before Christmas, so a move away was not out of the question. Forest needed their star striker to be firing for the run-in, but the criticism from management did not help. Everton's chairman Peter Johnson was not afraid to spend and a strike force of Duncan Ferguson and Collymore had the potential to provide European football over relegation battles.

At Stamford Bridge, there was fan disillusionment on both sides. Chelsea fans returned from Bruges battered and broken, but it was the Leeds fans who made their feelings known just 20 minutes into the game. Three fans broke ranks and hurled abuse at manager Howard Wilkinson. Their chants of 'Wilko out' earned them an early bath and a trip out of the stadium. Ironically, they missed out on one of Leeds' best away performances of the season. A double from Tony Yeboah and a Gary McAllister goal resulted in Chelsea fans departing the stadium in numbers well before the final whistle. Home form that had not produced a win since 23 October was not good enough. Mid-table looked like the most likely outcome for Hoddle's men.

Referees had taken centre stage at various times during the season and did the same again at Upton Park. This time it was a stand-in who did the damage. Martin Sims entered the fray when original referee Alan Wilkie pulled up injured. He mistakenly sent off Norwich midfielder Andy Johnson, instead of giving a second yellow card to defender Spencer Prior. The towering presence of Prior somehow blended into the pack of Norwich players after he had taken down Tony Cottee. Sims showed the red to Johnson and the game continued. It did not deter Norwich, however, who doubled their lead ten minutes into the second half. A two-goal lead away from home for a team with one of the worst runs of form in the league was priceless. The lead almost lasted the whole game. West Ham were guilty of missing far too many chances. Finally, with eight minutes left, Tony Cottee got a goal back. Then, with two minutes left, Cottee earned a point for the home side with his second of the game. Not an ideal result for either team, but if West Ham looked over their shoulder they could see Southampton and Crystal Palace with games in hand. Norwich could not turn draws into wins. Something needed to change.

The managerial job at Coventry was proving to be a much more positive experience for Ron Atkinson. A strong performance at home against the league leaders extended the Sky Blues' unbeaten run to six games. Dion Dublin gave his side the lead after half an hour. Blackburn were not themselves. Kenny Dalglish and Ray Harford were not happy with the performance and let rip in the changing room. Alan Shearer wrote that 'it was the worst 45 minutes of the season'. At this stage in the season, it was not always about performances. Results mattered the most. With three minutes left on the clock, Shearer got an equaliser. And, in a shock to no one, it involved a controversial refereeing decision.

Most officials will disallow goals for contact on goalkeepers. That had been the case for a number of years before this. It was certainly not invented with the arrival of the Premier League. There was much more physical pressure on goalkeepers in decades past, but decisions often went for them. Shearer tested the referee's decision-making skills with his equaliser.

A long ball played from just inside Coventry's half by Graeme Le Saux hung high in the air and reached the box, just past the penalty spot. Shearer and Coventry goalkeeper Jonathan Gould hung in the air. The striker led with his arm. Gould raised his arm out, too, ready to punch the ball clear. Shearer made the first contact on the goalkeeper with his arm, then headed the ball towards goal. A bounce on the bog of a goalmouth, a scuffed clearance by a Coventry defender and the ball somehow got over the line. Shearer celebrated. Referee Terry Holbrook, who Shearer 'always found to be one of the better officials', gave the goal. A point rescued. Blackburn sat four points clear, having played an extra game.

The FA Cup quarter-finals were split over the weekend, with the first two played on the Saturday. Liverpool faced

Tottenham at Anfield. Robbie Fowler had scored a goal in each leg of the Coca-Cola Cup semi-final to put Liverpool in the final, but his opener in this game was not enough to help his team progress. Teddy Sheringham and the irrepressible Jürgen Klinsmann scored important goals for Spurs all season and they did it again. A semi-final beckoned for Gerry Francis and his team.

The other tie to be played was Crystal Palace against Graham Taylor's Wolves. A 1-1 draw was the outcome, with a replay scheduled for 22 March. Palace had progressed well in the cup and it came as a welcome distraction to their dire position in the league.

Alex Ferguson wanted to win trophies. He would have loved to complete another double. The quarter-final against QPR was not a classic, but an efficient performance from Manchester United resulted in a 2-0 win with goals from Denis Irwin and Lee Sharpe. Roy Keane, an injury doubt before the game, only came on at half-time, for Ryan Giggs, who had a calf problem. Ferguson wanted to win every game, but he was acutely aware that he needed his best players as fit as possible for the run-in.

In a complete turnaround from the start the two teams had to the season, Everton triumphed over Newcastle to reach an FA Cup semi-final. Dave Watson got the only goal in a 1-0 win for the Toffees. After starting the season with a seemingly never-ending winless streak, they beat a side who had blown away all comers in the early months. The tables had turned under Joe Royle and it was a second consecutive semi-final for the manager, after losing in a replay with Oldham against Manchester United, and Everton fans hoped for a trip to Wembley.

Football almost made it to the middle of March without off-the-field incidents swamping the papers. Chelsea midfielder Dennis Wise appeared at Horseferry Road court to be sentenced, having been convicted of assaulting a taxi driver and causing criminal damage.

Magistrate Geoffrey Breen did not mince his words, calling Wise 'a bully' as he sentenced him to three months in prison. The verdict shocked Wise, his agent Eric Hall and his legal team, while Colin Hutchinson, Chelsea director, vowed to stand by the midfielder. Within minutes of the verdict being read out, Wise's legal team headed for Southwark Crown Court to lodge an appeal. Wise was taken to jail and spent a sobering two hours alone staring at the walls. The bail hearing was scheduled before the 1pm deadline and Wise was granted unconditional bail; relief for the Chelsea man, for now. On the pitch, it was clear that Glenn Hoddle had to take action, so he eventually stripped his star man of the captaincy.

The papers had a field day. The *Daily Mirror* had covered the 'Season of Sleaze' in detail, exclusively breaking the Paul Merson confession, devoting endless column inches to the Cantona kung-fu saga and publishing the details around George Graham's bung bust. The back pages reported Wise's predicament at length. Chelsea team-mate Nigel Spackman spoke of his concerns about how Wise would adapt to life in prison. Gordon Taylor, the PFA chief, worried that the same fate awaited Eric Cantona and Paul Ince for their part in the Selhurst Park carnage.

To add more fuel to the sleazy bonfire, news broke that police had raided the homes of Bruce Grobbelaar, Hans Segers and John Fashanu. The three men were arrested to be questioned about their alleged role in the match-fixing revelations. Fashanu's girlfriend, Melissa Kassamapsi, and Malaysian businessman Heng Suam Lim were also arrested after raids at two London addresses. At this point, police did not reveal to the public the games in question and the FA were clear in their opinion: they believed corruption was not rife within the sport. FIFA spokesman Keith Cooper had similar feelings and stated: 'We should not rush into feeling that it is a problem of endemic proportions when all we have is a few allegations which are not yet proven.'

Businessman Heng Suam Lim was known to Grobbelaar as Richard Lim. The two men knew each other and Grobbelaar had provided Lim with betting tips, but never against his own teams. In his autobiography, the player called it a form of punditry. He mentioned a similar arrangement that he had with a Norwegian newspaper, *Dagbladet*, so he did not see anything wrong with it. The police presented a case that Lim was at the heart of an organised operation to fix matches in the Premier League. All of the men firmly denied knowledge of the accusations and stated that they were in no way involved with any betting or match-fixing group.

Clearly, the reputation of English football had taken a battering. The accused appeared on the front pages of national newspapers, with *The Mirror* leading with an image of John Fashanu and his girlfriend next to the headline 'Fash in £1m bribe quiz'. The back pages revealed that Fashanu was ready to quit the English game and head to the United States. A delegation from the new professional league, Major League Soccer, headed to Europe to find big-name players to draw in the crowds and capitalise on the popularity of football after the World Cup. Fashanu's name was apparently on the list.

Before their home game with Coventry, Liverpool sat in fourth place with 54 points and games in hand. Win those three games in hand and they would leapfrog Newcastle and put pressure on Manchester United. A title bid was not out of the question, but a lot needed to go right. The first game they had to deal with was a home game against Coventry. Liverpool were unbeaten in six and Coventry in eight. A draw looked like the most obvious result. Peter Ndlovu had other ideas.

The Zimbabwean striker tormented many sides for Coventry. His unpredictable play complemented the strong, physical presence of Dion Dublin, who led the line as a classic No.9. Ndlovu became the first visiting player to score a hat-trick at Anfield since 1961. His opening goal was an opportunistic poacher's goal. A penalty after 35 minutes made it 2-0 and again Ron Atkinson's side performed like a completely different side to the one that could not get a win in the early part of the season. In the second half, Jan Mølby pulled a goal back from the spot, but Ndlovu scored his third with a great run and finish. The Anfield pitch did not help any player's ability to dribble, but Ndlovu proved that he had the ability for that not to become an issue. As the Liverpool fans applauded the goal, their team could only find a late consolation thanks to David Burrows's own goal. The home crowd booed off their team and waved goodbye to any late title challenge. It was a disappointing week for the Reds after defeat in the FA Cup. All that remained was a League Cup Final in April, a favourite competition for the famous Liverpool team of the 1980s, against Bolton.

Dennis Wise, in his suit at Stamford Bridge after being released on bail, celebrated a victory for his team, who were decked out in the unique grey and orange away kit, in the Cup Winners' Cup second leg against Club Brugge. Mark Stein levelled the tie with a goal after 16 minutes and his striker partner, Paul Furlong, got the second before half-time. Incredibly, Furlong had been involved in a goalmouth scramble in his own box from a Club Brugge corner before a quick counter-attack and great effort out wide by Stein found Furlong in the box and the expensive striker found the net. The atmosphere inside the stadium was euphoric after the final whistle, a far cry from the brutality of the away leg. Zaragoza were to be the next opponent, in the semi-final.

A night later, and putting the FA Cup exit behind them, QPR beat Norwich at Loftus Road to climb into the top half of the table with games in hand. Ray Wilkins settled into management confidently and his three star attackers, Les Ferdinand, Kevin Gallen and Trevor Sinclair, caused mayhem in the final third. Against a sorry Norwich team, Ferdinand and Gallen applied the finishes to chances created by Sinclair. The Canaries might have been four places above the dreaded drop zone, but only five points separated them from West Ham, who could only draw 1-1 with fellow strugglers Southampton.

Leicester had looked doomed for a long time, but another home defeat, this time to a Yeboah-inspired Leeds, did not give the players or fans much hope of safety. Hovering just above the relegation zone, Everton and Manchester City played out a score draw that did not do much for either team.

At the top end of the table, the pressure was just as intense. Manchester United's game in hand did not go to plan, with a goalless draw at home to Tottenham, who had impressed in their cup victory over Liverpool. The champions flew out of the blocks, with chances created from the kick-off. Mark Hughes and Andy Cole hit the woodwork, Ronny Rosenthal cleared one off the line and Ian Walker kept the United attack at bay. It was a fantastic display by Ferguson's side, but the manager was disappointed by the result. Spurs gave a much better account of themselves in the second half and earned their point. It was the first time United had failed to score at home all season. Ferguson was full of praise for Francis's transformation of his team, creating a physical, hard-running side that impressed the United boss. He may have praised his opposite number, but two dropped points in the title race was a blow, especially with Anfield next on the fixture list.

Blackburn moved into the transfer market to address the sale of Alan Wright – and the news that Jason Wilcox had suffered a season-ending cruciate ligament injury – by signing versatile full-back Jeff Kenna for £1.5m from Southampton. Days later, Alan Ball quickly reinvested the cash on a new striker to support Matt Le Tissier and Neil Shipperley in attack. Gordon Watson was the man tasked with scoring the goals to get Southampton out of trouble. The young striker christened himself 'Flash' when he met his new team-mates and quickly adjusted to fit into the squad, even if his room-mate had to put up with his smoking habits.

Arsenal were in midweek action in the Cup Winners' Cup, the competition their only solace in a turbulent season. Having drawn at home with Auxerre, who managed to score an away goal, Arsenal needed to win in France. As he had done many times, Ian Wright was the match-winner. Tony Adams's hopeful ball caused chaos in the right-back area for Auxerre and the ball squirmed free to Wright's feet. He dribbled inside and curled a shot with his left foot into the top corner. Falling to the ground as he shot, Wright was euphoric. So were the team by the final whistle. A hard-fought victory and progression to the semi-finals to face Sampdoria.

With new signing Kenna in the starting line-up, Blackburn beat Chelsea despite a scare inside the first three minutes of the game when Mark Stein's purple patch continued with the opening goal. Normality resumed when Alan Shearer scored his 100th league goal. An incredible achievement. The goal was also his 30th league goal of the season. He was the first striker since Jimmy Greaves in the early 1960s to record 30 league goals back-to-back. Shearer also made time to link up with his captain, Tim Sherwood, to lay on the winning goal for the midfielder. Six points clear at the top of the table ahead of Manchester United's game against Liverpool the following day, Blackburn and Shearer could not have asked for a better Saturday.

A vital comeback win for Manchester City against Sheffield Wednesday gave them breathing space from the relegation pack. Everton performed a similar feat at Loftus Road, trailing by 1-0 and then 2-1 to QPR before an own goal from Alan McDonald and a last-minute winner from Andy Hinchcliffe earned them three points. Poor results continued for Leicester and Crystal Palace, with defeats at Spurs and Wimbledon respectively. Safety looked a long way away for those two sides. Southampton did themselves no favours with a 3-0 defeat away to Nottingham Forest; they simply could not contain Stan Collymore and Bryan Roy, who displayed the early-season form that had Forest challenging at the top of the table. One team who did help their cause were West Ham, who beat Aston Villa 2-0 at Villa Park. A vital win for Harry Redknapp and a reminder for Villa about how quickly fortunes can change. The Brian Little revival had initially pushed the team up to ninth place, but they sat 15th after the home defeat.

Based on early-season form, Newcastle would have been expected to have still been in the title race deep into March, but poor form and the consistency of Blackburn and Manchester United meant that European qualification was the aim. Arsenal's season was difficult to put into words: Paul Merson a self-confessed drug and gambling addict, George Graham sacked after accepting illicit transfer payments and heavy investment risked on players unproven at the highest level. They faced each other at St James' Park, with a last-minute, long-range strike from Peter Beardsley giving Newcastle their first league double over the Gunners for 28 years. A great result for the home side and third place still in their sights.

The northern juggernauts, Manchester United, who had just announced an enormous building project at Old Trafford to increase the capacity to 55,000, and Liverpool had been rivals for decades. They met at Anfield for *Super Sunday,* live on Sky Sports. It was Manchester United's turn to play after their title rivals and they needed victory to keep the pressure on Blackburn. The gap stood at six points and they could not afford to keep it that way.

It was a day to forget for United. They did not perform anywhere near the level they had set in the previous two seasons. Liverpool, Jamie Redknapp especially, put in a strong performance and, although it was certainly not their best of the season, it was enough to ensure that United could not play their own game. Goals from Redknapp and an own goal from Steve Bruce gave them a 2-0 victory. The Anfield fans sang 'You've lost the league on Merseyside' as they had when United could not stop Leeds winning the title in 1991/92. It was a hammer blow for Ferguson, who was not happy.

In his diary, he wrote that, tactically, his players did not carry out his instructions. Paul Ince came in for criticism for not drifting left to monitor the free role that Roy Evans allowed Steve McManaman. Andy Cole started from the bench due to injury concerns, but Ferguson pondered whether his star striker should have started. He was less than enthused with Andrei Kanchelskis, who had recently asked for permission to leave Old Trafford, and singled out the winger for criticism and wondered, 'What's going on in the boy's head?' Whatever the reasons, they had to dust themselves down and get ready for another game three days later at home to Arsenal.

Finally, Norwich ended their 11-match winless run and got their first league win of 1995 in the best way possible – beating Ipswich in the East Anglian derby. A 3-0 victory with goals from Jamie Cureton, Ashley Ward and Darren Eadie at least prevented John Deehan from explaining another defeat. For Ipswich, it was another nail in the relegation coffin. They had struggled all season and change did not look like it was coming any time soon.

Liverpool dipped into the transfer market just before the 23 March deadline with the signing of highly rated Millwall teenager Mark Kennedy. Aged just 18, the Irish winger arrived at Anfield for £1.5m and added to the youth ranks in the Liverpool changing room. Roy Evans spent money on younger players and had undone a lot of the poor transfer deals sanctioned by his predecessor.

Wimbledon continued to defy expectations of a club working on a miniscule budget by recording a win over Manchester City. The home crowd had to wait until the second half for their team to get ahead thanks to a goal from Andy Thorn. The win was confirmed with a goal from Gary Elkins 15 minutes from the end. Eighth place in the league with eight games to go, Joe Kinnear had worked wonders with his squad despite high-profile players leaving and limited funds to replace them.

QPR had finished highest of all the London clubs in the inaugural Premier League season. That was followed up with ninth place in 1993/94. That was exactly where QPR sat in the league table after a 1-0 win over Chelsea thanks to another goal from Kevin Gallen. The 19-year-old striker was in brilliant form. The 62nd-minute winner meant he had scored three goals in consecutive games. His partnership with Les Ferdinand was one of the reasons QPR found themselves in the top half of the table. Gallen had nine goals and nine assists at this point in the season, which was a fantastic return for a prodigious talent. Chelsea's league form was dreadful and the defeat was their third in a row, leaving them in 15th place. The Cup Winners' Cup semi-final was all they had left to look forward to in their season.

After a difficult start to the second half of the season, Bryan Roy continued his good form with two goals in a

3-0 victory against Leeds. Three first-half goals meant Leeds had no chance of getting back into the game. Stan Collymore found the back of the net for the fourth consecutive game and proved why he was the most wanted striker in the game. Leeds' new star man, Tony Yeboah, had notched five goals in the last three games, scoring in them all, but Forest's defence held strong and kept him at bay. The defeat was a blip for Leeds, who had been in great form since the striker's arrival.

In the early part of the season, Newcastle were known for their explosive goalscoring. Blowing teams away early in games helped them rack up wins. At The Dell, the exact opposite happened. A perfectly executed Paul Kitson bicycle kick looked to have set Newcastle on course for a win by a single goal until an incredible last four minutes. Three goals in quick succession, helped by some generous goalkeeping from Pavel Srníček, rescued Southampton and gave them an improbable win. More incredible was the fact that Matt Le Tissier was not among the scorers.

Old Trafford was primed for an epic encounter between Manchester United and Arsenal. There had been some bad blood between the sides in the past, but there was none of that in this Wednesday evening game. A nervy start was calmed by Mark Hughes's goal after 26 minutes. He answered questions from the manager about his performances in the most emphatic way. A brilliant display from Paul Ince, who was about to stand trial a day later, and goals from Lee Sharpe and Andrei Kanchelskis capped a great night for United. The gap stood at three points, with Blackburn having played a game less. Into the final six weeks of the season, there was a lot of football left to play.

Crystal Palace had their cup replay alongside the busy midweek Premiership schedule. They had a much more straightforward game against Wolves this time with a 4-1 victory. They reached the semi-finals of the FA Cup for the first time since 1990 and would face their final opponents from that year: Manchester United. Chris Armstrong was happy to be back and playing football again after his recreational drugs transgression. He had the first and last Palace goals of the night.

Thursday, 23 March would be remembered as the day Eric Cantona faced judgment for his actions at Selhurst Park. Everyone was at Croydon Magistrates' Court ready for the story of the year. Numerous television crews and photographers gathered to capture a view of the suspended star. Paul Ince was also there alongside Cantona. The two men had travelled down the night before and probably did not help their cases with a night out captured in its full glory by the tabloids.

Cantona arrived in court dressed only the way he could. No shirt and tie, but instead a relaxed blue jacket and grey T-shirt, a tiny pin badge of the Statue of Liberty on his lapel. He did not look like a man about to take the justice system seriously. The court, however, was about to give a verdict that shocked everyone involved.

As Cantona stood in the dock, his sentence was read out. Fourteen days in jail.

Club director and solicitor Maurice Watkins told the BBC more than 20 years later that 'you could have heard a pin drop when the sentence was imposed'. The magistrate told him: 'You are a high-profile public figure with undoubted gifts and, as such, you are looked up to by so many young people.' To say both legal teams were shocked was an understatement. At the same time, Ince pleaded not guilty to a charge of common assault, with his trial to be held later.

To compound matters for Cantona, he was denied bail. He headed straight to the cells with his security man, Ned Kelly.

His lawyers raced to the Croydon Crown Court where they eventually secured the Frenchman's release on bail pending an appeal. During his three and a half hours in the cells, he had eaten a Big Mac and fries, paid for by Kelly and delivered by officers. A meal befitting a king.

With an appeal lodged, Cantona was back in court in little over a week. In the meantime, the vultures circled, with São Paulo and Inter Milan ready to bid for the star.

While Cantona was in court, his manager was at Buckingham Palace for his CBE investiture. Ferguson was told of Cantona's sentence after the ceremony had been completed. He could not believe it. Even more shocking, in his eyes, was that a great deal of the public supported the decision. The outcome of the appeal was of great importance to Cantona, Ferguson, Manchester United and the Premier League.

A day after Cantona's sentencing, Matthew Simmons was in the dock to face charges of his own. He pleaded not guilty to two charges that resulted from his part in the Cantona affair. The press may have focused their attention on the professional footballer, but Simmons was certainly not exempt from revelations about his private life. After his plea, a date was set for the Crystal Palace fan to appear in court in May.

Compared to all of the courtroom drama, a relatively quiet deadline day in the Premiership did not hide the fact that spending in the English game had increased exponentially. Expenditure on transfers had reached £135m, according to *The Independent*, almost doubling the previous season's total. The game had truly changed, with far more players arriving from outside the domestic game and an upward trend in fees for British players.

Blackburn added to the stars in their squad with the loan signing of Richard Witschge from Bordeaux. A promising player in the Netherlands, he earned a £3m transfer to

Barcelona but never managed to hold down a role in Johan Cruyff's 'Dream Team'. Kenny Dalglish hoped some extra quality would help his team get over the line.

There were few notable deals completed, but some interesting ones that did not get over the line. Aston Villa moved on from the experienced Ray Houghton, but Brian Little failed in a £3m raid on his former club to sign highly rated midfielder Mark Draper. The deal would have made a good profit for Leicester, but they held firm.

Everton were desperate for a striker, although it was not Stan Collymore on their shopping list. A £2.3m deal for Brian Deane was rejected by Leeds, who wanted closer to £3m. Joe Royle did manage to move on a striker when he sold Brett Angell to Sunderland for £600,000.

The biggest move of deadline day came from the First Division. Bryan Robson's Middlesbrough, backed by generous chairman and local lad Steve Gibson, spent £1.3m on Swindon striker Jan Åge Fjørtoft. Manchester United and England's former 'Captain Marvel' had his team pushing for promotion and needed goals to take one of the two places available for the 1995/96 Premiership season. The Norwegian had already proved he could score goals at the top level, so it seemed a shrewd investment from Robson.

With a break from domestic football, plenty of column inches were devoted to Cantona. He had to wait until the end of the month, once England had played a forgettable draw against Uruguay at Wembley, for his appeal hearing on 31 March.

This time, Cantona turned up at court in more traditional attire: a suit, with tie and jumper. He looked the part and hoped that the three-man appeal panel made up of two magistrates and a Crown Court judge felt the same way.

Reaction to Cantona's sentence had been one of complete shock, so when Mr Justice Ian Davies read out the panel's verdict, there was relief for some and ecstatic cheers from United fans. The prison sentence had been quashed and the sentence became a 120-hour community service order. In Cantona's mind, justice had been served and he had not been treated differently to the ordinary man over his offence. The sentence also massively increased the chances of Cantona remaining in England with Manchester United. He was no longer an outcast set to serve time in jail. While serving the remainder of his suspension from football, he would spend his days coaching younger players who were desperate to follow in his footsteps.

What happened next transformed the whole event into that of legend.

A press conference was organised after the appeal had been heard. Cantona sat behind a desk, glass of water in front of him. Maurice Watkins sat beside him. Ned Kelly hovered in the background. Cantona was told by the lawyer and club officials. So he did. In the only way he knew how to make a statement:

'When the seagulls follow the trawler, it's because they think sardines will be thrown into the sea. Thank you.'

He stood up and, amid the constant flicker and chatter of camera bulbs, he walked out of the room, Ned Kelly's arm around him. Maurice Watkins was startled in his seat. He looked around, puzzled by what he had heard. One of the Premiership's biggest stars, who had just won an appeal for assault against a fan during a game, had given a single-sentence statement that seemed to make absolutely no sense to a room of journalists who sent their story to every news outlet in print and on screen. An incredible moment.

Pos	Team	P	W	D	L	F	A	GD	Pts
1	Blackburn Rovers	34	23	7	4	70	29	+41	76
2	Manchester United	35	22	7	6	66	24	+42	73
3	Newcastle United	34	18	9	7	56	36	+20	63
4	Nottingham Forest	35	17	9	9	56	38	+18	60
5	Liverpool	32	16	10	6	54	26	+28	58
6	Leeds United	33	14	10	9	44	33	+11	52
7	Tottenham Hotspur	33	14	10	9	52	42	+10	52
8	Wimbledon	34	14	6	14	41	54	-13	48
9	Queens Park Rangers	32	12	8	12	50	50	0	44
10	Sheffield Wednesday	35	11	10	14	43	46	-3	43
11	Coventry City	35	10	13	12	37	53	-16	43
12	Norwich City	34	10	12	12	33	38	-5	42
13	Manchester City	34	10	11	13	43	52	-9	41
14	Arsenal	34	10	10	14	36	40	-4	40
15	Chelsea	33	10	10	13	40	46	-6	40
16	Aston Villa	34	9	12	13	46	48	-2	39
17	Everton	34	9	12	13	37	46	-9	39
18	West Ham United	34	10	7	17	33	44	-11	37
19	Southampton	32	7	15	10	44	51	-7	36
20	Crystal Palace	32	8	10	14	23	34	-11	34
21	Ipswich Town	33	6	5	22	31	75	-44	23
22	Leicester City	34	4	9	21	36	66	-30	21

The Survivors (April)

AFTER THE international break, football returned on 1 April. Some of the results could easily have been part of an elaborate April Fools' Day prank.

Arsenal had lost four games in a row in the Premiership, scoring a single goal. Norwich had won their first game in 1995 last time out after 11 games without a win. Sometimes, games featuring teams in terrible form result in a bore draw or the narrowest of wins. Three goals in the first 13 minutes soon eliminated that outcome. A double from John Hartson and a rare Lee Dixon goal were followed by a Jamie Cureton goal for Norwich. In truth, there was no real threat from Norwich and two more second-half goals put the finishing touch on an emphatic victory. Norwich were in a desperate situation and hurtling towards the relegation zone.

Leicester and Wimbledon managed seven goals between them in a thriller at Filbert Street. The home side were hanging on for dear life in the bottom two league positions for most of the season. Their opponents continued their rise up the table. Three consecutive wins and no goals conceded was a far cry from Leicester's run of four games without a victory. A Mark Robins goal gave Leicester a half-time lead. It lasted until just after the hour mark when Wimbledon scored twice in quick succession. Jon Goodman and Øyvind Leonhardsen put the Dons in front and it seemed their good run would continue. Incredibly, Leicester managed to get themselves back in front after an equaliser from Jimmy Willis and a Jamie Lawrence header from a corner. They were barely ahead for a minute when Kevin Poole's sliced clearance found Dean Holdsworth and the striker headed the ball into the path of the Norwegian, Leonhardsen. He powered into the box and fired it past the helpless Kevin Poole. The game was level. In the final minute, wily target man Mick Harford flicked the ball into the path of the running Jon Goodman. Clean through on goal, Goodman struck the ball past Poole and won the three points for Wimbledon. Sixteen points from safety with only 21 available for Leicester. A mountain that seemed to grow taller each week.

So that's one game with six goals and another with seven goals. At Hillsborough, fans saw eight goals. The problem for the home fans was that seven of them were scored by the opposition.

Stuart Pearce opened the scoring with a powerful, curled free kick that flew past Kevin Pressman, who barely moved. Another goal, this time from Ian Woan, extended Forest's lead and gave them a 2-0 cushion at half-time. The second half belonged to one man – Bryan Roy. His first goal finished a flowing move that built through midfield and featured some one-touch football until Roy was released in the box. A neat finish from the Dutchman saw the floodgates open. A penalty from Mark Bright did not deter Forest from their attacking intentions and Roy hit his second to make it 4-1. He showcased his superb dribbling abilities by setting Stan Collymore free for his first goal, which was a great strike, and then gave him a relatively easy finish, made somewhat difficult by the Forest No.10, for Forest's sixth. The final goal was scored by Lars Bohinen, a superb curling effort with the outside of his right foot that beat Kevin Pressman. Another assist for Roy, who had a hand in all five second-half goals. Public criticism seemed to work for Frank Clark as his star strikers certainly took the bait and raised their game. Whether it made them happy off the field was debatable.

The flood of goals in those three games did not quite transfer to the other fixtures. A vital win for Blackburn over Everton, with goals in the first and seventh minutes from The SAS, pushed them to six points clear of Manchester United, who were to face Leeds 24 hours later. Shearer was on another scoring streak, with five goals in his last four games. For Sutton, it was his first goal since 26 November. – an incredible statistic after such a strong start to the season.

A last-minute goal at Portman Road gave Aston Villa a 1-0 win and denied Ipswich what would have been a vital point. Crystal Palace had better fortune and beat Manchester City 2-1 to put them two points behind Everton with two games in hand. It was still all to play for at the bottom of the table.

One team who did manage to claw their way out of the relegation zone were Southampton. In a thrilling early kick-off against Spurs, they emerged victorious with a memorable 4-3 win. Goals came in bursts, with Neil Heaney and Teddy Sheringham getting the scoring under way in the 12th and 16th minutes. Then, ten minutes apart, Klinsmann and Le Tissier, the stars of each side, scored to make it 2-2 at half-time. A kamikaze five minutes before the hour mark saw goals from Le Tissier and Jim Magilton either side of another for Sheringham. It was Spurs' third 4-3 scoreline of the season; a win over Sheffield Wednesday, a defeat to Aston Villa in Gerry Francis's first game and now this. Back-to-back wins for Southampton against two top-eight sides was massive.

Manchester United faced Leeds in the other earlier kick-off and drew 0-0. The team who had pipped them in 1992 succeeded in frustrating the champions. Leeds fans revelled in their team's performance with chants of 'You're not the champions any more'. Ferguson was not impressed with Wilkinson's team. 'They didn't go forward. They didn't make threats to us' was how he described the opposition's game plan at Old Trafford. It worked for Leeds, who stopped Manchester United scoring. Andy Cole and Mark Hughes had chances, but they could not make it count. Gary McAllister and Gary Speed worked hard in midfield and got the better of their opponents. The game was notable for an excellent performance from Gary Neville, who had doubters in the Manchester United camp, including his manager, but excelled in the right-back role. That did not matter too much when a vital two points had been dropped.

At Wembley, Steve McManaman inspired Liverpool to victory over First Division Bolton Wanderers in the Coca-Cola Cup Final. His two goals earned him the Man of the Match award and fulfilled the promise he had shown over the last few seasons. It was a first trophy as manager for Roy Evans, too. The Boot Room stalwart was now in the dugout and added a record fifth League Cup to the Anfield trophy cabinet.

Before his two goals, McManaman was the creative heartbeat of Liverpool. He made chances for Ian Rush and Robbie Fowler, but the two strikers were wasteful. Bolton held their own, too. Young stars Alan Thompson and Jason McAteer proved that they could compete against Premiership players with strong first-half performances.

The star of the show, though, was McManaman. His first goal was a masterclass in powerful and direct running. Dribbling straight at Bolton, he found the space on his right and, with a neat touch past the Bolton defenders, fired past Keith Branagan. In the second half, Bolton continued to compete. Attacking Liverpool with crosses, passes in behind central defenders and some excellent passing by the likes of Richard Sneekes, Bolton looked like they would find a goal. When David James plucked a cross out of the air with Liverpool under pressure, he started a counter-attack that resulted in McManaman's second goal. Another excellent show of dribbling and a cool finish into the bottom corner. But, within a minute, Bolton had a goal back thanks to a brilliant turn and hit from Alan Thompson. They continued to push, but Liverpool held firm. Jubilant scenes in the Liverpool end highlighted the feelgood factor that had swept back into the team.

There was no rest in the football calendar at this time of the year. Blackburn won at Loftus Road thanks to a Chris Sutton goal, which put them eight points clear at the top with six games remaining. They edged closer and closer to the title.

A Tony Yeboah hat-trick for Leeds helped dismantle Ipswich at Elland Road. Howard Wilkinson's team were solid and consistent. They had featured in the top eight for months. A late-season surge for Europe was not off the cards. Sixth place with eight games to go kept them in with a chance.

Unfortunately for Ipswich, the result meant they were relegated. It had been a torturous season, with the only bright spot coming from a three-game unbeaten run at the turn of the year. There was hope. George Burley had the opportunity to reset the side with younger players and bring the club back stronger. It would be difficult to do outside the riches of the top flight, but the manager gave the fans and club hope.

Leicester prevented their relegation being confirmed, beating freefalling Norwich. The Canaries' alarming slide down the table continued at pace. Defeat against one of the worst-performing teams in the league did not help the cause. Incredibly, 22 February was the first time Norwich had been in the bottom half of the table since the second game of the season. Seventh place at the end of 1994 suggested a run for a European place was possible. Instead, they were now constantly looking over their shoulder.

A 3-1 win at Anfield against Southampton proved that there was no hangover for Liverpool after their cup success. Ian Rush hit two and Robbie Fowler got one of his own to cancel out an opener from Richard Hall. Southampton stood perilously close to the relegation zone but, with four more games to come in April, there were plenty of points to play for.

There was barely a break in football over the first week of April, with Thursday night European fixtures in the Cup Winners' Cup for Chelsea and Arsenal. Glenn Hoddle took his side to Zaragoza, where they were soundly beaten. The 3-0 loss gave them a huge deficit to erase at Stamford Bridge two weeks later. Arsenal took on Sampdoria at Highbury. A quick-fire brace from the most unlikely source, Steve Bould, gave the Gunners a 2-0 lead before Vladimir Jugović struck for the Italian side. Ian Wright restored the two-goal cushion for Arsenal only for Jugović to notch his second of the game. Despite the two away goals conceded, Arsenal had a lead to take into the second leg. With the trials and tribulations they had suffered all season, this was a real positive.

A single day without a Premiership side in action started a run of eight consecutive days of Premiership fixtures. Space in the football calendar was tight and the sheer amount of games played in April had the chance to impact the talent on a huge scale. Four teams also had FA Cup semi-finals to contend with.

There was an inevitable feeling at St James' Park when Peter Beardsley scored a penalty after eight minutes; Newcastle were going to win the game. The probability of victory increased exponentially when the opponent was Norwich. Another Beardsley goal before half-time put another nail in John Deehan's coffin. Paul Kitson's goal hammered home the point that Norwich's spiral to the relegation zone accelerated.

Manager Deehan was powerless to turn around his team's fortunes. The sale of Chris Sutton, Efan Ekoku, Mark Robins and Ruel Fox a season earlier certainly did not help, but the drop off in form since the first half of the season was stark. Bryan Gunn's injury meant promising goalkeeper Andy Marshall was thrust into the first team, but the fortunes of Deehan's side could not be put down to a change in goalkeeper. The manager left the club with player-coach Gary Megson, aged 36, stepping into the dugout. Five games to save the season.

Leicester had changed their manager much earlier when Brian Little left for Aston Villa. It had not gone to plan. Their opponents, Sheffield Wednesday, moved between mid-table positions most weeks without threatening to move too far up or down the table. After a run of positive results in winter, losses became normal. The game against Leicester gave them only their second win in ten games. Guy Whittingham scored the only goal of the game, which was his seventh league goal for Wednesday and his ninth of the season. The writing was on the wall for Leicester. If results did not go their way, that was the end of their season.

The only league game on the FA Cup semi-final weekend was between Liverpool and Leeds at Anfield. Brian Deane got the winner, which earned Leeds their first victory at Liverpool since 1971/72. The defeat was a blow to Roy Evans's European ambitions but if they won their games in hand, they had a chance of reaching the top three. Liverpool, Newcastle and Nottingham Forest, with Leeds not far behind, all had a chance of finishing as the next best to Blackburn and Manchester United.

While Leeds travelled along the M62 to Merseyside, Everton went in the other direction, with Tottenham headed north to Elland Road. Survival was crucial for Joe Royle, but a second consecutive trip to an FA Cup semi-final, after he masterminded Oldham's run the year before, was just what the team deserved. From being banned at the start of the competition to walking out in a semi-final, it was quite a turnaround for Spurs.

Everton's fans dominated the stands at Elland Road. They filled three sides of the ground, with Tottenham fans, although in equal number, housed in the huge new East Stand. It gave the feeling that it was a home match for Everton. A delay in some Tottenham fans arriving for the 1.30pm kick-off did not help either. Gerry Francis later revealed that his son had been ill all week, taking a toll on him. He also had to contend with being without a number of players; Justin Edinburgh, Sol Campbell and David Kerslake were all absent.

Matt Jackson headed Everton into the lead from a corner in the first half and it was clear that Joe Royle's side wanted it more than their opponents. A poor goal kick from Ian Walker gifted the ball to Paul Rideout, who charged in on goal, only to see the Spurs' goalkeeper atone for his mistake with a great save. Luckily for Everton, Graham Stuart had followed Rideout's run and tapped into the empty net. Two-nil to Everton, who had weathered the Spurs storm and now just needed to hold on.

Klinsmann got Spurs back in the game thanks to a penalty, with a bit of luck sprinkled on the ball due to a kiss from Teddy Sheringham. An equaliser almost arrived, but Stuart Nethercott hit the post and Everton broke away. Substitute Daniel Amokachi finished off a great cross to make it 3-1 and then finished another counter-attack, led by Gary Ablett of all people, with a sidefoot strike that hit the roof of the net. Amokachi and Everton were in dreamland. Wembley waited for Royle and his 'Dogs of War'.

In the Midlands, Manchester United and Crystal Palace faced each other at Villa Park. The 4pm kick-off meant that fans descended on pubs much earlier than they had before the other semi-final. Tensions ran high after the Cantona incident at Selhurst Park months earlier, but no one could have envisaged what happened before the game.

Paul Nixon, a 35-year-old Crystal Palace fan, died in the street after more than 100 fans brawled outside a Walsall pub. After being struck with a brick as he tried to get on a Palace supporters' coach, he was crushed under the weight of the coach carrying fans to the game. Reports from the day explained that both sets of fans were antagonising each other. The Palace fans repurposed United's 'Ooh aah Cantona' chant to 'Ooh aah prisoner', which did not go down well with Manchester United fans. One eye witness said the violence erupted after personal insults were exchanged between fans. Whatever the reason, fan violence had again left an ugly mark on football.

The game seemed somewhat inconsequential after those tragic events, but news had not spread into the ground by that point, so both teams gave it their all.

Palace took the lead with an Iain Dowie header from a yard out, before Denis Irwin scored what was a classic free kick: about 25 yards out and curled into the top corner. Neither side could find the net again and the match went into extra time. Within one minute of the additional period, Chris Armstrong broke through on United's goal and lifted the ball over Peter Schmeichel. It didn't take long for a response and Gary Pallister forced a replay with a header in the 96th minute.

Back to league action, Chelsea drew 1-1 with Wimbledon on Monday, 10 April. Premiership action continued the following night with a double header; relegated Ipswich lost 1-0 at home to QPR thanks to a goal from Les Ferdinand and

Tottenham beat Manchester City 2-1 at White Hart Lane with a late winner from Klinsmann. Elimination from the FA Cup meant that Spurs' best chance of European qualification had disappeared, but they were still confident of finishing in the top seven.

Due to the extreme fixture congestion, Chelsea were in action again, only 48 hours after the draw against Wimbledon, and they lost to Southampton at Stamford Bridge. Inconsistency had been a real issue for Glenn Hoddle over the course of the season. A two-goal deficit at half-time against a team who had struggled for a large part of the season summed it up. Neil Shipperley, who Chelsea had sold to the Saints, opened the scoring before the inevitable Matt Le Tissier goal put Alan Ball's team 2-0 up. It was a well-earned victory and lifted the away side above Chelsea in the table.

Two more teams followed Southampton's example and recorded away wins. Liverpool beat Arsenal 1-0 at Highbury thanks to a last-minute goal from perennial Arsenal pest Robbie Fowler. Nottingham Forest stayed ahead of Liverpool, having played two games more, with their own late winner as Steve Stone's 85th-minute goal inflicted yet another defeat on Norwich. It was their 16th loss of the season. An incredible statistic considering they had only lost seven up to the end of December 1994. They were firmly embroiled in the relegation battle now.

The focus of the night was the replay between Manchester United and Crystal Palace. Fans observed a minute's silence before the game in respect of Paul Nixon. Goals from Steve Bruce and Gary Pallister gave United a comfortable 2-0 lead and the game looked won. Injuries to Ryan Giggs and Roy Keane gave Alex Ferguson a half-time headache. He decided to take off Giggs and leave Keane on, despite the Irishman's bruised and cut ankle. The second half got under way and

Keane kept asking his manager for five more minutes on the pitch. Ferguson obliged. And then all hell broke loose.

A long ball over the top was headed away by the United defence and bounced into the path of Gareth Southgate. His touch did not trap the ball, but pushed it towards the onrushing Keane. The midfielder attempted to play the ball, but his studs were high. The whistle blew but Southgate slid straight through Keane. While the Irishman stayed on his feet, the tackle left the Palace player on the floor. Keane looked down and stamped twice on Southgate's chest. Players charged over to get involved. There were pushes and punches. Denis Irwin wagged his finger at the prone Southgate. Referee David Elleray had no choice but to send off Keane. Palace's Darren Patterson almost received his marching orders for steaming in and probably making the situation much worse.

The season just continued to get worse for Manchester United, with Keane now facing a suspension. All eyes turned towards Ferguson and his handling of discipline within the club. The news of Inter Milan's £4.5m bid for Eric Cantona, with the promise of a £25,000-a-week contract, did not help matters. Yet, even with all their problems, United were in an FA Cup Final and still had a chance to win the title. The season was not over yet.

A 3-0 win for West Ham helped in their battle against the drop – an uncharacteristic defeat for Wimbledon, who had a chance to finish seventh, only one place lower than the previous season.

Manchester City and Liverpool got the Easter weekend fixtures under way at Maine Road. Coming off a run of three consecutive defeats, City put in a great performance as they won 2-1. Nicky Summerbee's first league goal for the club opened the scoring but was cancelled out by Steve McManaman. The winner came thanks to German Maurizio

Gaudino, whose well-placed header beat David James to give City only their third win in 20 league games and lifted them to 11th in the table.

Crystal Palace's hopes of a welcome win were wrecked by a last-minute equaliser from Klinsmann's stunning free kick. The German striker also stunned his own club when he refused to commit his future to White Hart Lane for the 1995/96 season. Palace did not have any superstar dilemmas facing them. Points on the board were what mattered for them at this stage of the season, especially with some daunting fixtures ahead. Dropping two points at such a late stage of the game stung.

Buoyed by their emphatic cup win over Spurs, Everton recorded an excellent home victory over Newcastle, with Daniel Amokachi getting both goals. Newcastle drew a rare blank and put their top-four place at risk. Everton reached 42 points but knew this was not necessarily enough to secure their Premiership status. The result condemned Leicester to relegation. Sitting in 21st in the league with only 24 points, even winning all five games would only have drawn them level with Crystal Palace on 39. Palace also had a far-superior goal difference. Incredibly, Alan Smith's side had only conceded 36 goals by that point in the season; the fifth best in the league.

The title race had a month left to run and there had been a Premiership game every day for over a week. For various reasons, Blackburn had not played for ten days. They travelled to Elland Road and put in a great performance. Colin Hendry's goal just before half-time meant that Rovers led for almost all the second half until a corner was converted by Brian Deane to rescue a point for Leeds. Losing two points at this stage was crucial for Blackburn, especially as Manchester United won 4-0 against now-relegated Leicester. A brace from Andy Cole added to Lee Sharpe's opener and the scoring was completed by Paul Ince in the last minute. The gap was reduced from eight to six points. Alex Ferguson thought chinks were starting to appear in Blackburn's armour after letting their lead slip at Leeds. Both sides were at home on Easter Monday with everything to play for.

At the bottom, there were still two relegation places to be decided. Clearly, not every team was involved in a relegation battle, but Arsenal in tenth place were certainly not out of danger. Fifty points seemed like a reasonable target for guaranteed safety and Arsenal were on 43 points with five games to go. The first of these five was a comfortable 4-1 home victory over Ipswich that included a nine-minute hat-trick from Ian Wright. Not quite Robbie Fowler speed, but an impressive feat. It gave Arsenal, and caretaker boss Stewart Houston, some room to breathe.

Southampton recorded another impressive win. Alan Ball's decision to dip into the transfer market paid off when his two newest strikers, Neil Shipperley and Gordon Watson, scored the goals that beat Les Ferdinand and QPR. Four wins in the last five games had rescued Southampton's season. Relegation was still a possibility, but turning draws into wins was crucial. Coventry had made great strides under Ron Atkinson and victory over his former side, Sheffield Wednesday, continued their move up the table. Dion Dublin, now on 12 league goals for the season, opened the scoring early in the game and Peter Ndlovu notched with two minutes left on the clock. A well-deserved win and a step closer to safety.

A full set of fixtures took place on Easter Monday, with drama at the top and bottom of the table. Crystal Palace recorded a great victory against QPR to put them on 42 points and equal with West Ham and Norwich. Palace sat in the relegation zone on goal difference only. West Ham only managed a draw at Ipswich thanks to a last-minute equaliser from Jeroen Boere. A point was valuable in the circumstances, but a win would have made a huge difference. Norwich lost again, this time at Tottenham. Their descent into the relegation zone was jarring. At the end of March, they sat comfortably in 12th position. Now they were at risk of going down. Not a single point earned in the last five games, one goal scored and 11 conceded.

Having set the pace in the early part of the season, Newcastle tried to cling on to their top-four place, which looked difficult as Nottingham Forest surged and Liverpool caught up on games in hand due to their Coca-Cola Cup run. A defeat at home to Leeds, their first loss at St James' Park for 15 months, did not help. The goals came in a frantic six-minute spell in the first half after Leeds opened the scoring thanks to a Gary McAllister penalty. An unlikely goalscorer in Robbie Elliott took Leeds by surprise, the Newcastle man scoring with a left-footed shot that arrowed into the corner. His improvised celebration was a clear indication of how rare his goalscoring was. Tony Yeboah got the win as he raced on to a Gary Speed through ball, nudged the ball around the stranded Pavel Srníček and ran through to an empty net. Thirty-one minutes gone and it was 2-1 to Leeds, which was how the game ended. Fifth place for Newcastle, who hit a bad patch at the wrong time.

Nottingham Forest were desperate to secure third place and their home game against Coventry was done by half-time. Ian Woan and Stan Collymore earned the win and kept them in the hunt for third. Liverpool beat Leicester at home by the same 2-0 scoreline to keep the pressure on. Ian Rush and Robbie Fowler left their goals until much later. The sending-off of Mike Whitlow did not help Leicester's cause and they slumped to yet another defeat.

Stewart Houston was a happy man as his side hit another four goals with victory at home to Aston Villa, whose form had fallen dramatically. It was only the third time all season that the Gunners had recorded back-to-back victories. A truly desperate season for the team on and off the pitch was now much more likely to finish in mid-table mediocrity than the abyss of relegation.

Teams never want to help their local enemies in any way, but when Manchester City beat Blackburn, the main beneficiaries were Manchester United.

At first, it almost seemed like City tried to give victory to Blackburn. A shanked clearance from Tony Coton found Alan Shearer on the edge of the box. Without a thought, the newly crowned PFA Players' Player of the Year found the back of the net. An incredible 32nd goal of the season for Shearer. Two defenders took over the goalscoring duty next. A calm penalty from Keith Curle levelled the scores before Colin Hendry took aim from the edge of the box and, with some helpful deflections and generous goalkeeping, made it 2-1 to Blackburn before half-time.

Nicky Summerbee was the man who created the two second-half goals that earned Manchester City victory. The speedy winger was integral to the way City played and he caused problems for Blackburn all game. His deep cross into the box ended up dropping to the feet of Uwe Rösler, who curled a great finish past Tim Flowers for his 14th of the season. The winner came from strike partner Paul Walsh, who tucked away another Summerbee cross that had ricocheted around in the box.

Having been done a favour by their neighbours, Manchester United had a chance to close the gap on Blackburn. A miserable Manchester afternoon of rain only added to the tension at Old Trafford. Alex Ferguson was without the pace of Lee Sharpe, Ryan Giggs and Andrei Kanchelskis, so Chelsea's tactics were to sit deep and defend. Despite creating numerous chances, United could not find a way through. Andy Cole was supposed to be a difference maker, but he didn't prove to be as clinical as he or Ferguson would have wanted. In the last four home games, United had been held to 0-0 draws by Tottenham, Leeds and now Chelsea. In his *Captain's Log* video, Steve Bruce reflected on the last few weeks and said: 'It's been a bit of a disappointment really … when you're going for championships you need desperately to win your home games.' United had four games left, two at home and two away. To stand any chance of catching Blackburn, they really needed to win them all.

Three days later, Blackburn squeezed in another game to their fixture list when they hosted Crystal Palace. Jeff Kenna scored his first for the club to set Blackburn on their way. The story of the night was somewhat tragic. Kevin Gallacher made his first start for 15 months after nursing himself back to full fitness from a broken leg. He scored less than five minutes after Kenna to give Blackburn a 2-0 lead. Just after the hour mark, Gallacher was caught by a tackle from John Humphrey. It was another leg break. The same place and the same leg. Unbelievable bad luck, but a vital win for Blackburn.

In Europe, Chelsea faced Real Zaragoza in the hope of overturning a 3-0 first-leg deficit. They got off to a great start thanks to Paul Furlong, but a vital away goal by Santiago Aragon was a setback. Chelsea continued to push but, despite goals from Frank Sinclair and Mark Stein, it was not enough to overcome the Spanish side. Chelsea exited the competition and Zaragoza were through to the final.

Arsenal faced Sampdoria in their second leg and hoped they could reach a second successive European Cup Winners' Cup Final. Roberto Mancini, who beat the offside trap and nonchalantly lobbed the ball over Seaman, equalled the scores on aggregate in the first half before a trademark poacher's goal from Ian Wright brought Arsenal level on the night and gave them a 4-3 aggregate lead. Then, the last ten minutes produced some frantic football.

Substitute Claudio Belluci had barely been on the pitch for five minutes when he diverted Mancini's shot into the back of the net. Momentum back to Sampdoria; level on aggregate, ahead on away goals. When Belluci scored again, it meant the Italians were in the lead and Arsenal were going out. The scoring did not end there, though. Minutes before the end of the game, Stefan Schwarz lined up a free kick, complete with a run-up that must have been more than ten yards, and fired it past Walter Zenga to level the scores on aggregate.

The final whistle blew and the game was going into extra time. Both sides had won the home legs 3-2, so neither side had an away goals advantage.

No goals in extra time resulted in the dreaded penalty shoot-out. A virtuoso performance from David Seaman secured Arsenal's place in the final. The England goalkeeper saved three Sampdoria penalties, with the third, and winning, one-handed save from Attilio Lombardo the pick of the bunch. Incredibly, Arsenal had won the penalty shoot-out 3-2, which was in keeping with the scorelines from both legs. A fantastic night for Arsenal and one they could enjoy away from the controversy of their season.

The international break created a gap in the domestic fixture list, even though England did not manage to arrange a friendly. Instead, Terry Venables brought together a squad of fringe players for training. The players involved in the title race were exempt from the camp, so the likes of Steve Stone, Stan Collymore and others got to showcase their talent. Across the league, there was a growing pool of talent that Venables wanted to nurture before the European Championships in 1996. England usually had pressure from fans in tournaments, but one they were hosting carried a different burden.

Eric Cantona was back in the headlines as he started his community service at The Cliff, Manchester United's training ground, coaching young players. In news that disappointed many of United's rivals, he also signed a new contract to end speculation of a move to Italy and Inter Milan. It was a huge relief for Ferguson, who had stood by his star throughout the last four months. When news reached the papers that Cantona was in line for a pay rise, journalists' pens groaned with fury and Manchester United came in for more criticism. Ferguson decided to tackle the journalists' opinion head-on; he arranged a press conference with his French talisman by his side.

Looking relaxed alongside his manager, Cantona told of his happiness at staying at United. He wanted to win as many trophies as he could during his stay at the club. He had signed a deal that ended in 1998 and paid him £750,000 a year, a healthy increase on his previous contract. After the negotiations had been completed, he headed back to France to welcome his second child with wife Isabelle. His team returned to action with one thing on their mind.

The final weekend in April didn't produce too many surprises but, at Highbury, the North London derby proved again that controversy was never far away.

Always a game full of robust challenges, questionable fan exchanges and full-blooded football, Arsenal versus Tottenham embodied all of that as April came to a close. Already a tense atmosphere because of the Arsenal team's performance during the season, the feeling in the stadium was certainly not friendly. In another example of fans trying to get on to the pitch, some tried to charge on when Ian Wright won and then scored a penalty. He then had to pick up a whisky bottle that had been thrown at him. The game was halted and police continued to battle with Spurs fans, who were determined to make it on to the pitch.

That man Klinsmann got the equaliser for Spurs 13 minutes later to level the scores. The result did not help Spurs' European hopes or Arsenal's desire to secure a top-half finish. Thanks to their cup run, Spurs still had four games to play whereas Arsenal only had two. Gerry Francis hoped his side would be able to chase down Leeds and finish sixth, but Europe looked out of reach.

In another battle, this time at the bottom of the league, Leicester beat Ipswich 2-0. There was really only pride at stake at this point and at least the home fans got to see a victory. Struggling Norwich lost again, this time to a late Ian Rush winner in a 2-1 defeat by Liverpool. That result put them 20th in the table with 42 points. They had failed to win a single point in a calendar month of football, dropping from 12th to 20th in five weeks. Crystal Palace's situation was getting worse as the Roy and Collymore double act helped Nottingham Forest record a 2-1 win.

Sky Sports' *Super Sunday* cameras were at Upton Park for West Ham versus Blackburn. The home side desperately needed points to secure their place in the league and the away team wanted to extend their lead at the top to 11 points with a victory. At this time of the year, form goes out of the window and teams are just desperate for points. That was West Ham. Whatever Harry Redknapp said to his team worked wonders. Even though they were still in a relegation fight, West Ham had not lost for six games. They had grown stronger over the last few weeks and their counter-attacking was effective against the league leaders. Blackburn did have a goal disallowed thanks to a foul from Chris Sutton on the West Ham goalkeeper Luděk Mikloško which his team-mates were not happy about. It was West Ham's day – and possibly Manchester United's, too – and Blackburn needed to improve quickly, as four points from the last four games was not title-winning form.

Poor form aside, Blackburn had an eight-point cushion at the top of the table after 40 games, with only two remaining against Newcastle and Liverpool. Manchester United sat in second place having played two games fewer than Blackburn. Coventry, Sheffield Wednesday, Southampton and a final-day showdown with Blackburn's conquerors, West Ham, were the games left for the reigning champions.

At the other end of the table, Ipswich were rock bottom on 24 points, with Leicester three points above them and a huge gap to Norwich, who had 42 points in 20th place. Crystal Palace had the same points one place above them, with the out-of-form Aston Villa only a point outside the relegation zone. In truth, anyone up to Coventry on 46 points could have been dragged further into the battle to stay in the league.

While teams fought to stay in the Premiership, Middlesbrough emerged from a long and exhausting First Division campaign to win the title in Bryan Robson's first season as player-manager. In the final season at Ayresome Park before moving to a shiny new stadium by the river, Robson had masterminded a consistent promotion push with shrewd signings along the way. A return to the Premiership after two seasons away was well deserved and Captain Marvel had the chance to test himself against some of his old foes. How his old team would have loved to have had him for the run-in.

Pos	Team	P	W	D	L	F	A	GD	Pts
1	Blackburn Rovers	40	26	8	6	78	37	+41	86
2	Manchester United	38	23	9	6	70	24	+46	78
3	Nottingham Forest	40	21	10	9	69	41	+28	73
4	Liverpool	38	20	10	8	63	31	+32	70
5	Newcastle United	39	19	11	9	61	41	+20	68
6	Leeds United	39	18	12	9	53	35	+18	66
7	Tottenham Hotspur	38	16	12	10	60	49	+11	60
8	Queens Park Rangers	39	15	8	16	56	56	0	53
9	Wimbledon	39	15	8	16	46	63	-17	53
10	Arsenal	40	13	11	16	51	47	+4	50
11	Southampton	38	11	16	11	55	58	-3	49
12	Chelsea	39	12	13	14	44	50	-6	49
13	Manchester City	39	12	12	15	50	59	-9	48
14	Sheffield Wednesday	40	12	12	16	45	55	-10	48
15	Coventry City	38	11	13	14	39	56	-17	46
16	West Ham United	38	12	9	17	40	46	-6	45
17	Everton	38	10	14	14	40	48	-8	44
18	Aston Villa	39	10	13	16	47	54	-7	43
19	Crystal Palace	38	10	12	16	29	40	-11	42
20	Norwich City	40	10	12	18	35	51	-16	42
21	Leicester City	40	6	9	25	42	77	-35	27
22	Ipswich Town	39	6	6	27	33	88	-55	24

The Decider (May)

THERE WERE two weeks left in the 1994/95 season. The final day was set for 14 April, but there were still 34 games left to play. Similar to April, there were games almost every day until teams caught up on games in hand to leave the final day a fight for the title and, for others, a place in the league.

It seemed apt that the champions kicked off the final month of the season. An away match at Coventry might have looked an easier proposition earlier in the season, but Ron Atkinson had done a great job in edging the side closer to safety and making them more difficult to beat. Manchester United knew that a victory would close the gap to five points.

Goals were traded in quick succession. Paul Scholes drilled his finish past Jonathan Gould after great skill from Andy Cole in the 32nd minute, only to see it answered seven minutes later by Peter Ndlovu, who turned in Dion Dublin's shot in front of Peter Schmeichel. Ten minutes into the second half, Cole was involved again when a searching long ball deceived Steven Pressley and the striker latched on to it. With unerring accuracy, he struck his shot low and hard under Gould. Twenty minutes later, Pressley atoned for his error with a superbly taken header, which he guided past the motionless Schmeichel. The great Dane stood hands on hips. Coventry players mobbed the goalscorer. After the pinball nature of the goals, United did not have to wait long to go back in front. Another mistake, this time Kevin

Richardson's header back to his goalkeeper came up short, left Andy Cole through on goal. He nudged it past Gould, who had rushed out of his box, and, with the calmness and composure that United had invested so heavily in, tapped the ball into the empty net. Delirium on the bench. Ferguson and Kidd bounced up and down, euphoric. A chorus of 'Andy Cole, Andy Cole, he gets the ball and scores a goal' rang out from the away end and filled Highfield Road. The title race was on.

In the race to finish third, Liverpool wasted one of their games in hand over Nottingham Forest when they drew a blank against Wimbledon at Selhurst Park. Newcastle could not capitalise on that either when they thrilled fans, but not the managers, with a 3-3 draw against Tottenham at St James' Park. In a game reminiscent of their blistering start to the season, Newcastle found themselves two goals up after ten minutes with headers from Keith Gillespie and Darren Peacock. Spurs looked shell-shocked, but they responded in the best possible fashion. Three goals in four incredible first-half minutes put them ahead. Nicky Barmby finished off an intricate move to score the first and Jürgen Klinsmann, who had assisted the opener, volleyed in the second at the back post. Then came an incredible third. Darren Anderton picked up the ball a distance from goal. Maybe 25 yards out. He dribbled inside and unleashed a rocket from his right foot. The ball flew into the top corner and the whole ground applauded the brilliance. There had only been 26 minutes played.

Spurs continued to make chances in the second half and Barmby earned his side the best possible chance of a goal when he was taken down by Pavel Srníček for a penalty. The pain didn't end there for Newcastle, with Srníček sent off. Mike Hooper came on for Ruel Fox to face the Klinsmann penalty. With boos ringing around the ground, Klinsmann, not the usual penalty taker for Spurs, stepped up and fired the ball towards goal, but it was too straight and Hooper was able to get his legs to it and kick the ball clear. The German's penalty miss proved costly. After Colin Calderwood received his marching orders for a second yellow card, it was down to Peter Beardsley to score a brilliant goal to make it 3-3 and earn both teams a point. The game was a microcosm of the season. Both sets of fans had seen plenty of goals in their games, but it was points that mattered and a draw did not do much to help either finish as high as possible. Newcastle had work to do as they risked dropping out of the top five, which carried a European place, with the in-form Leeds United lurking behind them.

At Goodison Park, Everton, who had not scored in the last two games, faced Chelsea, who had kept three clean sheets in a row. It made perfect sense then that this ended up as a 3-3 draw. Goals bounced between the teams like a ping-pong game. Neither side could stop the other, so a draw seemed a fair result. It was another point closer to safety for Everton, but it was their third consecutive draw, which kept the focus on Premiership safety. There was no chance of even thinking about the cup final with next season's league status still up in the air.

Southampton continued their march up the table with a 3-1 win over Crystal Palace, who looked the most likely to fill the fourth relegation spot. Alan Ball had managed Southampton's star man brilliantly throughout the season. He had built the team around Matt Le Tissier and the team reaped the rewards. The Saints' No.7 had shown that he was a great goalscorer and a scorer of great goals, but he had now become the creative heartbeat of the side, too. The addition of strikers Neil Shipperley and Gordon Watson meant he had willing runners ahead of him. His new role dramatically reduced his work off the ball, so Southampton could use him more effectively in attack. The proof was on the pitch. In the Palace game, he scored one and made the other to give his side a deserved win.

Palace's defeat gave West Ham's draw at home to Wimbledon extra value; the point moved them up to 15th place with three games remaining. The Dons stayed ahead of QPR, who also shared the points with Arsenal the following night, by a point, as the two sides battled to finish eighth.

Mike Walker was back in the news with the revelation that he stood to earn a substantial windfall if Everton lifted the FA Cup. Granted compensation for the remaining two years on his managerial contract at Everton, Walker's lawyers were in the process of negotiating a £100,000 payment if the Toffees lifted the trophy and £25,000 if they lost. The total package discussed looked set to reach £350,000, based on a salary of £150,000 per year. For Everton, removing Walker was the best decision; Joe Royle had transformed the side and turned around the club. The whole affair was pretty embarrassing for Everton, as they had been charged with poaching Walker while he was still employed by Norwich. That decision resulted in a fine of £75,000 and £50,000 compensation to Norwich. The sooner Everton could move on, the better.

The penultimate Saturday of the season, 6 May, did not feature the title challengers, but two relegation places were still up for grabs.

Crystal Palace gave themselves an outside chance of staying up with a 1-0 victory at home to West Ham, who could not string a set of results together to get them clear of the bottom four. Chris Armstrong scored the winner, firmly putting behind him his off-field turbulence. Like West Ham, Aston Villa had not been able to put together a consistent run of form in the closing weeks of the season. A draw against Manchester City three days earlier stopped the losing streak but when Liverpool, intent on grabbing third place from Nottingham Forest, visited Villa Park there was not a lot of hope. However, in glorious sunshine, Aston Villa found their form and Dwight Yorke found his goalscoring touch. Two goals from the 23-year-old, now in a more central role alongside Dean Saunders, earned Brian Little a huge win. Liverpool, on the other hand, were so appalled by their performance that they refused a copy of the match video, content to never see the game again.

To further disappoint Liverpool, Forest continued their imperious form. Yet another win, a fourth in a row and ninth in the last ten, gave them the upper hand, despite having played one more game. With Liverpool in action against West Ham in the midweek fixtures, the gap stood at five points. Two wins and a collapse in form was Liverpool's only real hope. It didn't help that Leeds were breathing down their neck, too.

Leeds beat Norwich and relegated the Canaries. The win put Leeds on 69 points, two behind Liverpool, having played the same number of games. Behind for large parts of the game, Leeds rallied in the last ten minutes with the customary Gary McAllister penalty bringing the game level. Carlton Palmer hit a 90th-minute winner to confirm the inevitable for Norwich.

After a third-place finish and title challenge in 1992/93, relegation had seemed unthinkable for Norwich. A trickier second season, and the departure of Mike Walker, still ended with the Canaries in mid-table. But the sale of Ruel Fox to Newcastle and then Chris Sutton to Blackburn robbed the side of attacking quality. They did not replace like-for-like and suffered the consequences. The slide down the table was alarming, but poor results showed the true picture. Now it was time to plan for the next season and the long road back to the top.

Spurs' European dreams ended with defeat at QPR. It also looked like Klinsmann had been persuaded to leave Spurs by a large offer from Bayern Munich. Late-season form did not help the pursuit of European football but when the biggest club in Germany wants to sign you, it is difficult to say no.

There are plenty of cliches in football. Comments about not being able to write the drama that unfolds are used regularly. Often, situations present themselves and seem inevitable. Manchester United and Blackburn had their fair share of those in the two televised games that completed the round of fixtures.

Manchester United took on Sheffield Wednesday at Old Trafford. Two years earlier, Alex Ferguson and Brian Kidd had stormed the pitch, jubilant, after a pivotal win on the way to lifting the first Premier League title. In that game, it was 'Fergie time' that was needed for Steve Bruce to find a winner in the 96th minute. Ferguson noted in his autobiography that he had watched the game back and, with injuries and a change to the referee, there should have been 12 minutes added on. Fast-forward to Sunday, 7 May 1995 and another defender got on the scoresheet to secure victory against the Owls. This time, the goal was scored in the fifth minute of the game. Wednesday did not offer much in attack, but United could not find a way to increase their lead either. The winner was scored by David May, a summer signing from Blackburn Rovers. Who said they could not script it?

Alan Shearer could not watch. He decided that Middlesbrough versus Tranmere Rovers and Juventus versus Lazio were much more appropriate viewing. In his diary, he notes that he banished his father to another room to ensure the score did not filter through and spoil his Sunday. Of course, there was no way that Shearer would not find out the score. His dad entered after 90 minutes and informed his son of the narrow victory. United were now two points behind Blackburn, having both played 40 games. Blackburn's 41st game was the *Monday Night Football* showpiece on Sky Sports. The opponents were Newcastle United, Shearer's boyhood club. Those football writers were at it again.

Pressure was part of a footballer's daily life. Newspapers, fans, team-mates, family – all could exert pressure on players. Whether it was new contracts, transfers or underperformance, it affected people in different ways. Alex Ferguson seemed to revel in it. With the success he had had at Aberdeen, joining United and then winning the first two Premier League titles, he was well placed to deal with the forces that can cause teams to wilt. He also loved to exert pressure on others. So comments aimed at Blackburn after the Sheffield Wednesday win stoked the fire before the Newcastle game.

In the post-match television interview with Nick Collins, Ferguson alluded to the loss of form his side had at the end of the 1991/92 season that allowed Leeds to win the First Division title. That pressure was difficult for any team to handle. In a dig at Blackburn's current form, four points from the last four games, Ferguson said: 'You won't cure the title wobbles now.' He continued to prod at his rivals and stated: 'The fact that we are now just two points behind them is going to make it all the harder psychologically.' The United manager was always direct. He saw his comments as fair game at this stage of the season after Blackburn had done something similar in the 1993/94 title race. Now he was the challenger, he wanted to see how the leader reacted.

Cameras focused on a buzzing Ewood Park. An evening game live on Sky Sports with the title on the line was perfect for the increasing television audience. One of the main reasons for the huge bump in the television deal was to showcase games like this. Blackburn's fans played their part in building an incredible atmosphere. They were behind their team all the way. On the pitch before the game, Alan Shearer took the rapturous applause from the fans for his Golden Boot award, despite games still left to play, and the supporters' Player of the Year award, presented to him by Jack Walker.

From the start, Blackburn pushed Newcastle and started on the front foot. Shearer scored the opening goal with a back-post header, sending the fans into raptures. The goal was celebrated with some form of euphoric relief. Fans knew that they had the title in their grip and did not want to let it go. Newcastle upped the pressure and Blackburn had to hold firm. One man stood out from the rest – goalkeeper Tim Flowers.

Signed from Southampton for £2m-plus in November 1993, Flowers's consistency had put him in a position to challenge David Seaman for the England No.1 shirt. Terry Venables certainly rated the goalkeeper and had included him in his squads to prepare for the European Championships. He was a crucial part of Blackburn's strong rearguard and made saves that earned the team points. Against Newcastle, he had never been better.

Flowers made four world-class saves. The first was an incredible stop that denied Peter Beardsley from range, the second came after Ruel Fox's run into the box and the third was to keep out another long-range effort, this time from Rob Lee. In the 79th minute, Flowers bettered them all with an astonishing save from John Beresford.

Keith Gillespie had shown all season that he was a winger with great talent. When he sprinted down the Newcastle right-hand side, he manoeuvred himself into position to cross. Blackburn had men back in the box. Newcastle had men in the middle desperate to keep up with the young winger. Flowers guarded his front post. As Gillespie curled the ball across the face of the goal, it seemed like no one was there. Flowers scurried across his goal to the back post. There was John Beresford, ready to slide the ball in the net. He did everything right – tried to make a good contact and direct the cross back where it came from. Beresford did not bank on Flowers's agility. Somehow Flowers twisted his back down to the ground, pushed out his arm and stopped the shot. Shrieks in the crowd could be heard as the drama unfolded. Commentator Ian Darke's voice lifted as the shock of what Flowers had done sank in. A hero for Blackburn when they needed one most. After the game, the hero became a legend.

With a microphone from Nick Collins under his nose, Flowers unleashed a blazing response to Alex Ferguson's comments. 'Don't talk to me about bottle,' the goalkeeper said. 'Don't talk to me about bottling it, because that's bottle out there. That's quality players giving their all … we are going to fight to the death because we've got bottle.' Flowers's passion was clear. He expected the title to be won on the final day and his performance had given his team that opportunity. Blackburn had to wait two days before United played again. The opponents to face Ferguson's men were Southampton, the former club of both Tim Flowers and Alan Shearer. You couldn't make it up.

Before that huge game, other teams caught up on their games in hand. Everton beat Ipswich 1-0, which confirmed their place in the Premiership for another season. Joe Royle's appointment changed the fortunes of the club and, with the FA Cup Final on the horizon, there were smiles on the faces of fans. The final relegation place was still undecided, but it looked likely to be Crystal Palace, who felt the full force of Tony Yeboah. The striker scored twice as Leeds won 3-1 to keep them in the hunt for fourth, with rivals Liverpool in action at West Ham the following day. Another inspired performance from Peter Ndlovu, who scored twice, gave Coventry an excellent 3-1 victory at Spurs. Gerry Francis's team had not performed to their best for a few weeks and the defeat was not a surprise.

Liverpool still had a game in hand on Nottingham Forest and a win would mean the battle for third place would go to the final day. West Ham, who needed a victory to confirm their Premiership status for the following season, were the opponents and they did not let Liverpool settle into their rhythm all game. Matt Holmes opened the scoring with his first goal of the season from a tight angle before a Don Hutchison double in the second half sealed the win. Ex-Liverpool player Hutchison, who had his fair share of problems at Anfield, was a changed man at West Ham. His two goals, which came in two second-half minutes, showed the variety in his game. A long-range strike past a motionless David James was followed up with a classic striker's goal from a ball over the defence.

Celebrations at the end of the game were as much in relief as elation for Harry Redknapp and his players. Liverpool had gifted third place to Nottingham Forest. Winless in their last three games, Liverpool could not match Forest's spectacular end-of-season form. Both of these sides still had a part to play on the final day, as West Ham hosted Manchester United and Liverpool welcomed Blackburn.

Another team who had already celebrated safety for next season were Southampton, who sat comfortably in mid-table when they travelled to Old Trafford to face Manchester United. A win for the home side would mean the title would be not be decided until the final day.

After five minutes, Southampton ripped up the script. On the right wing, Gordon Watson spotted a run from Jim Magilton in midfield. He curled the ball around the United defence and Magilton was in on goal. He tried an audacious chip over the onrushing Schmeichel, but the Dane got a touch. It knocked the ball to the back post, right to Simon

Charlton. He had the simplest task and nodded it into the net. One-nil to Southampton and the start of an onslaught from United.

Gary Pallister hit the post and Mark Hughes and Andy Cole went close before the equaliser arrived in the 21st minute. It seemed apt that it was Cole who got the goal; he was playing well and scoring goals, despite some wasteful finishing. He hammered home the ball after some untidy Southampton defending gifted him the ball on the edge of the six-yard box. United continued to pile on the pressure, but the goal did not come. Goalscorer Charlton had a chance to increase Southampton's lead just after the interval, but wasted it. Dave Beasant, the Southampton goalkeeper, continued to repel shots from United and it looked like the goal would not come. Then came the controversy.

Denis Irwin played a great ball through the Southampton defence to Andy Cole, who was turning towards goal. As the ball came into the striker's feet, Ken Monkou lunged from behind and Dave Beasant darted out of his goal. The three players ended up in a heap on the floor as the ball was cleared. The referee blew his whistle. Penalty.

Beasant was furious. He charged towards the referee. Martin Tyler and Andy Gray, on commentary for Sky Sports, narrated the events. Tyler referred to comments made by Alex Ferguson about the lack of penalties given to this side at Old Trafford; this was only the second of the season for United. Praising the referee's decision, Gray spotted that Monkou's right arm had dragged Cole to the ground. Manchester United's penalty taker had been Eric Cantona; now it was Denis Irwin.

He stepped up, probably the calmest person inside the ground. His spot kick was brilliant, even though he slipped on contact with the ball. It rifled past a helpless Beasant, who guessed the right way, and gave United the lead. Irwin was mobbed by his team-mates. The Old Trafford crowd went ballistic. One of the most important wins of the season. Two points separated the top-two sides with one game left. The title hopes were still alive.

For Arsenal, the league season had ended long ago. Once the threat of relegation had been averted, all focus turned to the Cup Winners' Cup Final. They were the holders, after beating Italian side Parma a year earlier. This year, the opponents were Real Zaragoza of Spain. Having spent a large portion of the season in the top four of La Liga, Zaragoza sat in third place. A far cry from the struggles Arsenal had faced.

In the early part of the game, both sides had chances, not clear-cut, but the goalkeepers and defenders at both ends were certainly forced to work. After 67 minutes, it was Zaragoza who got the breakthrough thanks to a brilliant strike from Juan Esnáider, a volley with his left foot. Just eight minutes later, John Hartson managed to stab the ball into the net and bring Arsenal level. With no more goals, extra time arrived and David Seaman performed valiantly as he kept Zaragoza at bay. An incredible save to deny Xavier Aguado kept Arsenal in the game.

Time ticked on and it looked like a penalty shoot-out was the likely outcome.

Then, after 119 minutes of football, there was Nayim. The ex-Tottenham midfielder, who said he used to practise his long-range shooting with Paul Gascoigne on the Spurs training ground, saw an opportunity when an Arsenal clearance set the ball bouncing towards him. He didn't hesitate and struck the ball high towards the goal. Seaman backpedalled and got a hand on the ball. It wasn't enough. He pushed the ball into the top of the net and the Zaragoza players celebrated. A winning goal in the dying seconds. Heartbreak for Arsenal. The only light that shone in an awful season was extinguished by an ex-Spurs player. It summed up the season so far.

'This has been the most difficult decision of my entire career, at the age of 31, I had to give serious consideration to my final career move.' Words that no Tottenham fan wanted to hear. Alan Sugar was not impressed. The two-year deal he had made on that yacht in Monaco was, in his eyes, not honoured as it should have been by Klinsmann. A star player was lost and difficult to replace. On a brighter note for Sugar, and Spurs, manager Gerry Francis signed a contract to continue as manager for another season. He had transformed the side over the course of the season and a new contract was richly deserved.

The day before the final day of the season saw Wimbledon and Nottingham Forest play out an entertaining 2-2 draw at Selhurst Park. Only three minutes into the game, it looked like Forest would lose star striker Stan Collymore after lengthy treatment, but he carried on and created the first goal for David Phillips. Both sides had plenty to be positive about after great seasons. Wimbledon continued to defy expectations and finished in the top half of the table, while newly promoted Forest surprised many with a third-place finish. An incredible achievement by Frank Clark and his side. The star of the team was Collymore, who scored 23 league goals and created six more. He was likely to leave in the summer, with interest from the biggest and wealthiest clubs in the league. For now, Forest could celebrate a brilliant campaign.

When the final day of the season arrived, all the focus was on Upton Park and Anfield. But there was still one final relegation place available for one unlucky side. Three clubs were in danger. Crystal Palace were away at Newcastle, who themselves were looking to beat Leeds and Liverpool to fourth place, Aston Villa visited relegated Norwich and

Sheffield Wednesday were at home to bottom-of-the-league Ipswich.

Aston Villa needed only a point to stay up, unless there was a ten-goal swing in goal difference in Crystal Palace's game. Wednesday also only needed a point. Even if they lost, it would take a Palace win and a four-goal change in goal difference. For Palace it was simple: win.

Six minutes into the game at St James' Park, Ruel Fox gave Newcastle the lead after a mazy run and long-range effort, deflected into the Palace net. At Villa Park, just a minute later, Steve Staunton scored. In the same minute, Guy Whittingham also put Sheffield Wednesday ahead against Ipswich. Palace looked doomed. They certainly had their work cut out.

It didn't get any better for them when Newcastle, back in early-season form, scored two goals in two minutes before half an hour had elapsed. Rob Lee, with a header from a Ruel Fox cross, and Keith Gillespie, with a long-range effort, found the back of the net.

At half-time, Palace were going down. Aston Villa and Sheffield Wednesday both led 1-0, but their results did not matter if the score in the North East stayed the same.

The second half brought more goals. At Hillsborough, there were three goals in eight minutes. The first got Ipswich back in the game, but another from Whittingham and one from Michael Williams gave the home side a 3-1 lead. Palace also found the net with a goal from Tyneside-born Chris Armstrong, who headed past Pavel Srníček. Fans at Carrow Road saw Jeremy Goss equalise against Villa, too.

With ten minutes left to play, and after some great work by Bruce Dyer out wide, Palace did get a second when Ray Houghton finished in the box. It was 3-2 with ten minutes to play. The only problem for Palace was that they still needed to win and score a flurry of goals or hope that Norwich got an equaliser. Sheffield Wednesday were home and dry, so did not come into the equation.

Predictably, Palace proved that their poor form in front of goal was not going to change in the last game of the season. The final whistle blew in their game and relegated them to the First Division after a single season in the Premiership. Villa and Wednesday, who ended up in 13th place after other results went their way, had done exactly what they needed. Improvement was needed for both sides if they wanted to get back to competing for European places. Palace, and Alan Smith, had proved that they were capable of mounting a promotion push, but the possibility of losing Chris Armstrong made that much more difficult.

The win for Newcastle had given them a great chance of finishing fourth but it was not meant to be, as other results did not go to plan. A sixth-place finish after a swashbuckling start to the season was difficult to take. Kevin Keegan had fashioned a side built to attack but the sale of their star striker did not help matters. What he did have was money to spend and top of the shopping list was someone to fill Cole's goalscoring boots.

In the battle of the London clubs, Chelsea leapfrogged Arsenal and finished in 11th with a 2-1 win over the Gunners, who had experienced one of their most difficult seasons on and off the pitch. After the heartbreaking loss in the Cup Winners' Cup Final, Arsenal needed to go back to the drawing board. Chelsea's league position was a reflection of their inconsistency. Improvements were needed on the pitch and a big summer of transfers was a possibility.

The main event was, of course, the race for the title. Blackburn and Manchester United had battled for top spot in the last two seasons and it had never been closer than this.

Blackburn travelled to Anfield, Kenny Dalglish's football home for 14 years which brought 25 trophies. Liverpool were also the arch rivals of Rovers' rivals for the title. There was no love lost between Manchester United and Liverpool and, even before the game, Alex Ferguson addressed comments that suggested Roy Evans's side would not play to their best to ensure a Blackburn win. Nothing like some psychological warfare before a big game.

Manchester United were also away. A visit to Upton Park was never easy, let alone when a title was at stake. The fact the Hammers had secured their league status already could have helped or hindered United. For Paul Ince, matches against his old club turned unsavoury quickly. Having not anticipated a death threat on the eve of the game, he stayed in the team hotel all day in the lead-up to the game. In the Blackburn camp, Kenny Dalglish, Tim Flowers and Tim Sherwood had also received messages posted from Scandinavia that they would be killed if Blackburn won the title.

The atmosphere inside Anfield has always been special. On that final day of the season, Sunday, 14 May, as the two teams strode out on to the pitch, there was something surreal going on. Both sides were roared out on to the pitch for the warm-ups, not just the start of the game. There were Blackburn scarves scattered among supporters in the home end and there were even rumours of Liverpool fans buying Blackburn shirts. Scousers did anything for 'King Kenny'.

Sky Sports had longed for this day. Both games live on their channels and updates from the alternate games in a handy little box on the screen. Forty-one games played and it all came down to this. That alone was dramatic enough to build up the game but, when the action during the games created its own tension and drama, television was a big winner.

Alex Ferguson had decided to go for five in midfield and drop Mark Hughes to the bench to ensure his side controlled possession. Andy Cole led the line and wanted to add to his 12 goals in 16 games for United. Veteran Brian McClair had been a reliable performer all season when called upon. The team was strong and was confident.

The early exchanges in both games were tentative. Liverpool looked strong in the opening minutes at Anfield. Nigel Clough had an early chance and Alan Shearer missed one of his own. United were finding things more difficult at Upton Park, with few openings. Things changed when Alan Shearer scored after 20 minutes.

It was a classic goal. Great wing play from Ripley on the right created space for a cross, which was cut back into the box. Shearer found space about 12 yards out. How the top scorer in the Premiership stood open and had a free shot at goal is another story. He fired it into the bottom-left corner and left David James with no chance. Kenny Dalglish grinned like a Cheshire cat. Blackburn ahead and in the driving seat.

At Upton Park, things got even better for Rovers.

From the left wing, Matt Holmes whipped a fantastic delivery into the box. Running on to the cross, unmarked, was Michael Hughes, who volleyed the ball into the corner past Schmeichel. West Ham fans were delirious. They had delighted in chants of 'Judas' directed at Paul Ince as the United team bus headed into the stadium; now they played their part in the title decider.

Before the half-time whistle, Andy Cole had a chance of his own when he sprung forward and got in on goal. His powerful strike hit the post and rebounded out. The record-breaking signing knew he would get more chances. In fact, he later wrote in his autobiography of his mentality in that game: 'Give me the ball again. I wasn't going to hide. I have never hidden. Another chance. Give me another chance.' His determination, even desperation, to score was crucial to the best strikers.

The interval came and Blackburn were in the driving seat. Ferguson had to make a change to get back into the game, so he swapped young midfielder Nicky Butt for Mark Hughes to join an onslaught on West Ham's goal.

Manchester United had won two consecutive league titles. They knew what it took to get victories when it mattered. Everyone had to contribute to earn the right to be a league champion. Goals could come from anyone. Brian McClair had been prolific at Celtic and through his first four years at United. He was no longer a preferred option up front. Cantona and Hughes, then Hughes and Cole had taken the mantle. McClair had reinvented himself as a wily midfield veteran. He knew when to run, when to pressure the ball and when it was time to let his goalscoring instincts take over.

When Gary Neville stood over a free kick in the 51st minute of the game, McClair made his move and got United back in the game. A free header from just outside the six-yard box was simple for the Scot. Scores level. Game on.

In the dugout that he knew so well at Anfield, Dalglish checked the Sky Sports monitors behind him during the game. He knew he needed to get messages to his players if the scores changed. Near the dugout was a Liverpool fan who changed his shirt to a Blackburn one for the second half. They really did want a Blackburn win.

Tension turned to anxiety when John Barnes finished a Mark Kennedy cross to make it 1-1, ten minutes after the McClair equaliser at Upton Park. Blackburn knew they would be champions if United could only draw, but that goal had increased the strain on fans and players alike. News then reached Upton Park that Liverpool had equalised and United, who exerted huge pressure on West Ham all game, turned the screw.

One factor that United did not consider in their plans was Luděk Mikloško putting in a goalkeeping performance for the ages. He had been a consistent performer for West

Ham and a veteran of the team. No one saw this inspired performance on the horizon.

The second half was all United's and that included the game at Anfield. West Ham defended their goal as best they could but it was Mikloško who was the main protagonist. Chances came for Lee Sharpe, Denis Irwin and Mark Hughes but there was no way past the Czech keeper. The final throw of the dice for Ferguson was Paul Scholes. The 21-year-old forward had impressed all season and his introduction meant United effectively played with four strikers.

Chances kept coming for United and Scholes created probably the best. His perfectly weighted, intelligent through ball into the box released Cole on goal. The striker's touch set him up perfectly. Mikloško stayed big and low. Cole chose power over placement and the ball struck the big keeper, bounced back on to the United No.17 and out for a goal kick. It summed up Cole's afternoon.

Someone who had not missed many key chances all season was Alan Shearer. His opportunity to wrap up the league title came in the 87th minute. Strong play from Chris Sutton in the box knocked the ball down to Shearer. He chested down the ball and took aim on the half-volley. The shot flew over the bar. The look on Shearer's face said it all. In his season's diary, he wondered how costly the miss could be.

Another chance came for United. Cole's attempted overhead kick hit a defender, the ball bounced around the box and eventually made its way to Ince's feet. A goal for him would have been an incredible turn of events. A swarm of black shirts covered the box as the ball ricocheted through to Cole again. Mikloško sensed the danger. He moved out towards Cole and spread himself. Cole made contact with the ball. The keeper dived low and managed to block the shot as the ball broke to a West Ham defender.

Ferguson paced up and down on the bench. Another chance had gone begging. Cole could not believe his luck. He shook his head in disbelief. United did not let up and it was a siege on West Ham's goal. Still no second goal, but there was to be one final twist.

On Merseyside, the game continued with a free kick awarded to Liverpool outside the box. It was a good 25 yards out. Jamie Redknapp, a player brought to Liverpool by Dalglish, stepped up and curled in an incredible strike with his right foot. Tim Flowers had no chance, his despairing dive was just that. Two-one Liverpool. There was almost a polite celebration from the Liverpool fans for the strike. As it stood now, a Manchester United goal would keep the title at Old Trafford.

Yet, all of a sudden, before the celebrations for the goal had even finished, an incredible roar lifted Anfield. A stadium and a crowd that makes a sound like no other. Sky cut to Dalglish on the bench. He was startled. He looked to The Kop, unaware of what was going on. Behind him, a steward, in bright orange, broke into a smile and started to clap. A Liverpool fan, in a red shirt and blue scarf, leapt forward from his seat and embraced Dalglish. Blackburn had done it.

The final whistle blew. Blackburn Rovers were champions of England.

Shearer and Sutton embraced. Dalglish celebrated with his staff on the bench, and the Liverpool management team he knew so well hugged their former boss. The Blackburn manager looked like he had tears in his eyes. It was an incredible achievement to build a side and play at such a consistent level that they toppled a great side in Manchester United. All over the pitch, the Blackburn players celebrated and the fans were ecstatic. Only three years earlier, they had seen their team win a play-off to reach the first Premier League season. Now they were champions.

In the stands, Jack Walker wiped away tears, the boyhood Rovers fan made good had invested his money to bring his team success. No one would ever take that away from him.

Sky commentator Martin Tyler uttered the words that every fan in blue and white wanted to hear: 'Blackburn Rovers are champions.' John Motson, who commentated for the BBC that day, said: 'I don't think I have ever seen anything like that in 25 years of commentating.'

In the chaos of the 1994/95 season, the controversy of alleged match-fixing, illegal payments, questionable refereeing moments, horrific violence and that kung-fu kick, the nail-biting ending to one of the most dramatic seasons of all time was one for the history books.

Pos	Team	P	W	D	L	F	A	GD	Pts
1	Blackburn Rovers	42	27	8	7	80	39	+41	89
2	Manchester United	42	26	10	6	77	28	+49	88
3	Nottingham Forest	42	22	11	9	72	43	+29	77
4	Liverpool	42	21	11	10	65	37	+28	74
5	Leeds United	42	20	13	9	59	38	+21	73
6	Newcastle United	42	20	12	10	67	47	+20	72
7	Tottenham Hotspur	42	16	14	12	66	58	+8	62
8	Queens Park Rangers	42	17	9	16	61	59	+2	60
9	Wimbledon	42	15	11	16	48	65	-17	56
10	Southampton	42	12	18	12	61	63	-2	54
11	Chelsea	42	13	15	14	50	55	-5	54
12	Arsenal	42	13	12	17	52	49	+3	51
13	Sheffield Wednesday	42	13	12	17	49	57	-8	51
14	West Ham United	42	13	11	18	44	48	-4	50
15	Everton	42	11	17	14	44	51	-7	50
16	Coventry City	42	12	14	16	44	62	-18	50
17	Manchester City	42	12	13	17	53	64	-11	49
18	Aston Villa	42	11	15	16	51	56	-5	48
19	Crystal Palace	42	11	12	19	34	49	-15	45
20	Norwich City	42	10	13	19	37	54	-17	43
21	Leicester City	42	6	11	25	45	80	-35	29
22	Ipswich Town	42	7	6	29	36	93	-57	27

The Aftermath

THE PARTY started on the pitch for Blackburn. Winning a league title was a moment to be savoured. Once that trophy was lifted, all the pressure was off and it was time to unwind after a long, tense season.

After lifting the trophy, Blackburn started their lap of honour to cries of 'Are you watching, Manchester?' from around the ground. Success for Dalglish at Anfield, against his old side and his title challengers' bitter rivals, made the celebrations even sweeter. Especially in the dressing room where the players enjoyed the copious amounts of champagne on offer. Once everyone had tasted the victory in the ground, all the players, coaches and wives headed north to Preston to celebrate long into the night.

The following evening, the champions returned home, this time for another trophy presentation at Ewood Park, so the fans who had supported them all season could see their heroes lift the Premiership trophy. Before that, fans were treated to a legends game. Kenny Dalglish took centre stage, in full Blackburn kit, as his side took on a team of Blackburn veterans. The only problem was that most of the players were somewhat past their best and, according to Alan Shearer, the 'gaffer was embarrassing'. He could say that now the title race was over.

Earlier that day, the brutal reality of football struck Alan Smith, who was out of a job when Crystal Palace sacked him.

Promotion a year earlier had thrilled fans but, after a season of struggle in the Premiership, the time for change had come. Tensions between Smith and chairman Ron Noades did not help and the move was probably the best for everyone.

After a season of uncertainty on and off the pitch for Brian Horton, he knew that Francis Lee wanted to bring in his own manager over the summer. The good start to the season faded and a 17th-place finish was the end result. Horton had started to build a good side with a range of attacking options and pace out wide. He had blooded young players into the squad and, with more time, might have achieved more. Lee started his search for a new manager immediately.

The next man on the move was Jürgen Klinsmann, who joined Bayern Munich for a reported £1.3m, almost half the price Spurs had paid. He wanted to build his life after football and that revolved around being in Germany. A move to the biggest club in the Bundesliga clearly appealed to Klinsmann, but he had loved his time in the Premiership. His record of 20 goals and ten assists in 41 starts was impressive. Spurs had a huge hole to fill, not just on the pitch but off it, where Klinsmann had added real value to the club.

Another expensive international recruit followed Klinsmann out of the exit door at White Hart Lane. Gheorghe Popescu joined Barcelona for a rumoured £2.8m, although chairman Alan Sugar said the fee was £4m, which represented a good profit for the player. Although he did not have the same impact as Klinsmann, he was another who was hard to replace. Whoever came in to take his position was unlikely to come from abroad. With these two players leaving after only a season, Sugar had no interest in funding high wages for a year, only to see his players depart at the first time of asking.

Before he left the country, Klinsmann lifted the Football Writers' Association Footballer of the Year award. It was a fitting reward for the excellent football he showed. If Spurs had a functioning defence at the start of the season, maybe they would have finished higher in the league.

Klinsmann had scored goals regularly over the course of the season but he was not the top marksman. That honour fell to Alan Shearer, who scored 34 goals and matched Andy Cole's tally from the previous season. Robbie Fowler had truly exploded and finished nine goals behind Shearer with 25. Liverpool had developed an incredible talent and the transition from Ian Rush to Fowler was complete.

Two in-demand strikers came next: Les Ferdinand and Stan Collymore. Transfer rumours circled both of these players throughout the season and continued into the summer. Ferdinand hit the back of the net 24 times for QPR and impressed managers and opposition defenders with his all-action style. Collymore had made the transition from Division One to the Premiership seem easy. His 22 goals was an impressive tally and helped Nottingham Forest to third.

Andy Cole had been involved in the biggest transfer in English football and still managed to notch 21 goals, despite playing for two teams. His combined total for both Newcastle and Manchester United was impressive, if a lot less than the previous season. Once Cantona returned to the side, the striker would have another partner to feed off.

News came thick and fast in the week after the title decider, with a different news story every day. While the newspapers were filled with sackings and sales, Manchester United tried to pick themselves up after the disappointment of the final day and prepare for the FA Cup Final against Everton. The Cup Final week took in another Youth Cup victory for Eric Harrison that showed the future was bright for the club. Suit fittings constituted one of the most famous pre-match rituals before a cup final, so that took up another day. By the middle of the week, United headed to Old

Trafford to train and Ferguson checked on the fitness of Ryan Giggs, who looked like he had a chance of making the bench. Rumours also swirled around the future of Ferguson's assistant, Brian Kidd, who had been linked with the Manchester City job. Pure paper talk as far as the United manager was concerned. One departure that also reared its head was that of Andrei Kanchelskis, who seemed to be on his way out of Old Trafford in the near future.

Another post-season sacking saw Trevor Francis's four years as manager of Sheffield Wednesday come to an end. He had a good record in the dugout. Third place in his first season, followed by consecutive seventh-place finishes. Thirteenth in 1994/95 was a fair drop but his team were only a win or two away from the top half. Rumours suggested that Chris Waddle might be the man to take over as manager.

When Joe Royle arrived at Everton, they were in a relegation scrap. On Saturday, 20 May, they walked out for an FA Cup Final against Manchester United – an incredible turnaround that promised a positive future at Goodison Park. The fantastic semi-final performance at Elland Road to defeat favourites Spurs 4-1 was a huge moment in the season for Everton and gave them belief that they had a chance. In the league, a 2-0 defeat at Old Trafford was followed up later in the season with a 1-0 win at Goodison Park.

Everton's Dogs of War approach to the game might not have promised a spectacle for the neutral, but that was Royle's plan. Show the power and passion that prevented them from going down and they had a chance. Set pieces from the left boot of Andy Hinchcliffe provided Everton with a huge threat and the 11 assists that Hinchcliffe recorded during the league season was proof that he had the delivery to match.

No Andy Cole, Andrei Kanchelskis and Eric Cantona for Manchester United. Veterans Mark Hughes and Brian McClair provided the attacking threat, with Lee Sharpe and Roy Keane supporting from midfield. Giggs and Paul Scholes, who were on the bench, had proved during the season that they had the ability to change games. But, on Cup Final day, anything could happen.

Twenty-nine minutes had passed when Everton got the breakthrough. A passing move from United broke down on the edge of the box and the ball fell to captain Dave Watson. He rode Paul Ince's challenge and the ball broke for Anders Limpar, who had impressed already. The counter-attack was on. Wembley's huge pitch opened up as the men United had committed forward were left stranded on the edge of Everton's box.

Limpar drove through the open space. It was four against two. He chose right and Matt Jackson faced Gary Pallister in the box and managed to turn him inside out. Graham Stuart waited patiently at the back post and received the pass from Jackson. Stuart's fierce strike hit the bar, and even looked like it may have crossed the line, before it bounced on to the ground and up. Paul Rideout rose and powered his header into the top right-hand corner of the net with expert placement. Everton were 1-0 up and their fans, who were behind that goal, erupted.

The rest of the game played out with United in total control and Everton's defence the stars of the game. United could find no way past the determined Everton rearguard. Dave Watson was in imperious form and 36-year-old Neville Southall superb. The Everton goalkeeper made point-blank saves from substitute Paul Scholes and Gary Pallister. Both were stalwarts of the Everton side that lifted the title in 1987 but there had been little success since. Now they had their moment. Both at the veteran stage of their career, the trophy was well deserved. When the final whistle sounded, Everton players looked to be in disbelief at what they had achieved. The men in red fell to their knees.

An incredible turnaround from Everton. The first league victory did not come until 1 November and when Joe Royle took over, they had collected only eight points from a possible 42. Now, he had not only kept them in the Premiership, he had masterminded a Wembley victory over Manchester United, after suffering against them with his previous side Oldham, and secured qualification for the Cup Winners' Cup.

Manchester United finished the season empty-handed for the first time since 1989. More than that, the Cantona saga had dogged the club since January. A summer reset was needed.

Once the actual football had finished, transfer season started. The first rumours surrounded Paul Gascoigne, who looked destined to end his Serie A nightmare and return either to England or north of the border with Rangers. Everton were also busy, with a £7.5m offer to Nottingham Forest for Stan Collymore rejected. Frank Clark wanted to hold out for a transfer-record deal for his star striker.

The first domino to fall in Manchester United's summer plans was Paul Ince's court case on a charge of assaulting a Crystal Palace supporter. A verdict of not guilty was returned and Ince was relieved. He pulled out of the upcoming Umbro Cup with England to recover from what had been an emotionally draining period for the midfielder.

Duncan Ferguson was not so lucky. His date in court came and a sentence of three months in jail was given. An appeal was quickly lodged, standard practice in 1994/95, which meant that Ferguson was able to start the season with Everton.

A final flourish to the season came at Wembley in the First Division play-off final between Bolton and Reading. In a thrilling contest that featured second and third place in the league, Reading led 2-0 from the 12th minute and saw a first-half penalty saved by Bolton keeper Keith Branagan before Owen Coyle pulled one back after 75 minutes. Fabian de Freitas drew the sides level with only four minutes left to play. Extra time produced more goals. A Mixu Paatelainen goal and another from De Freitas made it 4-2 with 118 minutes played. Incredibly, the Reading player-manager Jimmy Quinn found the net a minute later but it was too late. Bolton were promoted to the Premier League.

Manager Bruce Rioch spoke after the game about his contract situation. After the final, his deal officially ended. He had lived away from his family for the three years he had been at Bolton and it was time for him to make a decision. The family home was located in Hertfordshire, not a bad commute to Highbury where he was tipped to take over.

Ten months after Jürgen Klinsmann arrived in England, another superstar arrived from Serie A – Ruud Gullit. The bright lights of London, and manager Glenn Hoddle, had attracted the iconic Dutchman to Stamford Bridge. A free transfer signing after leaving Sampdoria, Gullit commanded a £20,000-a-week salary from Chelsea for a one-year deal. Hoddle imagined his new signing in the role of sweeper. Gullit's vision and football intelligence allowed him to see the whole game and dictate play from the back.

Gullit's arrival was a catalyst for more spending on international imports. The Premier League was changing. Money flowed into the English game and clubs wanted to compete at the top end of the table and the best way to do that was to spend on the best players. As May turned into June, there were endless headlines about which new superstar was about to join the league. As long as they behaved themselves and performed on the pitch, clubs would be happy.

There was still a shadow cast over the game from the events of 1994/95, with Dennis Wise still waiting for his appeal to be heard as the season ended.

Bruce Grobbelaar, Hans Segers and John Fashanu (along with Richard Lim) were charged with conspiracy related to match-fixing in July 1995. A trial date was set for 18 months later, but a retrial was required when a jury was unable to reach a verdict. In a second trial that started in June 1997, the same result was reached. The men walked free in August that year. For Grobbelaar, a £10,000 fine was issued by the FA for breaking betting regulations. He pursued *The Sun* in court and sued them for libel, winning damages of £85,000 and his legal bills covered. The story continued when *The Sun* appealed the decision and won. Now Grobbelaar was awarded just £1 and ordered to pay the paper's legal costs, which bankrupted the goalkeeper.

Disgraced manager George Graham waited on news of his punishment after being found guilty of misconduct. When it arrived, the Scot was banned from football for a year.

And then there was Eric Cantona, still suspended and working with youngsters at The Cliff, who hoped to get himself fit and ready for his October return to football.

Football had, more than ever, become part of everyday life since the advent of the Premier League. Wall-to-wall coverage of games and news beamed into the homes of Sky subscribers. Terrestrial television tried to keep up. Newspapers dedicated front and back pages to the incredible stories from the season and passed down their own judgments.

The years ahead came to define the Premier League as the best in the world. After the incredible events of 1994/95, there was still work to do.

Acknowledgements

WRITING A book is a long and challenging process. There are some people I would like to thank that have helped make this project happen.

First, I want to thank my wife, Dora, for her endless patience at being surrounded by football books and magazines around the house, and putting up with endless days and nights spent writing. My son, Arthur, was not allowed anywhere near the writing process but he has caught the writing bug. His books will definitely not focus on football. Watch out for him in the future.

At Pitch Publishing, I would like to thank Paul Camillin for the late-night email exchanges that started with a book about 1996 and ended up deciding that a book about 1994/95 with an impressively long title would be so much more entertaining. He was right. Thanks to Jane, too, for all the hard work in supporting the marketing and publication of the book and everyone that works behind the scenes at Pitch; thank you for all your help in getting the book on the shelf.

An enormous thank you to Alex Ireland (author of *Pretty Poly* and *Double Diamond)* for answering the endless WhatsApp messages he received from me riddled with self-doubt and word counts. Having someone to share the process with has been incredibly valuable. We have learned a lot from each other and long may that continue.

Thank you to Tony Gale and Brian Horton, who gave up their time to discuss the season from their point of view in the early stages of my research. They were able to give real insight into life in the dressing room and the changes in the game more widely.

Another thank you to anyone that has supported my writing and podcasting endeavours over the last year or so. The whole gang at *These Football Times* podcasts, who have inspired and supported me during the book-writing process, whether directly or indirectly. Particularly a big thanks to Steven Scragg and Gary Thacker, who got me a slot on the podcast talking about *1992: The Birth of Modern Football* (still available in all good bookshops), which started off that partnership. Also to Rob Smyth and Martyn Ramsay from the *Nessun Dorma Podcast*, who share the 90s football passion, and all the team who have worked on *Boro Mag* over the years.

A final thank you to the people who supported my obsession during the 90s football boom with sticker books, pogs, football kits and following Middlesbrough.

To my Mam, Dad and sister, Lorraine, Rob and Kirsty. Without you, this book would not exist.

Bibliography

Adams, Tony with Ridley, Ian, *Sober: Football, My Story, My Life* (Simon & Schuster, 2017)

Auclair, Philippe, *Cantona: The Rebel Who Would be King* (Pan Books, 2009)

Beard, Brian, *The Breedon Book of Premiership Records* (Breedon Books, 2004)

Blickensdörfer Hans, *Jürgen Klinsmann* (Klinsmedia, 1998)

Cole, Andrew, *Fast Forward: The Autobiography* (Hodder and Stoughton, 2020)

Collymore, Stan with Holt, Oliver, *Stan: Tackling My Demons* (Collins Willow, 2004)

Cox, Michael, *The Mixer* (Harper Collins, 2017)

Dalglish, Kenny, *Dalglish: My Autobiography*, (Hodder and Stoughton, 1996)

Duerden, John, *Rovers Revolution: Blackburn's Rise from Nowhere to Premier League Champions* (deCoubertin Books, 2019)

Ferguson, Alex edited by Bell, Peter *A Year in the Life: The Manager's Diary* (Virgin Publishing, 1995)

Francis, Gerry and Slegg, Chris, *The Team That Dated to Do: Tottenham 94/95* (Pitch Publishing, 2017)

Graham, George, *The Glory and the Grief* (Andre Deutsch, 1995)

Grobbelaar, Bruce, *Life in a Jungle: My Autobiography* (deCoubertin Books, 2018)

Horrie, Chris, *Premiership: Lifting the Lid on a National obsession* (Pocket Books, 2002)

Keegan, Kevin with Taylor, Daniel, *Kevin Keegan: My Life in Football* (Macmillan, 2018)

Le Saux, Graeme, *Left Field: A Footballer Apart* (HarperSport, 2007)

Le Tissier, Matt, *Taking Le Tiss: My Autobiography* (HarperSport, 2009)

Lovejoy, Joe, *Glory, Goals & Greed: Twenty Years of the Premier League* (Mainstream Publishing, 2011)

Lynch, Tony, *The Official F.A Premier League Special* (Grandreams Ltd, 1995)

McCarthy, Paul, *Fever Pitch: The Rise of the Premier League 1992-2004* (Sphere, 2022)

Merson, Paul, *Hooked* (Headline Publishing Group, 2021)

Neville, Gary, *Red: My Autobiography* (Corgi, 2011)

Robinson, Joshua and Clegg, Jonathan, *The Club: How the Premier League Became the Richest, Most Disruptive Business in Sport* (John Murray, 2019)

Schmeichel, Peter, *One: My Autobiography* (Hodder and Stoughton, 2021)

Shearer, Alan in collaboration with Harrison, Dave, *Alan Shearer's Diary of a Season* (Virgin Books, 1995)

Shearer, Alan with Harrison, Dave, *Shearer: My Story so Far* (Hodder and Stoughton, 1998)

Sutton, Chris with Guidi, Mark, *Paradise and Beyond: My autobiography* (Black & White Publishing, 2011)

Various, *Manchester United: Official Review of the 94/95 Season* (Virgin Publishing, 1995)

Whitworth, Tom, *When the Seagulls Follow the Trawler: Football in the 90s* (Pitch Publishing, 2021)

Williams, Michael (Ed.), *Sky Sports The Ultimate Football Guide 1996*

Newspapers & magazines
90 Minutes
Birmingham Mail
Daily Mirror
FourFourTwo
Guardian
Independent
Liverpool Echo
MATCH!
Newcastle Evening Chronicle
Observer
SHOOT
Telegraph
The Times
When Saturday Comes
World Soccer

Websites
bbc.co.uk
britishnewspaperarchive.co.uk
englandfootballonline.com
fbref.com
premierleague.com
transfermarkt.co.uk
worldfootball.net
youtube.com